Developing Language Teachers
for a Changing World

Developing Language Teachers for a Changing World

Edited by Gail Guntermann

In Conjunction with the American Council
on the Teaching of
Foreign
Languages

National Textbook Company
a division of *NTC Publishing Group* • Lincolnwood, Illinois USA

Published by National Textbook Company, a division of NTC Publishing Group.
© 1993 by NTC Publishing Group, 4255 West Touhy Avenue,
Lincolnwood (Chicago), Illinois 60646-1975 U.S.A.
Manufactured in the United States of America.

3 4 5 6 7 8 9 0 VP 9 8 7 6 5 4 3 2 1

Contents

Foreword

As long as teachers continue to teach as they were taught, the past is perpetuated into the future. Yet tomorrow's schools will not be the same as yesterday's, and the old knowledge and skills will not suffice. The current demands for change in American education can be seen as an opportunity as well as a challenge. ACTFL is taking the leadership in its efforts to define the language teaching profession and its goals and to prepare for the tasks that lie ahead. This volume, a flagship in ACTFL's teacher-education agenda, was first discussed at the Summer Seminar on Language Teacher Education in Denver in 1991. Immediately thereafter an advisory committee was formed and met to map out the topics, organize them into chapters, and suggest potential authors. Then came the long, stimulating process of creating a coherent overview of the current situation, needed changes for the future, and alternate means for achieving them.

I am particularly grateful to the authors for their cooperation and patience with receiving constant input while they were writing, to the Center for Applied Linguistics for providing a search of the ERIC documents, and to Ed Scebold and ACTFL for setting me up with electronic mail, without which I wonder how we managed before. And without the patient help of Peter Lafford, manager of Arizona State University's Humanities Computing Facility, the editing would have been much more difficult.

The members of the advisory committee are also much appreciated for their constant willingness to review chapter drafts on a moment's notice. They are Ray Clifford, Gilbert Jarvis, Elizabeth Joiner, and Lynn Sandstedt, along with June Phillips, chair of the ACTFL Publications Committee and general adviser for the project. As usual, she was always available, knowledgeable, and articulate.

In addition, several other experts agreed to review the outlines and chapter drafts: Kathleen Bailey, Kenneth Chastain, Susan Colville-Hall, Gerard Ervin, Daniel Fallon, Robert LaBouve, and Alice Omaggio-Hadley. This volume has definitely been a team effort, and the collaboration, collegiality, and dedication of all involved bodes well for our ability to continue to progress as a profession.

Developing Language Teachers for a Changing World: Prospects for Progress

Gail Guntermann
Arizona State University

"Do you believe in progress?" my freshman humanities professor used to growl as he pointed his forefinger at my nose. Although at that time I would have preferred to avoid his impassioned challenge, his words have come back to me often, and they ring especially true as we examine educational reform in general and teacher education in particular in the 1990s. Are we making progress? On the positive side, Jarvis and Taylor (1990) note that "we have learned just enough about teaching and learning to recognize that we are on the brink of dramatic progress" (p. 160), and further point out that teacher educators in the institutions that graduate large numbers of teachers now tend to hold advanced degrees in language education. Without this cadre of leaders in the field, one wonders what the role of foreign languages would be in the education reform movement. The efforts of the profession to develop and measure proficiency and to link theory and research to practice must also be considered as progressive reforms; and finally, the authors of these chapters report on isolated instances of remarkable reforms in teacher education. Yet most of the recommendations that Elizabeth Joiner made at the first ACTFL national conference on professional priorities (Joiner 1980) remain to be addressed.

The major purpose of this volume, one of the first in a series of ACTFL projects on teacher education, is to serve as a catalyst for change. It should describe the current status of the national agenda and the place of language teaching within it; clarify standards for the content of language teacher development and suggest steps for meeting them; outline what we know and do not know about language teachers and teacher development and present the principal paradigms, constraints, and avenues for research; and, pulling it all together,

Gail Guntermann (Ph.D., The Ohio State University) is Associate Professor of Spanish at Arizona State University, where she teaches advanced Spanish courses and methods of teaching foreign languages at the undergraduate and graduate levels. She has worked in teacher training, education, and supervision in the United States and for the Peace Corps here and abroad. She has published articles and monographs on curricular topics, culture, and Spanish language acquisition. She is a member of ACTFL, the American Educational Research Association, AATSP, and AFLA, the Arizona state association.

point to further directions for action, searching out emerging models that can provide guidance. Although the book does not contain a complete review of the events and publications of the educational reform movement, most chapters refer to them, and the reader who requires this background information is directed to the original sources listed at the ends of the chapters.

The chapter authors help to clarify the context as well as the content and processes of language teacher development, and they describe examples of progress in selected sites in this country and abroad, within both foreign languages and other disciplines, while at the same time calling attention to the challenges that lie ahead. They have recognized the need to end the isolation of *foreign* languages and replace the traditional emphasis on teacher *training* with teacher *development,* if we are to play the leadership role in education that the changing world should require of us.

Penelope M. Earley, in the first chapter, describes the events, entities, and conflicting ideals that affect educational policy-making today and presents examples of the changes that are taking place in the influence arena. She shows how various types of interest groups are developing policies and taking on other new responsibilities that once belonged to the government.

This chapter is valuable for understanding the context and importance of the efforts of ACTFL and the AATs (American Associations of Teachers of French / German/Spanish and Portuguese) to establish standards and guidelines and other ACTFL teacher development initiatives. Several authors suggest that unity is the key to influencing the directions change will take, and Earley makes it clear that of equal importance is our acceptance of responsibility for safeguarding the quality of education by scrutinizing all reforms for the real effects that they may have.

In chapter 2 Sarah Hudelson and Christian Faltis—who together work in teacher development for multicultural and bilingual education as well as English as a second language at the elementary, secondary, and adult levels—share a vision for all teacher education based on Cochran-Smith's collaborative reso-nance model (1991), which engages the universities and the schools in the collaborative endeavor of critiquing and transforming education and prepares teachers to be researchers and developers of instructional strategies (e.g., for infusing culture into all teaching—something that heretofore has eluded most language educators). Teacher education, like all learning, takes place through social interaction, with the learner constructing his or her own knowledge. Hudelson and Faltis submit that this model is particularly necessary for meeting the needs and the potential of the multicultural, multilevel classrooms of tomorrow. In outlining five essential areas of generic teacher education, they provide the beginnings of a plan for a reformed program for colleges of education and a basis for dialogue on the relationships between general ped-agogical preparation and the content areas.

The five authors of chapter 3, who represent widely varied emphases and experience in language and culture teaching, follow Hudelson and Faltis's line of thinking and extend it further, to suggest that the many related fields that make up second language education should work together in an integrated manner as leaders and agents of change, given the power of language and culture for tomorrow's pluralistic school population. As Daniel Fallon, codirector of Project 30, pointed out at the ACTFL Summer Seminar on Foreign Language Teacher Education, the curriculum of U.S. schools has not changed much in fifty years with regard to multiculturalism or internationalism, in spite of advanced communication, the globally interdependent economy, and the fact that the United States is a world power without adequate experience for the role.

The authors of chapter 3 describe second language education for minority and majority learners and identify problem areas that need to be addressed if second language education programs are to reach their full potential. They point the way to integration of second language instruction within the total school. The chapter ends with a series of questions to be answered in the quest for a multiculturally literate citizenry—questions that invite reflection, dialogue, and research.

Research is the topic of chapter 4, by JoAnn Hammadou. Having reviewed the literature with Elizabeth Bernhardt only recently (Bernhardt and Hammadou 1987) and having found very little research reported, she was not surprised to discover that the situation has not changed drastically. She notes that among foreign language teacher educators there are simply too few researchers; and one might add that there are fewer yet who are not overextended: charged with all teacher preparation, supervision, and program coordination for their departments. This situation reflects the general lack of attention to language teaching that several authors decry as a major obstacle to progress in teacher development.

Hammadou reviews the characteristics and requirements of the principal research paradigms and critiques examples of each. She also suggests some important research questions that could be investigated using each paradigm, although she does not attempt an exhaustive list, in view of the fact that nearly every aspect of teacher development begs for empirical support. Her goals are (1) to stimulate teachers and teacher educators to conduct carefully conceived research on questions of concern to them, and (2) to provide a menu of inquiry paradigms from which to select the most appropriate for a given study. Those who wish to seek answers to local problems only will find the end of the chapter of most interest. The chapter can also serve as an aid in reading and interpreting articles that report research results.

Once again, Hammadou mentions the relatedness of foreign language, second language, ESL, bilingual, and immersion education, but she reminds us of the differences that can cause misinterpretations if one tries to generalize research results from one of these fields to another.

Leslie L. Schrier, in chapter 5, reflects on the occupation of teaching and the prospects for its becoming a true profession. She notes several barriers to progress in this area, related to the attractiveness of teaching as a career, the lack of a knowledge base on teachers and teacher preparation, and the compromising of standards in order to provide the numbers of new teachers that will be needed in the years to come. She also discusses the fragmentation of the occupation and the urgent need for visibility as a unified profession if we are to influence policy decisions. Schrier provides interesting information on the demographics and other characteristics of today's teachers and concludes with an overview of the elements that must be in place for language teaching to be considered a profession. Chapter 5 serves as an introduction to the topics of the next two chapters.

Chapters 6 and 7 together paint a picture of tomorrow's teacher's knowledge base and the means to evaluate it, and they make recommendations for future action in order to give substance to educational reform. In chapter 6 Robert C. Lafayette provides a comparative overview of the contents of the teacher-education guidelines and standards of ACTFL and the AATs, stressing the subject-matter content. He also reviews the work of other professional organizations, in order to demonstrate various effective approaches to specifying standards for the education of students and teachers. He critiques the characteristics of current and traditional programs, pointing to specific areas where change is needed if we are to improve the proficiency and cultural knowledge of teachers, changes that will entail major revisions in the foci and course work of language departments. Lafayette's chapter is a thorough treatment of emerging approaches to language teachers' content preparation and evaluation, including descriptions of new proficiency tests.

Chapter 7 provides an equally thorough and cogent view of the pedagogical content knowledge that language teachers will need. Although some reformers, primarily those who work outside of education, would like to abandon all pedagogical preparation for teachers, Barbara H. Wing argues that it is imperative that teachers understand the content from the standpoint of the learner and that they examine past and current practices in the light of up-to-date information on the processes of learning and teaching, if we are to operate from a vision for the future rather than perpetuating ineffective practices from the past. Wing reviews briefly the pedagogical section of the ACTFL program guidelines as well as the AAT documents, analyzing the major essential components of pedagogical content knowledge and how they can best be acquired, assuming that we can solve the problems that will arise along the way. As the chapter developed, it became increasingly clear that this aspect of teacher preparation requires far more attention than it can receive in one methods course (as was noted by Jarvis in 1983), and that the process must continue throughout a teacher's professional life. Wing discusses models and challenges for redesigning the pedagogical preparation of language teachers.

The final chapter of this volume is meant to tie together the threads that run through the chapters that precede it and to provide models and inspiration for future action. Elizabeth G. Joiner proposes a model for teacher development similar to that recommended in chapter 2, in that it promotes the active participation of all concerned—teacher educators, teachers, and teacher candidates—in analyzing and reforming existing practices and in designing new ones. In Wallace's (1991) reflective model, teachers are involved in reflecting on all aspects of teaching. In Cochran-Smith's collaborative resonance model, teachers are prepared specifically to foment change. Joiner has chosen to apply her preferred model personally, leading the reader to reflect on several extant programs in foreign languages and other fields, and from the United States and abroad, to assess the appropriateness of their various qualities in the light of our own knowledge and experience as well as the information gleaned from all the chapters of the volume. She asks us to look beyond the surface structure of these programs to consider the contents, the substance of reform. Finally, she reflects on the factors that are essential for effective change to take place, and, once again, the challenges that we need to overcome if long-recommended reforms are finally to be realized.

While actual progress in improving teacher preparation to date has not been very impressive, ACTFL has made a commitment to treat teacher education with as much serious attention as it devoted to proficiency in the 1980s. The effort began with the ACTFL Provisional Program Guidelines in 1988, the Summer Seminar in Denver in 1991 (Knop 1991), and the formation of a Special Interest Group that met for the first time at the 1991 annual meeting in Washington, D.C., under the leadership of Leslie Schrier. Standards for schools as well as for teacher education are being developed by the professional organizations, and the National Board for Professional Teaching Standards is considering a project to include foreign languages by 1997. A series of ACTFL proposals for projects in research and development is currently in the planning stages.

It is evident that the crisis in education demands basic changes rather than superficial re-forming and expansion of existing elements that have been shown to be inadequate in the past (Phillips 1989). Yet judging from the contributions to this volume, it would seem that progress, defined as change in predetermined desirable directions, requires collective identification of problems and needs and visionary approaches to meeting them, followed by professional, collaborative action, taking into consideration an understanding of the forces and processes of change. It is hoped that the chapters of this book provide the background and inspiration that are necessary for the profession to work through this process to make considerable progress in the years to come.

References, Prospects for Progress

Bernhardt, Elizabeth B., and JoAnn Hammadou. 1987. "A Decade of Research in Foreign Language Teacher Education." *Modern Language Journal* 71: 289–98.

Cochran-Smith, Marilyn. 1991. "Learning to Teach against the Grain." *Harvard Education Review* 61: 279–310.

Jarvis, Gilbert A. 1983. "Pedagogical Knowledge for the Second Language Teacher," pp. 234–41 in James E. Alatis, H. H. Stern, and Peter Strevens, eds., *Applied Linguistics and the Preparation of Second Language Teachers: Toward a Rationale.* Georgetown University Round Table on Language and Linguistics. Washington, DC: Georgetown Univ. Press.

_____, and Sheryl V. Taylor. 1990. "Reforming Foreign and Second Language Teacher Education," pp. 159–82 in Diane W. Birckbichler, ed., *New Perspectives and New Directions in Foreign Language Education.* ACTFL Foreign Language Education Series, vol. 20. Lincolnwood, IL: National Textbook.

Joiner, Elizabeth G. 1980. "Preservice Teacher Education: Some Thoughts for the 1980s," pp. 78–80 in Dale L. Lange, ed., *Proceedings of the National Conference on Professional Priorities.* Yonkers, NY: ACTFL Materials Center.

Knop, Constance K. 1991. "A Report on the ACTFL Summer Seminar: Teacher Education in the 1990s." *Foreign Language Annals* 24: 527–32.

Phillips, June K. 1989. "Teacher Education: Target of Reform," pp. 11–40 in Helen S. Lepke, ed., *Shaping the Future: Challenges and Opportunities*. Report of the Northeast Conference on the Teaching of Foreign Languages. Middlebury, VT: Northeast Conference.

Wallace, Michael J. 1991. *Training Foreign Language Teachers: A Reflective Approach*. Cambridge, Eng.: Cambridge Univ. Press.

1

The Teacher-Education Agenda: Policies, Policy Arenas, and Implications for the Profession

Penelope M. Earley

American Association of Colleges for Teacher Education

Introduction

This is a time of fundamental and far-reaching change in teacher education. As policymakers at the local, state, and federal levels attempt to chart a new course for schools and children, the process by which persons are recruited into, and prepared for, careers as teachers will be transformed. Much of this change will be driven by forces external to the colleges and universities engaged in the preparation of elementary and secondary school educators.

New players and stakeholders have entered the policy debate and those traditionally involved in making decisions about teacher recruitment, preparation, licensure, and remuneration have reasserted their roles. To appreciate the functions of these various stakeholders, it is important to know who they are, how they relate to one another, and the direct or indirect ways in which they are involved in the policy process. In this chapter, two frameworks for studying public policy actions are introduced and applied to teacher-education policy decisions. Included is a brief description of the evolution of teacher-education governance with attention to how this history complicates the implementation of a teacher-education reform agenda.

Penelope M. Earley (B.A., University of Michigan; M.Ed., University of Virginia; Ph.D. candidate, Virginia Polytechnic Institute and State University) is Senior Director for Governmental Relations and Issue Analysis with the American Association of Colleges for Teacher Education. She established and directs AACTE's State Issues Clearinghouse, a nationally recognized information source on state government policies relative to teacher education. Earley has written extensively on federal and state policy issues related to teacher education.

Teacher-Education Policy Frameworks ————————————

Teacher education is subject to many masters. The curriculum for potential teachers and the requirements they must meet for licensure are influenced by federal, state, and local governments, by institutions of higher learning and school districts, and by the actions of unions and professional organizations. Education analyst Willis D. Hawley (1990) suggests that the content and delivery of teacher education, and the institutions of higher education in which teacher preparation generally occurs, are subject to governmental, organizational, and ecological influences. Figure 1-1 illustrates these three domains and how he suggests they relate to each other.

Hawley's framework is helpful for identifying and pigeonholing groups of influencers. Policy-making is more, however, than the classification of interests and their power relationships; it is the process by which our society attempts to identify paradoxes and resolve dilemmas.

Thomas Green (1983) approaches policy studies from a different perspective. He submits that we rely on public policy tools to resolve the conflict between societal ideals. Green's framework provides us with a lens to scrutinize the consequences of policy actions in the domains of influence in Hawley's model.

Green suggests societal ideals may conflict in three ways. First, they may conflict because ideals have multiple meanings. As an illustration, one of the National Education Goals states that "By the year 2000, all children in America will start school ready to learn" (*America 2000* 1991: 19). School readiness is a societal ideal that may mean mental readiness, physical readiness, social readiness, or a combination of the three.

Green's second type of conflict involves level of aggregation. He maintains "some ideals make sense only when we consider large aggregations and others only when we consider small ones" (1983: 319). When the *Exxon Valdez* accident polluted Alaskan waterways, the U.S. government was faced with problems related to restoring the environment and preventing other such spills in the future. The prevention problem may be framed at a low level of aggregation: the need to ensure that captains of supertankers are sober while in command of their ships. Or, the problem may be framed at a high level of social aggregation: the need to address citizens' demands for inexpensive and readily available oil.

Green points out that Americans want educational systems that embody both excellence and equity, but that educational equity is a societal ideal best achieved at a high level of social policy aggregation while educational excellence can best be pursued at a low level of social aggregation. Attempts to design and implement federal programs to guarantee that each child receives an "excellent" education may result in mandates and regulations that hamper individual teachers' creativity. Thus, committing to a course of action at an inappropriate level of social aggregation may lead to a policy whose goals are thwarted by the programs designed to achieve it.

Green's third source of conflict involves policy implementation. When public monies are expended, there is an expectation that government will account to its

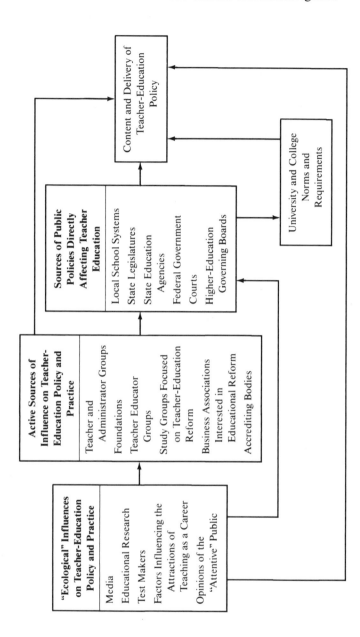

Figure 1-1. Patterns of Influence: Public Policies Directly Affecting Preservice Teacher Education

From "Systematic Analysis, Public Policy-Making, and Teacher Education," by Willis D. Hawley. Reprinted with permission of Macmillan Publishing Company from HANDBOOK OF RESEARCH ON TEACHER EDUCATION, W. Robert Houston, Editor. Copyright 1990 by Association of Teacher Educators.

citizens for the use of these funds. He notes that to "track the federal dollar" and to ensure that federal funds are used to supplement rather than supplant state or local resources, children receiving compensatory services (such as English-language instruction, therapy, or special tutoring) are commonly pulled out of their regular classroom or segregated into special classes. If the goal of a special-services program is to bring children with special needs into the classroom mainstream, however, pull-out programs may not work to that goal. In addition, a child who is routinely removed from a classroom for tutoring or to receive compensatory-education services loses other class time and may never catch up to children in his or her age cohort. Mechanisms to guarantee accountability for the receipt of government funds may, paradoxically, conflict with the ideal of what is a good education for an individual child or the broad goals of the government program.

Teacher-Education Reform and Influence Arenas

In this section, each of Hawley's three policy domains—governmental, organizational, and ecological—are explored. Within this discussion, situations are identified when one or more of Green's three sources of conflict enter the policy debate.

Government Arenas

Consideration of teacher-education policy in this arena begins with a brief review of the history of state and federal governments in the preparation of public elementary and secondary school teachers. The implications of this history on teacher-education policy are then discussed.

Historical Context.   Historically, we think of education in the United States as decentralized. The Tenth Amendment to the Constitution provides that "The powers not delegated to the United States by the Constitution, nor prohibited by it to the States, are reserved to the States respectively, or to the people." Since the Constitution is silent on the education of its citizens, states and localities have assumed primary responsibility for organizing and operating public schools. For the most part, the federal role in education has been limited to responding to education needs that other units of government have been unwilling or unable to address (National Teacher Development Initiative 1978; Stedman 1990).

Public governance or control of teacher education is also decentralized. When common schools were established in the nineteenth century, local school offi-cials who managed them would oversee the hiring of teachers. In certain localities, applicants needed to pass an oral or written test; some districts used course counting, a process by which a transcript review documenting the completion of course work establishes a person's qualifications to teach; in other situations, public school teaching was considered a patronage position (Roth and Pipho 1990; Tyack 1967).

States began to exert influence over who became a teacher in the early part of the twentieth century by establishing state guidelines for course counting (also known as transcript review) and through approval of teacher-education programs. Under a program-approval system, the state officially recognized programs to prepare teachers in one or more institutions of higher learning. Upon completion of an approved program, a student was awarded a document by the institution, and this document was recognized by public schools in the state for purposes of employment.

As states increased their regulation of teacher education, it was common for state education agencies (SEAs) to be given jurisdiction over teacher-education policy. SEAs assumed responsibility for (1) determining categories of teaching licenses (including alternative or emergency licenses), (2) setting the standards for individual licensure, (3) testing individuals prior to licensure, and (4) extending state recognition to collegiate-based teacher-education programs. Thus, many SEAs now regulate teacher supply and demand by tightening or relaxing licensure standards and by deciding which institutions of higher learning will or will not be in the business of preparing teachers.

State Authority.   The evolution of teacher-education governance in the United States has been predicated on the belief that state governments are the appropriate level of policy aggregation to regulate educator preparation. As a consequence, we have fifty systems for licensing educators and approving their preparation programs. Although similar in many ways, no two are identical. Each of these fifty state systems is supported by state agency bureaucracies that—in addition to their licensure and program-approval functions—justify their existence on the basis of the unique regulations and laws of their state.

An effect of this governance structure is that faculty and administrators in institutions of higher education with teacher-education programs have a unique relationship with state governments. The state, rather than just the college or university, is often the judge of what education courses should be required of potential teachers, whereas courses in the subjects to be taught are more often determined by faculty in specific collegiate departments. As a result, tension has developed between education faculty and faculty in other disciplines. In attempting to satisfy the dictates of the state—without which the teacher-education program could not exist—education faculty were placed at odds with colleagues responsible for instruction in the subjects future educators would teach (Hawley 1992: 3). Consequently, attempts to change teacher education at the institutional level have been difficult and slow. Strains on the teacher-education governance system are the result of conflict over the level of aggregation. Institutions of higher education believe curricular decisions rest with the college or university faculty and that state involvement in this matter violates institutional autonomy. The state, however, acts as an agent of its citizens and in that role is expected to protect its citizens from harm. The argument follows, then, that the state's authority to set standards for the preparation and licensure of its public employees—such as teachers—overrides issues of college or university autonomy.

State functions vary, but it is common practice for states to require potential teachers to pass a standardized test as a condition for receiving a teaching license. Teacher testing has its roots in the early history of education in the United States. As control over teacher education moved to the state level, however, the notion of teacher testing—first seen in the nineteenth century—shifted from individual schools or districts to the state. According to the Office of Educational Research and Improvement, by 1987 44 states had implemented or decided to initiate requirements that teachers pass a written test before receiving a teaching credential (Rudner 1987). Establishment of testing standards and the responsibility for administration of an assessment measure generally rests with the state board of education, state education agency, or an autonomous professional standards board.

State-mandated teacher testing further reinforced the relationship between education faculties and state governments. Teacher educators not only had to worry about whether their curriculum was aligned with the state's licensure test, but also were faced with the possibility that their teacher-education program would lose its state approval if students did not perform well on the mandated licensure examination.

During the past decade, state legislatures have challenged the authority and responsibility of state education agencies by including teacher-education decision making in the legislative arena. Laws have been passed to require tests for teacher licensure—sometimes even specifying the assessment instrument and cut score; to set credit-hour caps on teacher-education programs; and to establish licensure waivers (often called alternative certification). The introduction of state legislatures into the teacher-education policy arena has further solidified the position of the state in the matter of teacher preparation and licensure.

Hawley (1992) points out that the state's prominence in teacher-education governance has been problematic. He observes that because the fifty states and District of Columbia have not identified a common teacher-education curriculum, there is skepticism among those in the policy community over whether there is professional consensus on the knowledge base for teacher education. In this instance, what may appear to be a problem born of indecision about the components in the teacher-education knowledge base (a conflict of meaning) is actually an outcome of an unresolved governance conflict (conflict of level of aggregation).

Federal Authority.   Federal interest in teacher recruitment and preparation, which began in the early 1950s with the passage of the National Defense Education Act, has been modest. Although teacher inservice or preservice are allowable activities in many large discretionary education programs such as special education, bilingual education, vocational education, and compensatory education, the one major federal program that provides support for teacher education is Title V of the Higher Education Act.

Conflicts of implementation may occur when federal government policies do not mesh with state or district goals or needs. In many states, holding a vocational education license is based on possession of certain technical skills.

Because schools often need teachers with very specialized abilities for their vocational education programs, some states have waived academic require-ments—such as a bachelor's degree—that would be considered a minimum for teachers of other subjects. In recent years, however, the federal government's policy regarding vocational education has changed. To receive federal funds, school districts must integrate instruction in reading, mathematics, and writing into their vocational education courses. Current vocational education teachers are expected to teach these basic skills, notwithstanding the fact that little federal money is available for teacher inservice education.

When Ronald Reagan became president in 1980, he entered the White House with a pledge to downsize the federal government's role in education and other social-service areas. Eight years of policies designed to move domestic programs to the state level had two consequences for teacher education and its governance, namely:

1. State and local units of government, through their professional organizations, became more aggressive advocates at the federal level. Groups such as the Education Commission of the States, National Governors Association, Coun-cil of Chief State School Officers, National Conference of State Legislatures, and National Association of State Boards of Education maintain a presence in Washington, D.C., and are active in setting and influencing the federal education agenda.
2. Although the absolute size of federal agencies—in terms of personnel and budget allocations—didn't shrink, the type of work done by the agencies changed. Federal departments reduced their research, analysis, and evalua-tion functions and focused more on the mechanics of program administration and compliance. (The Center for Statistics in the Office of Educational Research and Improvement is a notable exception.) Consequently, policy development and research moved from government to professional and trade organizations. By 1990, most education organizations and interest groups retained a research and policy capacity and policy analysts turned to these entities for career options rather than to the federal government.

The notion that the post-Reagan years have seen a trend toward the centraliza-tion of education policy is a favorite topic of discussion among policy analysts (see for example, Smith, O'Day, and Cohen 1990). They point to *America 2000,* the National Education Goals, attempts by the U.S. Congress to legislate alternative teacher licensure, and the federal government's support for the national certification of teachers as indicators of this trend. States' involvement in education governance is strong and well-established, however, and there is no indication that states intend to relinquish their authority over teacher licensure and program approval.

On the surface, it may appear that presidential and congressional pressures for national goals, standards, and assessments present an irreconcilable conflict with traditional tenets of state control over education. This is not necessarily the case. Weiler (1990) points out that societal functions are subject to territorial centralization or decentralization (from one unit of government up or down to a higher or lower unit of government). They are also subject to functional centralization or decentralization, which involves the movement of certain government functions to nongovernmental or private agencies (p. 433). Functional centralization is what we are experiencing in the United States in regard to teacher education—and possibly other education activities. Groups representing citizens, units of government, education professionals, business, and others have assumed the policy development and agenda-building roles traditionally associated with government. As Smith et al. (1990) point out,

> dozens of foundations; quasi-governmental organizations such as the American Association for the Advancement of Science (AAAS) and the National Academy of Science (NAS); and various businesses and education groups [are] sponsoring reports about the condition of education. They are also conceiving and financing initiatives . . . designed to change the character of American education. (p. 12)

The functional centralization proposed by Weiler (1990) is driven by the activities of organizations with nationwide memberships or constituencies and thus have the effect of raising educational debate to the national—although not necessarily the federal—level. As a result, an understanding of education policy-making must give attention to the activities Hawley (1990) characterizes as part of the organizational arena.

Organizational Arena

Hawley (1990) claims that education organizations and groups directly or indirectly sway teacher-education policy, and he classifies influencing organizations into five broad categories:

1. *Foundations.* This category includes both those that have education as a major focus and those with eclectic portfolios, of which education is one component.
2. *Ad hoc or semiformal study groups on teacher education.* Such groups may be composed of private individuals or designated representatives of professional organizations. In many cases, they are supported and sanctioned by a unit of government. The National Goals Panel fits this model. It is not unusual for study groups to formalize their activities and become a professional organization. The Holmes Group is such an example.
3. *Professional organizations.* This category includes associations of educators, administrators, government officials, and citizens.
4. *Business groups.* These may also be special study groups and may be linked to one or more foundations.
5. *Accrediting bodies.* For teacher education, this refers to regional accrediting bodies or to the National Council for the Accreditation of Teacher Education.

The focus of this section is on the role of foundations, ad hoc study groups, and professional organizations in shaping education policy. It also considers quasi-governmental organizations, a category not included in Hawley's model. It is not possible to describe the activities and spheres of influence of the hundreds of organizations with educational interests. Those included for this discussion were selected because they present interesting examples of organizational influence in the world of teacher-education policy. The depiction of organizational activities is generally limited to their policy impact. Readers interested in pursuing the substantive agenda of a particular group will find rich descriptions elsewhere in the teacher-education literature. The bibliography accompanying this chapter and chapters 6 and 7 of this volume may be useful starting points.

Organizations and ad hoc groups of individuals may influence the policy arena directly or indirectly, and often it is the indirect effect that is the most interesting and has the most profound impact. As an example, the National Education Association (NEA) has been a vocal advocate for the national certification of teachers through the National Board for Professional Teaching Standards (NBPTS). As expected, the NEA used its considerable leverage to lobby the U.S. Congress to provide funds to support the work of the NBPTS. In this manner, the teachers' organization has directly swayed the federal policy agenda to include government support for the national certification of teachers.

In addition, the NEA expects all its member teachers to earn an NBPTS certificate. Accordingly, it has attempted to influence the standards and internal policies of the National Board to preclude actions that would greatly limit the number of NBPTS certificates issued each year. The relationship between the NEA's belief that all its million-plus membership should earn a national teaching certificate and education policy is indirect. The consequences of the organization's actions, however, are far-reaching. If all, or the majority of, public and private school teachers are expected to earn an advanced certificate offered by the National Board for Professional Teaching Standards, this credential could ultimately replace existing state licenses and, therefore, temper the role of state governments in setting teaching standards. Teacher-preparation institutions would be expected to peg their curriculum to NBPTS specifications rather than state requirements. In this situation, the level of aggregation for policy decisions on educator licenses moves from the state to the national level (but not necessarily the federal level). If the NBPTS elects to restrict the number of certificates it issues, state licensure policies will be little changed and institutions of higher education will continue to respond to state guidelines. The vast majority of teachers will hold a state license, but a select few also will have earned the NBPTS certificate. It is probable that school districts will be pressured to recognize teachers holding the additional credential through special assignments or additional pay. In this manner, decisions by a private national organization may drive policy actions at the school or district level.

Foundations.   The influence of private foundations on teacher-education policy is largely uncharted territory, yet foundations are important players in setting the policy agenda for education through their ability to provide financial support for new or untested programs and activities. Commonly, foundation boards, staff, or both identify areas in which proposals will be solicited and resources directed. In recent years, the Ford Foundation elected to support programs to recruit minority students into teaching careers. In 1992, the Danforth Foundation announced plans to redirect a portion of its grant programs to support services for preschool children. For nearly a decade, the Carnegie Corporation has supported activities related to establishing educational standards such as the National Board for Professional Teaching Standards. The Teach for America program received contributions from nearly fifty corporations and foundations to provide alternative routes to teaching for young college students. In this manner, foundations are able to draw attention to issues that have not yet moved onto the public policy agenda.

The amount of money foundations may direct to particular issues is a significant factor in their influence. The Danforth Foundation awards nearly $8 million each year—more money than the federal government appropriates for the entire system of ERIC Clearinghouses. The National Board for Professional Teaching Standards received a $5 million award from the Carnegie Corporation, and the MacArthur Foundation and Pew Charitable Trusts provided $2.5 million for the New Standards Project. By comparison, the Department of Education's Office of Educational Research and Improvement awards less than $1 million a year for field-initiated research.

It is not uncommon for foundation activity to go beyond agenda building to policy development and implementation. The Exxon Foundation gave the University of Washington's Center for Educational Renewal $250,000 for a study of teacher education to be directed by John Goodlad. The study and a set of recommendations to reform teacher education were published in *Teachers for Our Nation's Schools* (Goodlad 1990). Exxon then awarded the Center $2.5 million to support projects in twelve states based on Goodlad's work. This generated interest from state policymakers and the Education Commission of the States. Subsequently, the Southwest Bell Foundation awarded over $300,000 to stimulate similar education reforms in other parts of the nation.

Study Groups Focused on Teacher Education.   A common response to a perceived societal problem is to appoint a group to study it. Study groups may be generated by foundations or nonpublic organizations. The Carnegie Task Force on Teaching as a Profession was a nonpublic initiative supported by the Carnegie Corporation. A study group may, like the National Goals Panel, be appointed and supported by a government agency. In addition, study groups may be self-styled and self-appointed, such as the Holmes and Renaissance Groups—two efforts spotlighting teacher-education reform.

The Holmes Group was established in 1986 by deans of education from major research universities. Their initial discussions focused on frustrations associated with teacher-education program accreditation and concerns about teacher education's low status in their universities. The Holmes Group's recommendations for revising teacher-education programs in their institutions were published in *Tomorrow's Teachers* (Holmes Group 1986). A key to implementing these recommendations involved garnering support from the member institutions' presidents and provosts. This required a relatively high profile set of activities. To accomplish this, the Holmes Group requested and received support from the Ford, Johnson, and New York Foundations and the Carnegie Corporation.

Over time, the Holmes Group changed from an ad hoc group to a professional organization. Members are assessed dues, and like most organizations, it publishes a newsletter and sponsors an annual conference. Although the Holmes Group has offered a number of suggestions for revising the preparation of teachers and for organizing elementary and secondary schools, they are most associated with proposals to shift teacher education to the graduate level and the establishment and administration of professional development or teaching schools.

Frustrations over the status of teacher education in institutions of higher education also led to the establishment of the Renaissance Group, an alliance of presidents and deans of education from institutions of higher education with large teacher-education programs: generally, regional or state universities. Begun in 1989, the Renaissance Group adopted twelve principles to guide the preparation of teachers in state colleges and universities (Renaissance Group, 1989).

The Holmes and Renaissance Groups are similar in their belief that reforming teacher education cannot go forward without the involvement of college and university presidents. They also agree on the importance of in-depth subject-matter preparation and general and content-specific preparation in teaching methodologies.

The colleges and universities that created the Holmes and Renaissance Groups were reacting to circumstances that originated with a clash between state requirements and professional norms—a conflict between levels of policy aggregation. In these situations, each group of institutions chose to cast their lot with other teacher-education professionals and to enlist the support of their institutions' presidents and provosts.

Professional Organizations.   There are a range of professional organizations with primary or secondary interest in teacher education. They can be grouped into four categories:

1. *Organizations that focus exclusively on all aspects of teacher education.* The Association of Teacher Educators, the American Association of Colleges for Teacher Education, and now the Holmes and Renaissance Groups are examples.
2. *Organizations that include attention to teacher education as one of multiple priorities.* The National Education Association, American Federation of Teachers, American Association of School Administrators, and the elementary and secondary school principals' associations are examples.
3. *Organizations that concentrate on activities in a particular teaching field.* The National Council of Teachers of Mathematics, National Council of Teachers of English, American Council on the Teaching of Foreign Languages, National Council for Languages and International Studies, National Council for the Social Studies, and National Council for Geographic Education are examples.
4. *Organizations with memberships made up of elected or appointed public officials.* The Council of Chief State School Officers, National Association of

State Directors of Teacher Education and Certification, National Governors' Association, National School Boards Association, and National Association of State Boards of Education are examples.

All these organizations have a defined membership (such as mathematics teachers, teacher-education faculty, or school board members) and they exist to represent the concerns of these individuals and institutions in public forums and before governmental and nongovernmental bodies. They are funded, at least in part, by membership dues, giving them the stability ad hoc groups lack. Many attempt to influence federal and state governmental policies and speak out on behalf of their members in the media. Although concern about the recruitment, preparation, and continuing professional development of teachers is a common value, these organizations may disagree on the specifics of standards for licensure, teacher assessment, and teacher preparation. As a result, on occasion they lobby one another as a means of gaining support for a particular position or activity.

Most professional associations with interest in teacher education have nationwide memberships and their purposes and activities tend to be of a national, rather than local, nature. Many are involved in the development of curriculum guidelines and standards for the preparation and licensure of educators. The National Council of Teachers of Mathematics (NCTM), for example, has developed curriculum standards for elementary and secondary schools. When the federal government's National Council on Education Standards and Testing (an ad hoc study group) considered what mathematics content should be taught in schools, they endorsed the NCTM standards (National Council on Education Standards and Testing 1992).

However, adoption of a specialty group's standards by the federal government, or even national agreement on these standards by the membership of the group, do not guarantee that their implementation will occur without controversy or problems. A recent NCTM survey found that "standardized testing, curriculum mandates, and parent opposition prevent many teachers from applying the innovative instruction envisioned in national math standards" ("State, Local Controls" 1992). This is an instance of a policy conflict over implementation. In this situation, national standards were developed by a professional organization (and later endorsed by the federal government). Yet using the standards is problematic because their implementation conflicts with state and local policies as well as with parental expectations of teachers and schools.

Quasi-Governmental Organizations.   Smith et al. (1990) note the growth of quasi-governmental organizations in the education policy world, offering the National Academy of Science and the American Association for the Advancement of Science as examples. In teacher education, the National Board for Professional Teaching Standards may be similarly classified.

The NBPTS has an interesting history. The establishment of such a board— with authority to grant a national teaching certificate—was a recommendation of the Carnegie Task Force on Teaching as a Profession (1986). After releasing their report, *A Nation Prepared: Teachers for the 21st Century,* the Carnegie Corporation provided start-up funds to hire NBPTS staff and to begin work on assessment prototypes. To supplement foundation support, the NBPTS appealed to the U.S. Congress for a special appropriation. An initial award was made by the Department of Education and authorizing legislation is pending to direct additional funds to the Board. A sole-source award of this nature is de facto endorsement of the Board and its activities, placing the NBPTS in a special relationship with the federal government.

The creation of the NBPTS raises a definitional issue. If the NBPTS offers teachers an opportunity to earn an advanced teaching credential and calls that credential a "certificate," how will it be differentiated from "certificates" awarded by many states to new teachers?

The terms *teaching license* and *teaching certificate* are often used interchangeably. Some states call the teaching credential they issue a certificate and others use the term *license,* even though the processes and authorizing agencies may be parallel. At present, 11 states use the term *license* and 40 states and the District of Columbia use the term *certificate* (American Association of Colleges for Teacher Education 1991). On occasion, the terminology is even further befuddled by the use of *accreditation* to describe the process by which an individual meets the requirements to be a teacher (see, for example, the 1988 Republican Platform, "An American Vision" 1988).

Whether the credential a beginning teacher earns is a certificate or a license is more than a semantic issue. In general, states issue licenses and that credential advises the public that the holder of the license has met standards for safe practice. A certificate, on the other hand, is usually issued to individuals who have met advanced standards developed by the profession of which they are a member. Although educators recognize the distinction, many teachers, and those who educate them, believe that certification denotes professional preparation while licensure has a vocational connotation. Nevertheless, calls for national certification of teachers have brought attention to the need for more precise use of the terms *certification* and *licensure* (Jordan 1988; Lilly 1991; Shive 1988). The key issue in this conflict of meaning is whether a teacher's *initial* preparation has professional status.

Ecological Influences

Hawley's model (1990) identifies five sources of influence on teacher-education policy and practice that are a function of the societal environment. In this section, two are discussed: the media and educational research. These are selected because when policymakers are asked to identify sources of knowledge that inform their decisions, the first one is frequently named and the other rarely cited.

Policymakers draw on a variety of information. When they are asked to rank information sources by frequency of use, the media is generally near the top (Kapel and Gallia 1991: 49). Examples of decisions made as the result of television, radio, or the print media are abundant. In the 1980s, a member of Congress introduced legislation to "warranty" teachers, an idea he picked up from an airline in-flight magazine. During a 1992 House of Representatives hearing on several education and juvenile justice bills, a congressman cited the television program *Unsolved Mysteries* as evidence to support a particular piece of legislation. Congressional staff persons suggest the best way to get the committee chairperson to pay attention to teacher education is to get a good article in the *Washington Post* or the *New York Times*.

Carlson (1990) asserts that positive press helped garner support for the New Jersey Alternative Certification program for teachers announced in 1983 by Governor Thomas Kean. He notes that the proposal was backed by the state's largest paper, the *Star-Ledger* (Newark, NJ) and a review of articles from the *Star-Ledger* confirms this. In the months following the announcement of the New Jersey alternative route, numerous stories favorable to the governor's plan were published in the New Jersey and East Coast press (see, for example, Braun 1983, 1984a, 1984b; Cooperman 1984; Maerhoff 1985; Van Tassel 1983).

In their study of sources of decision-making information, Kapel and Gallia (1991) found that policymakers report that they make use of educational research. As it happens, however, the research they use is generally provided by interest groups and has significance because it reinforces what they already believe. A legislator who believes teachers should pass a standardized examination before licensure will respond more positively to data and studies by test manufacturers than an advocacy organization that opposes such assessments.

Airasian (1988: 301) asserts that virtually none of the remedies suggested by the federal government to improve schooling were designed and developed on the basis of empirical evidence. He suggests three reasons for this. First, most education initiatives are the result of a crisis situation, such as publication of *A Nation at Risk* or launching of the Sputnik satellite, giving little time for sophisticated research efforts. Second, he observes that policymakers want to be seen as decisive problem-solvers. Lengthy studies of alternative solutions would likely negate the political benefits of posing new initiatives. Finally, he suggests that innovations are framed "in such general terms that pretrial studies are difficult to plan and carry out" (1988: 302). If there are no data from controlled studies to inform decision making, Airasian submits that policymakers look for solutions that conform to prevalent social norms and values. Thus, it isn't surprising that an elected official will seek out data from interest groups that he or she believes have a compatible perspective.

Of the influence domains suggested by Hawley (1990), the ecological influences on teacher-education policy are the most nebulous. They surround the policymakers and those who attempt to influence policy decisions, but, as in the natural sciences, subtle changes in the environment often go unnoticed.

Conclusion and Policy Implications

Hawley (1990) presents a comprehensive framework for identifying individuals and institutions that influence teacher-education policy. Green's (1983) notion that the public policy debate is a mechanism to resolve conflicts over societal ideals challenges us to look beyond political relationships to understand the power and influence of competing values in policy-making. Attention to competing societal values leads us to the consideration of some serious policy questions for teacher education. Given the amount of state control over teacher-education programs, to what extent can institutional pressures result in systemic change? Should state governments be urged to deregulate teacher education? If this is done, what safeguards are in place, or could be put in place, to assure citizens that teachers are qualified to enter the profession? Can or should a national system of teacher education—with common standards and regulations—be constructed? Who should be the architects of such a system—the federal government? a confederation of states? professional organizations? What are the obligations of elected officials to seek out data and research that may not be consistent with their personal values? What are the obligations of professional educators to provide timely information to decision makers?

Suggestions for reforming and revising teacher preparation are not in short supply. Elected officials, educators, and the public have an abundance of ideas for recruiting teachers, educating them for their professional responsibilities, and structuring their work environment. All these ideas need to be scrutinized for their direct and indirect impacts on the education system. As educators, we have a special obligation to ensure that this occurs.

References, The Teacher-Education Agenda

Airasian, P. W. 1988. "Symbolic Validation: The Case of State-Mandated, High-Stakes Testing." *Education Evaluation and Policy Analysis* 10: 301–34.

American Association of Colleges for Teacher Education. 1991. *Teacher Education Policy in the States: A 50-State Survey of Legislative and Administrative Actions.* Washington, DC: AACTE.

America 2000: An Education Strategy. 1991. Washington, DC: U.S. Dept. of Education.

Braun, Robert J. 1983. "Kean Seeks Coalition to Aid State as Education Reform 'Laboratory.' " *Sunday Star-Ledger,* 7 August, pp. 1, 27.

———. 1984a. "State Seeks to Assume Larger Role in Training Public School Teachers." *Star-Ledger,* 6 June, pp. 1, 27.

———. 1984b. "Tinkering with Cooperman's Plan Will Only Weaken It." *Star-Ledger,* 4 May, p. 1.

Carlson, Kenneth. 1990. "New Jersey's Alternate Route to Teacher Certification." Paper presented at the Annual Meeting of the American Educational Research Association, Boston, Massachusetts, April.

Carnegie Task Force on Teaching as a Profession. 1986. *A Nation Prepared: Teachers for the 21st Century.* Rochester, NY: National Center on Education.

Cooperman, Saul. 1984. "Teacher Licensing Reforms Drawn to Raise Standards." *Sunday Star-Ledger,* 19 August, pp. 59, 65.

Goodlad, John I. 1990. *Teachers for Our Nation's Schools.* San Francisco: Jossey-Bass.

Green, Thomas F. 1983. "Excellence, Equity, and Equality," pp. 318–42 in L. S. Shulman and G. Sykes, eds., *Handbook of Teaching and Policy.* White Plains, NY: Longman.

Hawley, Willis D. 1990. "Systematic Analysis, Public Policy-Making, and Teacher Education," pp. 136–56 in W. Robert Houston, ed., *Handbook of Research on Teacher Education.* New York: Macmillan.

————. 1992. "The Conspiracy to Ensure the Failure of Teacher Education." Unpublished manuscript.

Holmes Group. 1986. "Tomorrow's Teachers: A Report of the Holmes Group." East Lansing, MI: Holmes Group.

Jordan, Forbis F. 1988. *State Professional Standards / Practices Commissions or Boards: A Policy Analysis Paper.* Washington, DC: American Association of Colleges for Teacher Education.

Kapel, David E., and Thomas J. Gallia. 1991. "Informing Legislation: Sources of Decision-Making Information." *National Forum of Applied Educational Research Journal* 4: 41–56.

Lilly, M. Stephen. 1991. "Research on Teacher Licensure and State Approval of Teacher Education Programs." Unpublished manuscript.

Maerhoff, Gene I. 1985. "Alternate Route Leads Teachers to the Classroom." *The New York Times,* 13 August, pp. C1, C9.

National Board for Professional Teaching Standards. 1990. *Toward High and Rigorous Standards for the Teaching Profession: Initial Policies and Perspectives of the National Board for Professional Teaching Standards.* 2d ed. Detroit: NBPTS.

National Council on Education Standards and Testing. 1992. *Raising Standards for American Education.* Washington, DC: U.S. Government Printing Office.

National Teacher Development Initiative. 1978. *Analysis of U.S. Office of Education Discretionary Programs Having a Professional Development of Educational Personnel Component.* Report submitted to U.S. Commissioner of Education Ernest Boyer.

Renaissance Group. 1989. *Teachers for the New World: A Statement of Principles.* Cedar Falls: Univ. of Northern Iowa.

Republican National Committee. 1988. "An American Vision: For Our Children and Our Future." Washington, DC: Republican National Committee.

Roth, Robert A., and Chris Pipho. 1990. "Teacher Education Standards," pp. 119–35 in W. Robert Houston, ed., *Handbook of Research on Teacher Education.* New York: Macmillan.

Rudner, Larry M. 1987. "Questions and Answers Concerning Teacher Testing," pp. 1–3 in Larry M. Rudner, ed., *What's Happening in Teacher Testing, An Analysis of State Teacher Testing Practices.* Washington, DC: Office of Educational Research and Improvement.

Shive, Jerald J. 1988. "Professional Practices Board for Teachers." *Journal of Teacher Education* 39,6: 2–7.

Smith, Marshall S., Jennifer O'Day, and David K. Cohen. 1990. "National Curriculum American Style." *American Educator* 14,4: 10–46.

"State, Local Controls Inhibit National Standards, Teachers Say." 1992. *Report on Education Research,* 15 April, p. 3.

Stedman, James B. 1990. *Teachers: Issues for the 101st Congress.* Washington, DC: Congressional Research Service. [CRS Report 90-117 EPW].

Tyack, David B., ed. 1967. *Turning Points in American Educational History.* Waltham, MA: Blaisdell.

Van Tassel, P. 1983. "State to Name Panel to Explore Teacher Quality." *The New York Times,* 4 December, pp. 1, 12.

Weiler, Hans N. 1990. "Comparative Perspectives on Educational Decentralization: An Exercise in Contradiction?" *Educational Evaluation and Policy Analysis* 12: 433–48.

2

Redefining Basic Teacher Education: Preparing Teachers to Transform Teaching

Sarah Hudelson and Christian Faltis

Arizona State University

Reforming Teacher Education in the 1980s

In the early 1980s, the National Commission on Excellence in Education, an arm of the federal government, issued *A Nation at Risk* (1983), a report in which the U.S. school system was depicted as declining in quality, particularly in comparison with other technologically advanced nations. According to the report, the culprit was a widespread capitulation to mediocrity throughout all levels of education. That same year, The Education Commission of the States (1983), The National Science Board (1983), and The College Entrance Examination Board (1983), among others, also published reports reaffirming the government's description of the deterioration of the nation's schools. In the next three years, at least five other major reports were issued, all decrying the sad state of affairs in U.S. education. In a single voice, all the reports recommended a total reform at all levels. Accordingly, the way to solve the nation's educational problems was to return to an emphasis on the basics, to implement higher standards for gradua-

Sarah Hudelson is Associate Professor of Multicultural Education in the College of Education at Arizona State University. She prepares teachers and works with graduate students in bilingual/second language education and researches native and second language literacy development of bilingual children. Her professional affiliations include TESOL, NABE (National Association for Bilingual Education), the National Council of Teachers of English, and the International Reading Association. She has published several books and numerous articles in her field.

Christian Faltis received his Ph.D. in Bilingual Cross-Cultural Education from Stanford University. He is currently an Associate Professor of Bilingual Education at Arizona State University, where he conducts basic research in bilingual secondary education. He has published several books and articles and supervises graduate students in bilingual, second language, and multicultural education. His professional affiliations include TESOL, NABE, and the American Anthropological Association.

tion and for entering college, and to hold schools and teachers accountable for their actions through greater use of testing. It was thought that these reforms would propel U.S. schools to a new standard of excellence.

Without exception, the reports indirectly placed major responsibility for implementing the newly-called-for reforms in the hands of teacher educators. At the same time, the reports also made teacher education itself a target of reform, citing a connection between how teachers are prepared and the general disregard for learning and schooling (Holmes Group 1986: 29). The reports described teacher education as having become so enamored with education courses that were heavy on technique and light on substance that teachers were being produced knowing myriad techniques, but lacking a subject-matter knowledge base to draw from for planning and implementing lessons. According to most reports, excellence in education could be restored by increasing course work in the liberal arts, math, and science; by eliminating nonessential electives; and by reducing the number of courses in teaching methods and general education. Moreover, as was the case for schools in general, the way to demonstrate openly that excellence was being accomplished was to make schools accountable for their programs of study through the use of tests. Accordingly, in the mid-1980s teacher-education programs began requiring prospective teachers to pass basic-knowledge entrance examinations, such as the Pre-Professional Skills Test, to be eligible to take courses in teacher education. Once students complete the teacher-education program, they are again required to pass a test on pedagogical and subject-matter knowledge.

The introduction of entry and exit tests for teacher education was complemented by a similar move in the field of foreign language education, with the development of oral proficiency testing (Hiple 1987). The most widely used speaking proficiency test in foreign language education is based on the ACTFL proficiency guidelines. Although the original purpose of the ratings was to provide "a common yardstick, a series of descriptors of foreign language ability that are based on real life performance" (Woodford 1979: 73), by the end of the 1980s, proficiency testing began to be used for accountability purposes, as entry and exit criteria, and as a criterion for employment as a foreign language teacher.

The early efforts to reform teacher education were characteristically top-down and driven by groups and individuals from outside education. Moreover, the reformers categorically disregarded input and information from the people most directly involved in research and practice in teaching and teacher education. For these reasons, and because the reforms themselves did not seek to transform the basic nature of how teachers learn to teach, the reform movement did not catch on at the national level (Phillips 1989). It appears that the most significant and widespread impact of the reform movement was the interjection of testing for gatekeeping purposes.

In fact, research has demonstrated that little has changed in teacher education in the United States since the early 1960s. In 1983, John Goodlad reported that teacher-education programs across the nation were "disturbingly alike and most uniformly inadequate" (1983: 249). He later reported (Goodlad 1990) the results of a nationwide study in which he examined twenty-nine institutions representing six types of teacher-education schools and departments. He found that practices then differed little from those reported in 1983, and that, by and large, there is little difference between the ways that students learned to teach thirty years ago and how they learn to teach today. Goodlad compared his findings with those reported by James Conant (1963). Both found that teacher education involved some sort of a social-foundations component, a component dealing with how children develop and learn as they grow, and a component on principles of teaching. Furthermore, the course work designed to socialize students to this basic content remains essentially the same. Teacher-education students continue to take courses in social foundations of education, educational psychology, child development, methods of teaching (reading and the content areas), and student teaching, usually sequenced in this order (Goodlad 1990). Today, as before, teacher-education majors are taught to teach using research-based teaching behavior competencies, and their cooperating teachers and their university supervisors are trained to provide systematic feedback and instruction in those same behavior competencies (Cochran-Smith 1991a).

Although Goodlad (1990) did not specifically mention foreign languages, it is fairly safe to assume that the above components and sequence hold true in general for foreign language teacher-education programs as well, since they are most often specializations within secondary education.

Transforming Teacher Education in the 1990s

Despite the relatively limited impact the reform-minded reports have had on how teachers are prepared to teach, they have encouraged significant research into teacher education, which in turn has led to important changes in teacher-education programs at some institutions. Two major changes in the ways that some students are prepared for teaching are (1) a shift toward a more socially oriented knowledge base in which students are exposed to a more critical perspective on language, literacy, technology, and pedagogy, and (2) the development of collaborative student-teacher experiences in which students learn to critique existing teaching and schooling practices as they learn to teach in schools. In this paper, we highlight both efforts, first through the introduction of the collaborative resonance model of teacher education, and second, through a general discussion of the major components of study for all teachers that follows from the features and goals of the collaborative resonance model. We believe that the knowledge base for teaching should prepare students for field experiences and student teaching and that what happens during field experiences and student teaching must be central in any discussion of reform in teacher education.

Cochran-Smith's Collaborative Resonance Model   ———

One teacher educator and researcher involved directly in the issue of transforming teacher education is Marilyn Cochran-Smith. She has argued that to effect fundamental changes in teacher education we must consider not only the knowledge base but also the ways in which university teacher educators, school practitioners, and prospective teachers relate to each other.

Cochran-Smith (1991a, 1991b) distinguishes among three models of teacher education, *the consonance model, the critical dissonance model,* and *the collaborative resonance model.* The consonance model operates under the philosophy that the university-based and field-based portions of teacher education are consistent with each other and agree upon the need to train teachers as informed decision makers, making extensive use of the literature on teacher effectiveness. The goal of this model is to improve existing practice by utilizing the teacher-education research of university researchers, but without examining and questioning the practice that exists. The vast majority of teacher-education programs in the United States currently operate under this model.

In contrast, the critical dissonance model suggests that there is a basic incongruity between prospective teachers' university training and what goes on in the schools, and deliberately sets up distinctions between the two. The major function of the university teacher-education program, then, is the critique of the status quo, the critique of existing teaching and schooling.

The third model, that of collaborative resonance, is based on what Cochran-Smith calls the "co-labor of learning communities" (1991a: 282), communities composed of university teacher educators, practicing teachers in the field, and future teachers who are students in teacher-education programs. What distinguishes this model from that of consonance is that the members of these communities work *collaboratively* to critique existing practices and to make substantive changes in the teaching and learning that occurs in schools. The goal of the collaborative resonance model is the transformation of teaching. We will argue that it is this third model that leads to fundamental changes in teacher-preparation programs and that such a model is particularly powerful as it applies to the preparation of foreign language teachers.

The collaborative resonance model, currently in operation at the University of Pennsylvania, has several features that make it a potentially powerful one for the transformation of teacher education, the first of which is collaboration, a critical requirement for this model to function. Cochran-Smith outlines various ways in which collaboration may occur, but central to collaboration is joint inquiry about teaching/learning and schooling, so that theory and practice are linked.

Another feature of the model is that the practicing teachers are chosen because they have already engaged in reforms, because they see themselves as change agents within their school communities. Cochran-Smith calls this stance, which focuses on change, "teaching against the grain" (1991a: 279). In addition, these teachers, admittedly in the minority of the profession, view themselves as inquirers who constantly ask questions about teaching and learning in their schools and work with other professionals to seek answers. These expert teachers are researchers within their own school settings, and they model this intellectual activity for the novices with whom they work. This model, then, takes into account that teachers themselves (and not just university teacher educators and outside researchers) have understandings about teaching that are valuable and that can inform teacher education. The perspective of the practicing teacher is at least as important as that of the university teacher educator.

Another feature of this model is that the university classes in methods and curriculum development are themselves focused on nontraditional instructional strategies and critical-theory-based curriculum study, moving away from the traditional transmission view of education. The university perspective thus challenges the status quo and argues for fundamental changes in classroom organization and instruction. What learners study in their university classes is reflected in what they see teachers in the field struggling to examine and to make real. Students also try out some of these alternative strategies in their placement classrooms and critique their work in both the university and the field setting.

In addition to their university course work, the student teachers work in the classrooms with these carefully selected teachers, participating in experiences and research projects that involve them in making changes in schools. So in their apprenticeships they view themselves as change agents, and in weekly seminars and journal writing they are able to reflect upon these experiences.

In this model, teaching is viewed as both a sociopolitical and an ethical-moral activity, in that it takes the perspective that the status quo in schools (and in society) should *not* be maintained; that teachers should be change agents working for both better schools and a more just and truly democratic society. In thinking of this model from the specific perspective of foreign language teaching, we believe that there is in collaborative resonance the possibility both for challenging and changing traditional pedagogy and for including in foreign language classes examples of the cultural and social diversity that reflects the reality of our country. For these reasons, we advocate the model of collaborative resonance as the appropriate one to use for reform in teacher education in general and foreign language teacher education in particular. We will now detail some of the specific aspects of a knowledge base for the nontraditional instructional and critical-theory-oriented curriculum study that Cochran-Smith advocates.

Components of Study for Teachers "against the Grain"

Studies in Human Development

The first essential kind of knowledge that teachers need is that of human development. In order to work effectively with children and adolescents, teachers need to understand how learners grow and develop, not only physically but socially, emotionally, and psychologically as well. Of necessity, views of human development present trends rather than specific instances, but knowledge of general features assists teachers in making sense of individual cases.

One of the most important aspects of human development for teachers to know is that of cognitive development, that is, how it is that humans learn and come to understand their world (and, therefore, by extension, how it is that we should teach). An examination of classroom practices in the majority of elementary and secondary schools in the United States (Goodlad 1983, 1990) might lead to the conclusion that we learn by being told what we need to know, that is, through lecture and demonstration and guided practice, through the transmission model of education (Cummins 1986). We might also believe that children and adolescents learn by having content broken down into myriad assumed components, so that bits of content are organized hierarchically or sequentially and are taught compartmentally, the assumption being that the teaching of each isolated part will add up to a coherent whole. This tends to be the view of teaching and learning that is offered by most educational psychology courses and instructional courses that make extensive use of the research on teacher effectiveness. This view of learning, however, which has formed part of the basis for commonly accepted methods in foreign language teaching and which continues to influence many foreign language educators, has been called into question from at least two other perspectives that we would like to consider briefly here.

The first is the constructivist view of learning, associated most closely with the developmental psychologist Jean Piaget. According to this view, rather than learning by being told and shown, people learn by doing for themselves. Learners are active in and responsible for constructing their own knowledge. From the beginning of life, learners act upon the world, formulating questions, researching answers, making hypotheses and predictions, testing out their ideas, manipulating objects, investigating their world, and imagining and inventing. In classrooms, it is the learners, *of whatever age,* who must construct their knowledge; no one else can do it for them. Learners must come to their own understandings and alter their understandings as they continue to act in the world (Duckworth 1987; Fosnot 1989). According to this perspective, teachers act as mediators for learners, not as dispensers of information (Fosnot 1989).

A somewhat different perspective, but one that also makes the learner active rather than passive, is what some might call the social interactionist perspective on learning, as exemplified by Lev Vygotsky (1978). While acknowledging the activity of the learner, Vygotsky's focus is on the interaction between the individual and others with whom she or he may be working. For Vygotsky learning occurs as individuals work in collaboration with others to solve problems before they work on similar problems alone. Because some students are more knowledgeable or expert in certain areas than others, individuals move beyond their present understandings as they collaborate with those more expert than they. The teacher may be one of the people in this expert position, as may peers. Vygotsky uses the term "the zone of proximal development" to define the student's potential for cognitive development, that is, what that person is able to do and understand when participating with others rather than working alone.

Each of these two positions emphasizes the active nature of learning, that learning requires involvement with people, materials, and ideas. Individuals preparing to be teachers need to work with these conceptions of learning and use them to examine and critique existing assumptions, including assumptions about the teaching and learning of foreign languages (Faltis 1990).

We would also suggest, as have others (e.g., Bayer 1989; Duckworth 1987; Fosnot 1989), that there is a need to examine the ways that we teach in our teacher-education programs. Many critics of existing teaching practices in university classes assert that adults learn most effectively when they, too, are actively involved in their learning, rather than when they are sitting through endless lectures and memorizing material to be written down on examinations.

Another aspect of human development that needs to be emphasized is that of language development or language acquisition. In the last twenty-five years, child-language-acquisition researchers have discredited the behaviorist position on language acquisition (as exemplified by Skinner 1957), rejecting the notion that language acquisition is essentially a process of imitation and reinforcement of gradually more accurate representations of adult models of language. Rather it is generally accepted that children are the creative constructors of their native language, cognitively generating and revising hypotheses about how it works (Dale 1976; Lindfors 1987).

But it also has become clear that language acquisition is a profoundly social phenomenon. Children acquire language as they use it in social interactions with others in order to accomplish their purposes in the world. They develop linguistic and communicative competence as they use language with others (adults and other children) who attend to their messages, respond to what they are trying to do, and provide linguistic data that they are able to use in their construction of language (Dyson and Genishi 1991; Genishi and Dyson 1984; Lindfors 1987).

It is also important, when considering language acquisition, to acknowledge that there is important cross-cultural variation in the ways that children are "taught" language. All normal children acquire their native languages, yet not all adults interact with children in the ways that the mainstream Anglo-American caretaker and motherese literature suggests that they do. (See, for example, Heath 1983; Ochs and Schiefflen 1983.) In addition, there is significant variation in what constitutes communicative competence within one's own speech community, since rules for successful participation in community life vary significantly across social and cultural groups (see, for example, Heath 1983; Philips 1983).

As in the case of cognitive development, an examination of language-acquisition research has led many researchers to critique existing instructional practices, to advocate significant changes in the interaction that occurs in classrooms, and to take cultural variation into account in planning for interaction. This is true for both native language and second language settings (Cazden 1989; Cazden et al. 1972; Edelsky et al. 1990; Ellis 1986; Heath 1983; Lindfors 1987). Given the growing number of settings involving Foreign Languages in the

Elementary Schools (FLES), this information has become increasingly influential in curriculum planning and instructional delivery (Met 1985). At the secondary level of foreign language instruction, comparisons of underlying similarities between first and second language acquisition (Ellis 1986; Long and Larsen-Freeman 1990) have led to changes in instructional strategies. We believe that prospective teachers need to struggle with these ideas throughout their course work and field experiences.

Multiculturalism

The chances are great that most prospective teachers will be placed in a school and community that is both linguistically and culturally diverse. Prospective teachers are more than likely to encounter African-American students, the largest ethnic minority group in the United States, and Hispanic students, the largest language minority group. Following Hispanics, the next-largest language minority population are students of Asian and Indo-Chinese origin; for example, Chinese from Taiwan, Hong Kong, and more recently mainland China; Korean; Filipino; Vietnamese; Cambodian; Khmer; Hmong; and Laotian.

Many children of Hispanic, Asian, and Indo-Chinese origins are reared through the native language of their parents and caregivers and maintain their cultural ways throughout their schooling experiences. Children from all three groups make up the largest number of learners of English as a second language in school. The population of students aged 5–17 for whom English is a second language is estimated to be between 2.6 and 3.0 million nationwide. The number is conservatively expected to swell to 6 million by the year 2020 (Pallas et al. 1989).

There are also many and various Native American communities in Alaska and throughout the other forty-nine states. Increasing numbers of Native American children are attending nonreservation public schools, particularly in urban areas.

Given the diversity that exists in the United States and the fact that the numbers of ethnic and language minority students are increasing rapidly, it is essential that prospective teachers gain knowledge of and experience in multicultural education through their course work and during their field experiences. The overall purpose of multicultural education is to help students gain cultural (ethnic, language, and gender) consciousness and to infuse cultural knowledge and practice in multilingual, multicultural classrooms through the study and practice of strategies that facilitate intergroup communication, integration, and cooperation (DeVillar and Faltis 1991; Faltis 1988). Multicultural education draws primarily from sociocultural research and emphasizes the importance of addressing head-on the issues of (1) racism and sexism in content and materials, (2) tracking and segregation in the classroom and at the school-site level, and (3) the roles of social interaction in the classroom (Nieto 1992).

The most conventional way of preparing prospective teachers for working in culturally and linguistically diverse settings is by requiring them, preferably toward the end of their program, to complete at least one course in multicultural education. One advantage of having a specific course on multiculturalism in education is that the instructor can tie together issues of culture, ethnicity, and gender, as these show up in the classroom, with the more general topics of inequality due to racism, classism, and sexism.

Another way of introducing prospective teachers to multiculturalism is to infuse multicultural topics throughout all courses having to do with teaching and schooling in general, including foreign language and foreign language education courses. This approach means that students are being asked to address multi-cultural issues in more specific contexts, and thus are being given examples and teaching strategies that are connected to various areas of interest. A variation of this approach is to offer a specific course on teaching in multicultural contexts, while at the same time encouraging all teacher-education faculty to address multicultural topics throughout their courses and during practicum experiences. This approach aims toward a more comprehensive preparation for teaching in culturally and linguistically diverse settings.

There are a number of ways to prepare prospective teachers to deal with culturally and linguistically diverse settings. Merino, Minnis, and Quintanar (1989) present three models. The first, labeled the *competency model,* focuses on teaching about minority cultures in the United States with a relatively limited emphasis on learning styles, values, customs, and traditions of a few major underrepresented ethnic groups. We believe that this model too narrowly defines the parameters of multicultural education, and that it tends to ignore individual and group variation, resulting in the creation of new stereotypes. In the case of foreign languages, it tends to separate languages from cultures. And there is no guarantee that successfully completing a course and the knowledge, attitudes, and skills gained from it will result in substantive changes in classroom practice. Furthermore, it may be unreasonable to ask all faculty members in teacher education to share the knowledge base addressed in this approach.

A second model, labeled *teacher as ethnographer,* advocates preparing teachers to conduct case studies and to use ethnographic techniques to generate descrip-tions and interpretations of "cultural scenes" (Spradley 1979). The case studies then serve as the basis for curriculum development and adaptations in instruc-tional strategies to build on the learning preferences and needs of the children and adolescents in the classroom. Nieto (1992) describes ways to use case studies to illustrate the "mosaic of the student body in U.S. classrooms" (p. 5). One of the main advantages of this approach is that beginning teachers learn an inquiry strategy to investigate any cultural group they may encounter in their teaching experiences. Moreover, this approach to learning about culture is transferrable to all teacher-education classes and can be incorporated as an essential assignment. It is challenging, however, because of the time it requires for students to learn ethnographic and case-study methodology.

A third model, labeled the *selective eclectic introspective model,* assumes that teachers must become reflective practitioners. The model is selective and eclectic because, while it draws primarily from studies in educational anthropology, it also incorporates research and methods from other disciplines, with an emphasis on what is known about effective ways of infusing culture into the teaching process as well as providing tools for investigating the background of students. It is introspective because student teachers must assess themselves and the way that they are planning to develop their own cultural consciousness, knowledge, and abilities. Students develop a portfolio in which they place a series of short self-assessment pieces designed to have them reflect about their own background and experiences with cultural diversity. The culminating project is to develop an action plan in consultation with the instructor on ways to continue developing their cultural consciousness and knowledge in the coming year. We advocate this approach because it treats students as professionals who can make decisions about engineering their own development as teachers. It also models a kind of assessment that we feel teachers should incorporate in their assessment repertoire.

Whatever approach is taken to preparing prospective teachers for multiculturalism in education, it is essential that students have opportunities to question and reflect, to have modeled for them what we expect them to become as teachers.

School Law and Policy Issues

Prospective teachers need to know their legal obligations and responsibilities to children, parents, and the school. Knowing about school law and policy empowers teachers to support the kind of classroom and school climate reflected in the collaborative resonance model. More specifically, this knowledge enables teachers to advocate for students and their families on several important issues. First, it provides teachers with the legal rationale to protect the rights of students who need special instructional services. For example, teachers who understand Public Law 94-142, which provides for the least restrictive environment for special-education students, know that they are responsible for accommodating students by making sure that the school is doing everything possible to meet these learners' needs.

Another important law that advocates for students with special needs is Section 1703(f) of the Equal Education Opportunity Act of 1974. This law requires a school with students limited in English proficiency to "take appropriate action to overcome language barriers that impede equal participation by its students in its instructional programs" (Public Law 93-380, 20 U.S.C. Sections 1701-1720). Knowing about this law provides teachers with the legal support to ensure that students limited in English proficiency are provided with language programs such as bilingual education and English as a second language (Cazden 1986).

Second, knowing about school law and policies prepares students to safeguard against censorship of reading series, controversial books, movies, and other forms of communication. Censorship in schools is a complex legal and social matter that often involves religious and moral beliefs (Burress 1989; Moffett 1988; Noble 1990; West 1988). In some cases, it may even concern language use. For example, prohibiting students who are learning English as a second language to use their native language in school is a form of censorship. In the collaborative resonance model, prospective teachers learn about censorship and about laws and policies that protect against it. Moreover, they can address the issue of censorship through case studies in collaboration with their practicing teacher during the student-teaching experience (Moffett 1988).

Third, knowing about school law and policy provides teachers with an understanding of the kinds of changes and innovations they are entitled to advocate as teachers within the given school organization. In the collaborative resonance model of teacher education, prospective teachers are given the challenge to transform the traditional classroom setting into a new climate for teaching and learning. Thus, it is important for prospective teachers to learn about how they can become actively involved in the political and social structure of school governance so that they can advocate for the changes that are necessary to transform their classrooms into active social learning environments. This knowledge is particularly critical for prospective foreign language teachers who wish to use authentic communicative and acquisition-rich language teaching within school environments that emphasize traditional approaches to language teaching.

Fourth, knowing about school law and policy enables teachers to take stands for and against certain practices, such as corporal punishment, retention, sexual harassment, search and seizure, and firearms on campus. Teachers need to be well informed about what they can and cannot do when a student transgresses a school policy. Moreover, they need to learn how to advocate for change when a school policy discriminates against certain students or conflicts with basic human rights. For example, we know of a teacher who placed students who did something wrong in class (talked to a neighbor, turned in a paper late, etc.) into a makeshift cage for a certain period of time. Although the cage was large enough so that the student did not suffer any physical damage, this practice is unjust, cruel, and unusual punishment, because no student deserves to be incarcerated in school. As advocates for children, we would teach prospective teachers how to address this kind of problem legally within the school system.

Helping prospective teachers become advocates for students and their families is a central goal of the collaborative resonance model of teacher education. Teachers who teach against the grain are constantly confronted with pressure from the status quo to think and behave in ways that conserve tradition. In summary, we are concerned with preparing teachers who question what schools have been doing, who work toward transforming their own classrooms, and who are equipped with legal and policy knowledge to support their continued development as practicing teachers.

Literacy Development in Childhood and Adolescence

In the last twenty years, research in children's acquisition of literacy (both reading and writing) has paralleled the work done in oral language acquisition. This research has demonstrated that, much as they creatively construct their oral language, children also figure out how the written language works. Children become readers and writers by experimenting with the written language, by using reading and writing to accomplish some of their purposes in the world, and by seeing demonstrations of literacy by those around them (Baghban 1984; Weaver 1988). Children develop working hypotheses about how reading and writing work (Chomsky 1971; Read 1975; Sulzby 1992). Their hypotheses change over time (Bissex 1980; Doake 1985; Ferreiro 1990; Harste et al. 1984; Sulzby 1992), as their understandings and renditions come closer to those of adults. But it is the children who are in control of their understandings, much as they are in control of their own learning in general (Goodman 1990).

Researchers also have discovered that literacy acquisition is a social phenomenon. Children experiment with and come to understand written language because they are engaged in literacy activities with other people and because others around them, both adults and children, demonstrate some of the uses of reading and writing (Baghban 1984; Daiute 1990; Dyson 1989). There is evidence of the social construction of literacy not only for mainstream children but for children from culturally and linguistically diverse backgrounds, including children in second language as well as first language learning situations. (See Edelsky 1986; Heath 1983; Hudelson 1989; Hudelson and Serna 1991.)

In school settings, researchers have discovered that classrooms can be places where children are engaged in reading and writing for multiple purposes (Calkins 1986; Hansen 1987; Peyton and Staton in press) and where children develop as readers and writers as they work with others (Dyson 1989; Hansen 1987); that children are able to reflect upon and make changes in pieces that they are writing, that is, engage in the craft of writing (Calkins 1986; Graves 1983); that children are able to engage in in-depth study of literature, both sharing the meanings that they have constructed and taking into account the meanings constructed by others (Eeds and Wells 1989); and that children are able to raise questions they want the answers to and use literacy as a means both to answer their questions and to articulate what they have learned (Altwerger et al. in press).

What has emerged from this work is substantive documentation about children's engagement with and learning of literacy through participation in such innovative instructional practices as dialogue journals; writers' workshop; reading with predictable, natural texts; literature study in many forms; and the utilization of thematic units to investigate topics, to name just a few. This documentation is now beginning to occur not only for native English speakers but for learners in bilingual and second language classrooms as well (Edelsky 1991; Freeman and Freeman 1992; Hudelson 1989; Peyton and Staton in press). Thus there are significant implications of this literature for foreign language teachers as well as for teachers in general.

As a result of this work, teachers themselves are carrying out research on their students' learning and reporting on it, thus learning about current research, theory, and innovative practice from each other (Bissex and Bullock 1987; Glover and Sheppard 1989). The teacher-researcher movement is especially strong among professionals involved in native and second language and literacy work and could easily move into foreign language classrooms as innovative teachers seek answers to questions about their own teaching and their students' learning.

At the secondary school level, too, there have been significant changes in our understandings both of the active roles that learners play in their own literacy and of the importance of the social context. Emig's now classic study (1971) of high school students' writing processes has influenced other research that has continued to demonstrate that learners employ various strategies as they work to express themselves in written language (see, for example, Perl 1979). The work of other writing researchers has demonstrated the importance of peer and teacher response to writers' efforts, with response focusing initially and primarily on the content of the work, putting off until final editing stages concern for surface level correctness. (See, for example, Freedman 1992; Freedman et al. 1987; Gere 1987; Sperling 1991.)

In reading, work in schema theory has demonstrated that readers make extensive use of prior knowledge (both content knowledge and knowledge of rhetorical patterns) when they are constructing meaning from text (Anderson and Pearson 1984; Mandler and Johnson 1977; Meyer 1975; Weaver 1988). Reading is not simply a process of understanding the writer's message, but a transaction between the text and the reader, who brings a background of prior knowledge to the text and constructs meaning from it, whether the text is an expository one or a piece of literature (Rosenblatt 1989). These views of literacy have influenced literacy practices in secondary schools.

In the study of literature, more attention has been given to encouraging varied reader responses to texts (Farrell and Squire 1990). There has been a focus on writing as process rather than strictly as product, so that learners are encouraged to craft their writing pieces, whether they are for English or another class. Across curricular areas, more attention has been paid to using literacy in the exploration of content (Perl and Wilson 1986). Teacher researchers are active at the secondary level (Schecter and Ramirez 1991). Again, work has been carried out in native language, second language, and even some foreign language settings. (See Barnett 1989; Bernhardt 1991; Grabe 1991; Raimes 1991; and Rigg 1991 for recent reviews of the literature.)

In addition to teaching strategies that reflect the perspective on literacy delineated here, there is also concern that assessment of student work reflect this view, which means a movement away from standardized testing and evaluation to an emphasis on assessment that is an integral and ongoing part of classroom work. One example of this kind of assessment is portfolios, where students collect their own work over time and choose the pieces that they consider the best for evaluation by the teacher (Gomez et al. 1991). Very often, too, learners are involved in self-assessment of their own work, reflecting, for example, on their preparation for and participation in various activities (Fournier et al. in press;

Peterson and Eeds 1990). In addition, teacher observation and documentation of student behavior and work within the contexts of the classroom become valued tools in assessment (Goodman et al. 1989). The discussions of classroom-based assessment focus on the educator's ongoing role as an informed observer, on the need to assess student learning by utilizing what learners are actually doing in specific classroom settings.

For educators who adopt the perspective that learners actively construct literacy and knowledge within a framework of social interaction, computer technology becomes an issue when considering the choice and utilization of computers. Teachers operating from the frameworks just described would not choose to use computers for practice on isolated skills, even though those kinds of software predominate in the market (both in the native language and in second and foreign languages). Rather, they would choose to use technology in ways that allow learners to construct their own knowledge and to do this in transactions with others. Word processing is one example of the kind of technology that fits this perspective. Computer networks, in which learners, often separated by time and space, write and respond to each other, are another example. Cummins and Sayers (1990) have described such a project *(De Orilla a Orilla),* which involves pairing classrooms from geographically separate locations (e.g., the United States, Puerto Rico, Argentina, English- and French-speaking Canada, and Mexico), allowing learners to write electronic mail messages to each other as they plan joint projects. They use word processing to plan, compose, revise, and edit their texts, and they use telecommunications to send their writings quickly to distant readers.

We contend that prospective teachers need to understand the constructivist and social interactionist research in literacy acquisition and development and need to be able to utilize the instructional strategies that come out of that research. They will best learn to utilize these strategies by participating in them in their university classes (which means that university faculty must engage their students in activities such as dialogue journals, literature study using multicultural literature, personal narrative writing, study of meaningful content through using literacy across the curriculum, and the like) and practice them in field placements and student teaching.

Curriculum and Organization for Teaching

For all prospective teachers, knowledge of curriculum and curriculum development is crucial. But there are many different definitions of the term and perspectives on what it means to develop curriculum and to organize oneself to teach. We believe that work in this area should examine a variety of definitions and perspectives and should challenge learners to examine their assumptions about how, what, and why to teach.

The traditional or conservative view of curriculum (Reynolds 1989) takes the current-skills-and-objectives-based approach to curriculum as a given and focuses on rearranging these sequences of skills and improving methods of delivery of content in order to achieve a higher level of content mastery. In this prescriptive, technocratic view, the work of teachers is to make delivery of content more efficient, through careful specification of learning objectives, a linear sequence of learning activities designed to teach to those objectives, the utilization of textbooks as the basis for content and for sequencing of the learning activities, and an evaluation of the learning of each objective. This approach to teaching, in evidence in schools since the nineteenth century (Finkelstein 1971; Shannon 1990), views the teacher as a skillful manager of learning who brings about high levels of student achievement (Fenstermacher and Soltis 1992).

Over the years, many theorists and practitioners have critiqued this traditionalist view of curriculum and proposed alternatives that have taken more of the constructivist and social interactionist views of learning discussed earlier in this paper. (See Shannon 1990 for a discussion of multiple alternative views.) One of the more recent alternatives has been presented by the critical theorists, whose basic theoretical premise is that schools, as they exist today, play an important role (through both the overt and the hidden curriculum) in the reproduction or maintenance of an unjust, unequal society (Apple 1982; Reynolds 1989). The aim of current schooling is to take control of the thinking of both teachers and learners, so that the status quo is perpetuated and not challenged. Critical theorists maintain that positivist, scientific, and technological approaches to the management of schools contribute to student and teacher passivity and acceptance of current realities, both in school and in society at large. They believe that schools should be organized to encourage teachers and learners to learn about themselves and their communities, to make connections between themselves and the operations of the larger social structure, and to use their knowledge to work for justice and equality (Shannon 1990: 157). According to some educators, a potential exists for collaboration between critical theorists and the proponents of constructivist and social interactionist positions on language and literacy learning (Edelsky 1991).

Classrooms and lessons organized from this critical perspective are distinctly different from those operating from other positions. Rather than sitting passively, learners are active in asking questions and seeking answers. Instead of teachers controlling all the topics or content, learners have some input into the topics to be studied. Efforts are made to move away from the domination of the textbook in the classroom. Multiple sources of information are used. Rather than the teacher exercising sole control over who talks and the order in which individuals talk, an effort is made for a balance of control between learners and teachers. Instead of working individually, learners work in pairs and small groups and there is a flexibility in grouping. Attempts are made to integrate content into units or topics. Assessment, too, needs to be viewed from a different perspective, so that it reflects process as well as product and so that the learners, as well as the teachers, are involved in the process. (See Walsh 1991 and Freeman and Freeman 1992 for examples of actual classroom practice.)

Practicum Experiences

In her collaborative resonance model, Cochran-Smith has emphasized the critical nature of students' field experiences and student teaching placements. We know that student teachers tend to be socialized into teaching by the professionals with whom they interact in field settings. In addition, teachers have a tendency to teach either the way that they were taught or the way that the teachers with whom they carry out field experiences teach. If we want to influence both students' views of the roles, stances, and behaviors of teachers and their understandings of nontraditional, nontextbook-dominated pedagogies, it is vital that the sites for field experiences reflect these perspectives. We believe that it is essential that students' field experiences be with teachers who work from a worldview of critique and change and who utilize innovative instructional strategies that reflect the ideas we have delineated in our knowledge base. In addition, it is absolutely essential that the practitioners have outstanding abilities in the languages that they are teaching. Student teachers must have excellent language models as well as pedagogical models.

Given the increasing social, cultural, and linguistic diversity of elementary and secondary school classrooms, it is absolutely imperative that the teachers with whom students work demonstrate an understanding of and appreciation for a variety of cultures, as exemplified by the ways in which they interact with culturally diverse students. Teachers also need to exhibit high expectations with regard to students' potential for achievement, regardless of background and socioeconomic situation. Ideally, too, exemplary teachers would demonstrate that they are able to incorporate aspects from multiple cultures into the content of their classes, being careful not to limit their inclusions to examples from the culture(s) of the language they teach (Faltis and Merino 1992).

Conclusion

In this chapter we have espoused the adoption of the collaborative resonance model in teacher education. We believe that this model is especially appropriate because of its collaborative nature and because it recognizes the need for university teacher educators and outstanding classroom practitioners to work together with prospective teachers to transform teacher education and our schools. We hope that this chapter will promote dialogue and a renewed spirit of collaboration among those involved in the critical undertaking of preparing elementary and secondary education teachers.

References, Redefining Basic Teacher Education

Altwerger, Bess, V. Resta, and G. Killar. In press. *The Theme Cycle: Creating Contexts for Whole Language Strategies.* Portsmouth, NH: Heinemann.

Anderson, Richard, and David Pearson. 1984. "A Schema-Theoretic View of Basic Processes in Reading Instruction," pp. 255–92 in P. David Pearson, Rebecca Barr, Michael L. Kamil, and Peter Mosenthal, eds., *The Handbook of Reading Research.* White Plains, NY: Longman.

Apple, Michael. 1982. *Education and Power.* Boston: Ark.

Baghban, Marcia. 1984. *Our Daughter Learns to Read and Write.* Newark, DE: International Reading Association.

Barnett, Marva. 1989. *More Than Meets the Eye.* New York: Prentice Hall.

Bayer, Anne. 1989. *Collaborative Apprenticeship Learning: Language and Thinking across the Curriculum, K–12.* Mountain View, CA: Mayfield.

Bernhardt, Elizabeth B. 1991. *Reading Development in a Second Language: Theoretical, Empirical and Classroom Perspectives.* Norwood, NJ: Ablex.

Bissex, Glenna. 1980. *GYNS at Work: A Child Learns to Write and Read.* Cambridge, MA: Harvard Univ. Press.

————, and William Bullock. 1987. *Seeing for Ourselves.* Portsmouth, NH: Heinemann.

Burress, Lee. 1989. *Battle of the Books: Literacy Censorship in the Public Schools, 1950–1985.* Metuchen, NJ: Scarecrow.

Calkins, Lucy. 1986. *The Art of Teaching Writing.* Portsmouth, NH: Heinemann.

Cazden, Courtney B. 1986. "ESL Teachers as Advocates for Children," pp. 9–21 in Pat Rigg and D. Scott Enright, eds., *Children and ESL: Integrating Perspectives.* Washington, DC: TESOL.

————. 1989. *Classroom Discourse.* Portsmouth, NH: Heinemann.

————, Vera John, and Dell Hymes. 1972. *The Functions of Language in the Classroom.* New York: Teachers College Press.

Chomsky, Carol. 1971. "Write First, Read Later." *Childhood Education* 47: 196–301.

Cochran-Smith, Marilyn. 1991a. "Learning to Teach against the Grain." *Harvard Educational Review* 61: 279–310.

————. 1991b. "Reinventing Student Teaching." *Journal of Teacher Education* 42: 104–18.

College Entrance Examination Board. 1983. *Academic Preparation for College: What Students Need to Know and Be Able to Do.* New York: CEEB.

Conant, James. 1963. *The Education of American Teachers.* New York: McGraw-Hill.

Cummins, Jim. 1986. "Empowering Minority Students: A Framework for Intervention." *Harvard Educational Review* 56: 18–36.

————, and Dennis Sayers. 1990. "Education 2001: Learning Networks and Educational Reform," pp. 1–24 in Christian Faltis and Robert DeVillar, eds., *Language Minority Students and Computers.* Binghamton, NY: Haworth.

Daiute, Collette. 1990. "The Role of Play in Writing Development." *Research in the Teaching of English* 24: 4–47.

Dale, Philip. 1976. *Language Development: Structure and Function.* 2d ed. New York: Holt, Rinehart and Winston.

DeVillar, Robert A., and Christian Faltis. 1991. *Computers and Cultural Diversity: Restructuring for School Success.* Albany: State Univ. of New York Press.

Doake, David. 1985. "Reading-like Behavior: Its Role in Learning to Read," pp. 55–71 in Angela Jagger and M. Trika Smith-Burke, eds., *Observing the Language Learner.* Newark, DE: International Reading Association.

Duckworth, Eleanor. 1987. *The Having of Wonderful Ideas and Other Essays on Teaching and Learning.* New York: Teachers College Press.

Dyson, Anne. 1989. *Multiple Worlds of Child Writers: Friends Learning to Write.* New York: Teachers College Press.

————, and Celia Genishi. 1991. *Visions of Children as Language Users: Research on Language and Language Education in Early Childhood.* Berkeley, CA: Center for the Study of Writing.

Edelsky, Carole. 1986. *Writing in a Bilingual Program: Había una vez.* Norwood, NJ: Ablex.

————. 1991. *With Literacy and Justice for All.* Philadelphia: Falmer.

————, Bess Altwerger, and Barbara Flores. 1990. *Whole Language: What's the Difference?* Portsmouth, NH: Heinemann.

Education Commission of the States. 1983. *Action for Excellence: A Comprehensive Plan to Improve our Nation's Schools*. Denver, CO: The Commission.

Eeds, Maryann, and Deborah Wells. 1989. "Grand Conversations: An Exploration of Meaning Construction in Literature Study Groups." *Research in the Teaching of English* 23: 4–29.

Ellis, Rod. 1986. *Understanding Second Language Acquisition*. New York: Oxford Univ. Press.

Emig, Janet. 1971. *The Composing Processes of Twelfth Graders*. Urbana, IL: National Council of Teachers of English.

Faltis, Christian. 1988. "Cultural Consciousness and Instruction in the Heterogeneous Classroom," pp. 27–32 in Carolee Gunn, ed., *Proceedings of the Holmes Group Far West Meeting. University of Colorado, Boulder*. Salt Lake City: Univ. of Utah.

————. 1990. "Spanish for Native Speakers: Freirian and Vygotskian Perspectives." *Foreign Language Annals* 23: 117–27.

————, and Barbara Merino. 1992. "Toward a Definition of Exemplary Teachers in Bilingual Multicultural School Settings," pp. 277–99 in Raymond Padilla and Alfredo Benavides, eds., *Critical Perspectives on Bilingual Education Research*. Tempe, AZ: Bilingual Press.

Farrell, Edmund, and James Squire. 1990. *Transactions with Literature: A Fifty-Year Perspective*. Urbana, IL: National Council of Teachers of English.

Fenstermacher, Gary, and Jonas Soltis. 1992. *Approaches to Teaching*. 2d ed. New York: Teachers College Press.

Ferreiro, Emilia. 1990. "Literacy Development: Psychogenesis," pp. 12–25 in Yetta Goodman, ed., *How Children Construct Literacy: Piagetian Perspectives*. Newark, DE: International Reading Association.

Finkelstein, Barbara. 1971. "Governing the Young: Teacher Behavior in American Primary Schools, 1820–1880." Ph.D. diss., Teachers College, Columbia Univ., New York.

Fosnot, Catherine. 1989. *Enquiring Teachers, Enquiring Learners*. New York: Teachers College Press.

Fournier, Julia, Beth Lansdowne, Zulema Pastenes, Pamela Steen, and Sarah Hudelson. In press. "Learning with, about and from Children: Life in a Bilingual Second Grade," in Celia Genishi, ed., *Ways of Assessing Children and Curriculum*. New York: Teachers College Press.

Freedman, Sarah. 1992. "Outside-In and Inside-Out: Peer Response Groups in Two Ninth Grade Classrooms." *Research in the Teaching of English* 26: 71–107.

————, with Carolyn Greenleaf and Melanie Sperling. 1987. *Response to Student Writing*. Research Report no. 23. Urbana, IL: National Council of Teachers of English.

Freeman, Yvonne, and David Freeman. 1992. *Whole Language for Second Language Learners*. Portsmouth, NH: Heinemann.

Genishi, Celia, and Anne Dyson. 1984. *Language Assessment in the Early Years*. Norwood, NJ: Ablex.

Gere, Anne. 1987. *Writing Groups: History, Theory and Implications*. Carbondale: Southern Illinois Univ. Press.

Glover, Mary, and Linda Sheppard. 1989. *Not on Your Own: The Power of Learning Together*. New York: Scholastic.

Gomez, Mary Louise, M. Elizabeth Graue, and Marianne N. Bloch. 1991. "Reassessing Portfolio Assessment: Rhetoric and Reality." *Language Arts* 68: 620–28.

Goodlad, John I. 1983. *A Place Called School: Prospects for the Future*. New York: McGraw-Hill.

————. 1990. *Teachers for Our Nation's Schools*. San Francisco: Jossey-Bass.

Goodman, Kenneth, Yetta Goodman, and Wendy Hood. 1989. *The Whole Language Evaluation Handbook*. Portsmouth, NH: Heinemann.

Goodman, Yetta. 1990. *How Children Construct Literacy: Piagetian Perspectives*. Newark, DE: International Reading Association.

Grabe, William. 1991. "Current Developments in Second Language Reading Research." *TESOL Quarterly* 25: 375–406.

Graves, Donald. 1983. *Writing: Teachers and Children at Work*. Portsmouth, NH: Heinemann.

Hansen, Jane. 1987. *When Writers Read*. Portsmouth, NH: Heinemann.

Harste, Jerome, Virginia Woodward, and Carolyn Burke. 1984. *Language Stories and Literacy Lessons*. Portsmouth, NH: Heinemann.

Heath, Shirley Brice. 1983. *Ways with Words: Language, Life and Work in Communities and Classrooms*. New York: Cambridge Univ. Press.

Hiple, David. 1987. "A Progress Report on the ACTFL Proficiency Guidelines, 1982–1986," pp. 5–25 in Heidi Byrnes and Michael Canale, eds., *Defining and Developing Proficiency: Guidelines, Implementations and Concepts*. ACTFL Foreign Language Education Series, vol. 17. Lincolnwood, IL: National Textbook.

Holmes Group. 1986. "Tomorrow's Schools: A Report of the Holmes Group." East Lansing, MI: Holmes Group.

Hudelson, Sarah. 1989. *Write On: Children Writing in ESL*. New York: Prentice Hall.

————, and Irene Serna. 1991. "Mira, teacher, escribí mi nombre en inglés: Beginning to Add On English Literacy in a Whole Language Bilingual Program." Paper presented at the Second Annual International Whole Language Conference, Phoenix, AZ.

Lindfors, Judith. 1987. *Children's Language and Learning*. 2d ed. New York: Prentice Hall.

Long, Michael H., and Diane Larsen-Freeman. 1991. *An Introduction to Second Language Acquisition Research*. White Plains, NY: Longman.

Mandler, Joan M., and Nancy S. Johnson. 1977. "Remembrance of Things Parsed: Story Structure and Recall." *Cognitive Psychology* 9: 111–51.

Merino, Barbara, Douglas Minnis, and Rosalinda Quintanar. 1989. "Models for Training Student Teachers for Cultural Diversity." Paper presented at meeting of the Commission for Preparing Teachers for Cultural Diversity, Davis, CA, May.

Met, Miriam. 1985. "Decisions! Decisions! Decisions: Foreign Language in the Elementary School." *Foreign Language Annals* 18: 469–73.

Meyer, Bonnie J. F. 1975. *The Organization of Prose and Its Effects on Memory*. Amsterdam, Neth.: North Holland.

Moffett, James. 1988. *Storm in the Mountains: A Case Study of Censorship and Consciousness*. Carbondale: Southern Illinois Univ. Press.

National Commission on Excellence in Education. 1983. *A Nation at Risk: The Imperative for Educational Reform*. Washington, DC: U.S. Dept. of Education.

National Science Board. 1983. *Educating Americans for the 21st Century*. 2 vols. Washington, DC: National Science Foundation.

Nieto, Sonia. 1992. *Affirming Diversity: The Sociopolitical Context of Multicultural Education*. White Plains, NY: Longman.

Noble, William. 1990. *Bookbanning in America: Who Bans Books?—and Why?* Middlebury, VT: P. S. Eriksson.

Ochs, Elinor, and Bambi Schiefflen. 1983. *Acquiring Conversational Competence*. London, Eng.: Routledge and Kegan Paul.

Pallas, Aaron, Gary Natriello, and Edward McDill. 1989. "The Changing Nature of the Disadvantaged Population: Current Dimensions and Future Trends." *Educational Researcher* 18: 16–22.

Perl, Sondra. 1979. "The Composing Processes of Unskilled College Writers." *Research in the Teaching of English* 13: 317–36.

————, and Gloria Wilson. 1986. *Through Teachers' Eyes: Portraits of Writing Teachers at Work*. Portsmouth, NH: Heinemann.

Peterson, Ralph, and Maryann Eeds. 1990. *Grand Conversations: Literature Groups in Action*. Toronto, Ont: Scholastic TAB.

Peyton, Joy, and Jana Staton. In press. *Dialogue Journals in the Multilingual Classroom: Building Language Fluency and Writing Skills through Written Interaction*. Norwood, NJ: Ablex.

Philips, Susan. 1983. *The Invisible Culture*. White Plains, NY: Longman.

Phillips, June K. 1989. "Teacher Education: Target of Reform," pp. 11–40 in Helen S. Lepke, ed., *Shaping the Future: Challenges and Opportunities*. Report of the Northeast Conference on the Teaching of Foreign Languages. Middlebury, VT: Northeast Conference.

Raimes, Ann. 1991. "Out of the Woods: Emerging Traditions in the Teaching of Writing." *TESOL Quarterly* 25: 407–30.

Read, Charles. 1975. *Children's Categorization of Speech Sounds in English*. Urbana, IL: National Council of Teachers of English.

Reynolds, William. 1989. *Reading Curriculum Theory*. New York: Peter Lang.

Rigg, Pat. 1991. "Whole Language in TESOL." *TESOL Quarterly* 25: 521–42.

Rosenblatt, Louise. 1989. *Reading and Writing as Transaction*. Berkeley, CA: Center for the Study of Writing.

Schecter, Sandra, and R. Ramirez. 1991. *A Teacher-Research Group in Action*. Technical Report No. 50. Berkeley, CA: Center for the Study of Writing.

Shannon, Patrick. 1990. *The Struggle to Continue: Progressive Reading Instruction in the United States*. Portsmouth, NH: Heinemann.

Skinner, B. F. 1957. *Verbal Behavior*. New York: Prentice Hall.

Sperling, Melanie. 1991. *Dialogues of Deliberation: Conversation in the Teacher–Student Writing Conference*. Technical Report No. 48. Berkeley, CA: Center for the Study of Writing.

Spradley, James. 1979. *The Ethnographic Interview*. New York: Holt, Rinehart and Winston.

Sulzby, Elizabeth. 1992. "Transitions from Emergent to Conventional Writing." *Language Arts* 69: 290–97.

Vygotsky, Lev. 1978. *Mind in Society*. Edited by Michael Cole, Sylvia Scribner, Vera Steiner, and E. Souberman. Cambridge, MA: Harvard Univ. Press.

Walsh, Catharine. 1991. *Literacy as Praxis: Culture, Language and Pedagogy*. Norwood, NJ: Ablex.

Weaver, Constance. 1988. *Reading Process and Practice: From Socio-Psycholinguistics to Whole Language*. Portsmouth, NH: Heinemann.

West, Mark I. 1988. *Trust Your Children: Voices against Censorship in Children's Literature*. New York: Neal-Schuman.

Woodford, Protase. 1979. "Foreign Language Testing Background," pp. 71–77 in *President's Commission on Foreign Language and International Studies: Background Papers and Studies*. Washington, DC: U.S. Government Printing Office.

3

Second Language Education in Tomorrow's Schools

Diane J. Tedick, Constance L. Walker, Dale L. Lange,
R. Michael Paige, Helen L. Jorstad

University of Minnesota

Changing Times

To be interested and involved in language education in the 1990s means that you are in touch with several of the most vital and fascinating aspects of education today. If you are of a certain age, and if your experiences as a teacher and graduate student span a certain era, you have witnessed great growth in the field

The authors of this chapter represent the Division of Second Languages and Cultures Education of the University of Minnesota's College of Education.

Diane J. Tedick (Ph.D., The Ohio State University), is involved in the preparation of ESL and foreign language teachers. Her research interests include teacher education, second language writing and reading, and second language writing assessment. Her memberships include ACTFL, AERA, NCTE, and TESOL.

Constance L. Walker (Ph.D., University of Illinois, Urbana-Champaign) works in the preparation of teachers for ESL, bilingual, and foreign language settings. Her interests lie in minority student achievement, multicultural education, and the preparation of teachers for diverse student populations. She is a member of the AERA, NABE, and TESOL.

Dale L. Lange (Ph.D., University of Minnesota) is Associate Dean for Academic Affairs in the College of Education. He was President of ACTFL in 1980 and participated in the development of the ACTFL Provisional Guidelines for Teacher Education Programs. He is currently working on a case study of the University of Minnesota College of Education for the Holmes Group. His affiliations include ACTFL, the AERA, and the AACTE.

R. Michael Paige (Ph.D., Stanford University) is an Associate Professor of Intercultural and International Education in the Departments of Educational Policy and Administration, and Curriculum and Instruction. A professional intercultural educator / trainer since 1968, he has edited books in the field and is Training Section co-editor of the *International Journal of Intercultural Relations*. He is active in SIETAR and the Comparative and International Education Society.

Helen Jorstad (Ph.D., University of Minnesota) is Associate Professor in Second Languages and Cultures Education. She has served on the ACTFL Executive Council. Her areas of special interest are language immersion education and language education in elementary settings. Her memberships include ACTFL, the AERA, and TESOL.

of second language education—a growth that has affected foreign language teaching, bilingual education, and English as a second language (ESL) instruction as well as introduced such concepts as international education, intercultural communication, and multicultural gender-fair curriculum. Today's language educator must be attuned to these major dimensions of education in order to fully integrate the burgeoning world of cultures and languages in U.S. schools.

As faculty members, our combined experiences in language and culture education have come together in a program of teacher education and graduate professional development that serves individuals with interests in everything from international development to immersion education, with room for those with a healthy interest, for example, in the cultural content of college-level Spanish texts, the academic needs of Southeast Asian refugee students, or undergraduate students' perceptions of international teaching assistants. While we don't profess to "do it all," we have learned that our division within the College of Education, Second Languages and Cultures Education, is an apt description for what we believe to be true: There are more commonalities in the process of becoming bilingual and bicultural across national boundaries, school cultures, and individuals than was previously believed. Our experiences as language learners, teachers, administrators, teacher educators, and researchers have brought us in contact with multiple language communities in which second language and culture education takes place: high school classrooms, urban bilingual schools, Talmud Torah schools, English teaching overseas, study-abroad programs, Peace Corps training, university language classes, and preservice and inservice teacher-preparation programs. While we have developed informed and carefully constructed opinions on our own particular areas of interest, we continue to find that our perspectives coalesce consistently where the basic issues of language and culture are concerned. We find that the human-development aspect of language learning forms the nucleus around which all other decisions must rest. Our experience and judgment find us attracted to those aspects of teaching and learning that are humanistic and hermeneutic, and therefore we continue to examine language education within a larger social and political context while seeking to maintain focus on the individual learner's need for enhancement. We find ourselves intrigued by the changes in the world and in our nation that highlight the importance and need for *communication* across cultures, and we believe that our field can provide key directions for the development of successful paths toward such communication.

The essence of second language education is embodied in its attempt to join individuals together so that they might communicate across linguistic and cultural boundaries. Whether the setting is a community classroom for adult learners of ESL, a Spanish immersion first grade, a Vietnamese bilingual social studies class, or a second-year German class at a high school, it involves efforts by individuals to master some aspects of a new code and means of expression so that other, more important goals can be attained. Foreign language education in the United States has long sought to offer students exposure to and some modicum of competence in another language and culture. Bilingual education and ESL blossomed in the 1960s and 1970s as a result of several social, judicial, and legislative imperatives; the absence of global awareness and intercultural competence underscored the need, in the 1980s, for international education; the shallowness of a monocultural curriculum spawned efforts in multicultural education that bring us into the last decade of the twentieth century.

In order to examine the nature of our changing population, the ways in which schools have met the challenge of those changes, and the attention to issues of language and culture that is required to prepare our citizens effectively for a multicultural society, we must first outline several major demographic characteristics. Changes in the school-age population over the past two decades reflect changes in the racial and ethnic composition of society at large—the relative ratios of African-American, Hispanic, and Asian-American students to European-American students in today's schools have changed considerably during this period ("Here They Come" 1986; Burstein and Cabello 1989). While the general population grew a total of 11 percent between 1970 and 1980, the Hispanic population grew by 61 percent. Major urban areas report increasingly nonwhite public school populations who come to school with languages other than English. Yet the population of U.S. teachers continues to be primarily white—89.7 percent in 1986 (Burstein and Cabello 1989; Gil 1989). While only 10 percent of the 2.5 million elementary and secondary teachers in the United States represent racial minority groups, one-third of today's public school students are from minority backgrounds. The underachievement of minority students has long been documented (Coleman et al. 1966; Manuel 1930, 1965; Oakes 1988; Ogbu 1978), with 5 percent of the total school population estimated to be limited in English proficiency, providing a major challenge in several urban areas. One-third of California's public school population is nonwhite, with a large number bringing first language competence in Spanish or a Southeast Asian language (Hmong, Lao, or Vietnamese) to the classroom ("Here They Come" 1986). Cultural differences are clearly an integral component of the face of today's schools; many districts work to meet the needs of students of a variety of immigrant groups in addition to those of African-American, American Indian, Asian-American, and Hispanic students. School districts in the state of New York serve more than 100,000 students limited in English proficiency, from 85 different language backgrounds (Burstein and Cabello 1989).

As we examine more closely these dimensions of schooling that involve languages and cultures beyond English, several important elements are clear: (1) school responses to language needs of students have come about due to the recognition of cultural pluralism of a global as well as a national nature; (2) the fields of second languages and cultures education have not sprung from a common source, nor have they grown toward common goals; (3) second language education has always reflected complex political and social issues related to majority/minority relationships within the United States; (4) educational decisions with respect to the language needs of majority and minority students have not always been based on a sound linguistic or pedagogic rationale; and (5) the power of language and culture within the educational setting of U.S. schools has long gone unrecognized and unexplored.

What does this mean for the choices we make in schools that concern issues of language and culture? How has the school found itself at center stage of this drama of cultural pluralism in U.S. society? In this chapter, in an examination of second language education for majority- and minority-language students, we describe a variety of language instruction efforts in elementary and secondary schools. We examine the social and political context of second language education, outlining three fundamental issues that we believe portray the dilemmas and the challenges that second language educators face. With those issues in mind, we seek to examine some of the major efforts to change schools and their importance for second language education. We focus on school reform as it relates to teacher development and multicultural education. Our goal in this chapter is to argue for the future of second language education as an agent of change, particularly in the area of multicultural literacy. Many unresolved questions for teachers and teacher educators are presented at the end as challenges for the profession.

Cultural Pluralism—
The Basis for Second Language Education

Cultural pluralism has long been the defining feature of U.S. society. The national response to heterogeneity, however, has changed significantly. Until recently, the "melting pot" concept was the dominant ethic. Within this acculturative model, those permitted to participate fully in the economic, political, and social life of the nation had to conform to essentially Anglo-European norms and, at least in public life, had to use the English language. Such conformity undoubtedly helped unify the European immigrants, as parochial loyalties and ancient identities, so divisive in the Old World, were set aside.

The major legacy of the melting pot is the presence today of a dominant, core culture in the United States, perhaps most accurately defined as European-American in nature. Schools, as agencies of cultural transmission and institutions created by society, reflect this core culture. *Valued* knowledge, patterns of behavior, social norms, civic attitudes, and so forth are those that are taught in the schools. They are predominantly European-American.

To the degree that second languages and cultures education in the United States still operates within a melting-pot ethos, and we would submit that it does, much of it has a distinctly assimilationist emphasis. ESL and bilingual education have generally been predicated on the idea of helping nonnative speakers make the transition to the mainstream, culturally and linguistically. Their own languages and cultures have received little explicit attention or support. For the majority, second languages and cultures education has been seen more as an optional form of educational enrichment than as a learning necessity.

The undeniable appeal of the melting pot in U.S. national life has resided in its unifying power, its capacity to promote a sense of oneness among the majority of its citizens through a shared language and culture. Its crucial flaw has been its exclusivity; full economic, social, and political participation has not been permitted to certain groups of Americans, most notably the indigenous peoples and those of African, Asian, and Latino origins. Not only have they been structurally excluded, but their cultures and languages have been ignored or worse, both in terms of their contributions to the nation and in their own right. Gender, social class, exceptionality, religious background, age, and sexual orientation have also been profoundly important determinants of equality of opportunity and outcome in national life.

As Nieto (1992: 195) points out, "power, knowledge, and resources are inevitably located in the norms of the dominant cultures and languages." These subordinated groups do not possess what Bourdieu and Passeron (1977) refer to as "culture capital," the cultural and linguistic norms of the dominant group and of the schools; hence, they are at a serious disadvantage. Reviewing the research evidence of the impact of race and culture on differential school achievement, Nieto (1992: 33) concludes that "racism and other forms of discrimination play a central role in the process of educational failure." In her analysis, the structure of schooling, tracking, testing, the curriculum, pedagogy, physical structure, disciplinary policies, and limitations regarding the roles of teachers, students, and parents all contribute to less than optimal learning for these students.

The concept of a multicultural society—a society that recognizes and values its diversity, broadens its concept of core culture in the structures of schooling, and is far more inclusive of second languages and cultures—is a more recent response to cultural pluralism. Referred to by some as the "salad bowl" approach, the multicultural society seeks to promote national unity through explicit support for diversity. It emphasizes the importance of understanding and respecting our different languages and cultures. The multicultural approach emphasizes that equality of opportunity should not be determined by race, gender, sexual preference, social class, cultural origins, and other birthright characteristics. It envisions "multiculturally literate" citizens: individuals who share a common language and guiding value system, while simultaneously possessing additional language and culture skills, be they those of their home communities or others. Education in the multicultural society would promote the shared language and culture as well as the second languages and cultures. It differs from education in the melting pot by valuing cultural and linguistic diversity. It extends the core culture by replacing monoculturalism with multiculturalism. It theorizes that loyalty to the nation is furthered far more effectively by inclusivity than by exclusivity.

As we consider second language education within the construct of a multicultural society of the future, it is clear that it plays a very prominent role. But where does it fit today? How is second language education a reflection of values, choices, and goals of the dominant culture, and what are the results for U.S. elementary and secondary students?

Second Language Education
for Majority-Language Students

Majority-language speakers, individuals with English as their primary language, are exposed to second language instruction through what has traditionally been termed "foreign language education." The term *foreign language* refers to any language that is not spoken formally in the linguistic community of the speaker; this is the term usually used for programs to teach European or Asian languages in U.S. schools.

Elementary Schools

Few potential additions to elementary-school curricula have had more tenacity than the idea of introducing languages to young children rather than waiting for adolescence (Curtain and Pesola 1988). Potential program additions span a variety of models whose goals range from simple introduction of another culture in English, without the introduction of much language, through the attainment of a higher level of proficiency in the language through enrollment in a full-immersion model.

Global education often takes the form of thematic units with a global focus, e.g., global pollution, rain forests, family life changes. Language goals are extremely limited or even nonexistent in a global education program.

FLEX (Foreign Language Exploratory) programs introduce a language component, often in conjunction with a global theme. The foreign language program, however, is not continuous throughout the elementary-school span; the language may not even be taught as a regular part of the school day. A FLEX program may be a short-term enrichment for the curriculum (e.g., daily for ten weeks). At middle-school levels, FLEX sometimes takes the form of a one-year or shorter class in which students may be introduced to all the languages that will be taught at higher levels in the district. Such programs are usually required rather than elective, and older students then may select one of the languages for secondary study.

FLES (Foreign Language in Elementary School) programs are both continuous and regular. Classes are included in the school day, although they may be very short and infrequent (e.g., 15 minutes twice weekly) or longer and more frequent. The content of the FLES program is usually language arts—ordinary listening, speaking, reading, and writing activities focused on daily-life topics such as foods, feelings, greetings, numbers, and colors, to name just a few. It is assumed that today's FLES programs are articulated from grade to grade and from level to level through an entire elementary and secondary sequence, even though not all students may continue with the same language that long. This assumption may not always hold true, however.

Content-enriched FLES classes have all the characteristics of FLES, but center the curriculum on one or more regular school subjects, for example, science or geography. The best teachers in both language-arts FLES and content-enriched FLES programs use only the target language in the classroom, and students become particularly skilled in comprehension of oral and written language, although their production skills may not be as well developed.

Partial-immersion programs teach about half the day in the target language and half the day in English. Typical subjects taught in the foreign language are math, science, and social studies. Students in partial-immersion programs usually begin initial reading instruction in their native language (English).

Full-immersion programs, finally, are the most intensive of the models. Children hear only the target language all day from teachers and other personnel, although children speak English to each other at times. They learn initial reading in the second language in what are termed "early immersion" programs, beginning at kindergarten or preschool levels. Or they may be in "late immersion" programs, which do not begin at all until after initial reading skills have been developed in the native language. English is introduced gradually into the curriculum in immersion schools as language arts, and by the end of middle-school levels some regular school subjects are taught in English. There are variations on partial and full immersion in some communities where an additional immersion language is offered to the same children, or where linguistic minority children may form half the population, with half a day in English and half a day in the minority language.

For partial- and full-immersion programs, in which some or all of the regular elementary-school curriculum is a focus, teachers must be prepared as regular elementary-school teachers—but they must also have excellent foreign-language proficiency. These requirements present a dilemma for potential immersion teachers, because in most institutions, elementary education certificate programs are separate from programs that certify language teachers. Special certification programs or endorsements for immersion teachers need to be developed.

Secondary Schools

Secondary-school program offerings in foreign language, ranging from beginning to advanced study, operate within basically the same structural framework as they have for decades. Some public schools offer as little as two years of a single foreign language, while others may offer six-year sequences in two or more languages. Dandonoli (1987) reports that in 1985, 32.3 percent of students in grades 9–12 enrolled in a foreign language, 10 percent more than in 1982, and the highest percentage since 1934. She attributes this increase to the report of the President's Commission on Foreign Languages and International Studies (1979), along with such factors as the reinstitution by some states and by some colleges and universities of requirements for foreign-language study and a positive environment for language study.

Fortunately, the structural framework of secondary foreign language programs has not hindered the opportunity for individual language programs and teachers to make some significant changes in the ways in which second language learning is offered at the secondary level. The focus on proficiency as a goal for L2 instruction has encouraged the development of reasonable communicative goals for secondary students and provided for some teachers the impetus to examine their curricular and instructional practices. Our work with inservice teachers has shown us the willingness of many to emphasize the active use of the language in their classrooms for listening, speaking, reading, and writing. As they share their experiences with other language teachers, many find new ways to bring in the real world of languages, emphasizing the study of language for communicative and culture-learning purposes. As more teachers have begun to be energized within their own field and seek additional professional development, we find that they acknowledge the limitations of curricula that put second language study within a very narrow box. District and school-site efforts that encourage cooperative planning and cross-disciplinary collaboration are allowing still more integration of language study with the total curriculum. We discuss in depth the potential for such integration in our section on school reform.

Second Language Education
for Minority-Language Students

Students with English as their second language, often defined as "bilingual" or "LEP (limited English proficient)" students, are those designated as requiring specific assistance with language and/or academic development within a school program due to a home language that is not English. Although bilingual schooling, education using the first language as a medium of instruction, has existed since the earliest history of the United States (Fishman 1966), legal mandates requiring specific language assistance for LEP students are of more recent vintage (Leibowitz 1982). *Lau* v. *Nichols* (1974) had the most impact on the education of minority-language students, requiring that schools provide language instruction (either bilingual education or ESL) for those individuals with a non–English language background. The number of students eligible for special assistance with language and academic development far exceeds the number of students actually served by such programs. Significant numbers of LEP students are left to "sink or swim" in the academic ocean. Of those receiving either ESL or bilingual assistance, many do not achieve desired academic outcomes (Collier 1987, 1989). Despite efforts at providing instruction within the mainstream school setting and attempts at large-scale ESL instruction, academic underachievement for minority-language students is pervasive (Cortes 1986; Walker 1987).

Approaches to instruction for LEP students have been pedagogic in nature, within a heavy sociopolitical framework that has obscured many fundamental issues that needed to be addressed over the years. Unfortunately, traditional perspectives on language and learning have rendered a pervasive view that the primary "problem" faced by LEP students is linguistic in nature. The compensatory and remedial nature of programs serving their needs (including federally and state-funded transitional bilingual education programs) has succeeded in limiting the potential for examination of the intricate relationships between bilingualism and learning. More important, the assumption that language needs are the first "hurdle" for LEP students has often allowed for a concentration on language instruction exclusive of academic development.

Educators have been able to agree on one fundamental principle with respect to the learning needs of minority-language students: they are both academic and linguistic. The differences lie both in the precise relationship between those needs and in the determination of which needs supersede the others in emphasis (Snow 1992). The relationship between first language (L1) and second language (L2) development and academic achievement lies at the heart of any discussion of how best to educate LEP students (Collier 1987, 1989; Cummins 1981, 1984). ESL instruction is based upon the principle of rapid acquisition of the second language as a precursor to academic achievement; bilingual education argues that academic learning needs to take place in the first language so that both cognitive and academic development can occur while English is acquired as the second language.

Bilingual Education

As stated earlier, bilingual education programs have existed since the early 1800s in the United States, but the most recent North American renaissance of bilingual education occurred in the 1960s. Since 1980, funding has decreased at both federal and state levels for instruction for eligible populations, and due to both political preference and a lack of trained staff and resources, school districts choose to offer ESL instruction over programs that utilize the L1 for instruction.

Bilingual education requires instruction in the first language (and includes ESL instruction as well). While it is possible to find a history of theoretical examples of bilingual education models (Kjolseth 1976; Mackey 1970), actual implementation and practice has rendered the field one of complexity and variety. *Transitional bilingual education* is a term used to describe the most common programs, those utilizing the first language to a limited degree until proficiency in English is attained. An occasional community will seek to implement a bilingual program that has as its goal the maintenance of the first language while developing English language proficiency, but these are extremely rare (Legarreta 1977). As a result of limited federal support for the active development of bilingualism, biliteracy, and biculturalism through bilingual education programs, services to students of limited English proficiency retain a compensatory and remedial flavor.

Bilingual programs vary with respect to the amount of L1 used for instruction. Generally, in the primary grades, language arts development and beginning reading are introduced in the first language, with ESL offered as well.

Mathematics and science instruction may be offered in the first language, if teachers are bilingual and instructional materials are available. The goals of the school community for L1 and L2 development, local community attitudes and educational goals, the availability of bilingual staff, resources allocated, and the language needs of students all determine the type of bilingual instruction that will be offered. More recently, the availability of national tests and texts in Spanish has helped to standardize bilingual instruction for many large urban school districts implementing bilingual education programs.

More recent research in bilingual education has helped to identify the complexity of language and academic development (Collier 1989; Cummins 1981, 1984), and has raised very real questions about the complexity of language learning in academic contexts and the variety of settings in which effective bilingual instruction can occur. Historically, misconceptions about bilingual education have arisen because of a tendency to consider it a curricular model rather than a concept. Educators question the acceptance of the term as a unitary phenomenon (Otheguy 1982), arguing that the real manifestations of bilingual schooling are as varied as the regions, languages, communities, and schools and often the classrooms in which it occurs. Recognizing the fact that the practice of bilingual education *depends* upon a number of political, social, linguistic, curricular, and contextual variables (e.g., Hornberger 1990; Skutnabb-Kangas 1984) helps one to understand the difficulties inherent in determining its effectiveness (Cziko 1992).

ESL Education

ESL programs are as diverse as their bilingual counterparts. The programs vary with respect to time, native language background(s) of students, heterogeneity of the student populations, and variation in proficiency levels, in curricular foci, and in program models. ESL program models are defined by the way in which LEP students are scheduled and grouped in the school or district. Whether LEP students are mainstreamed throughout the school or isolated in a special classroom and the portions of the school day allotted to instruction are functions of the program model chosen. ESL programs are distinguished further between those of elementary and those of secondary schools (Placer-Barber 1981; Ramirez 1985). The programs range from self-contained classrooms to pull-out and pull-in models, and variations exist within each.

Self-contained ESL classrooms primarily serve newly arrived students who have little or no proficiency in English and frequently contain a large number of students of many different ages and at many different grade levels. Pull-out programs are perhaps the most common; in these programs, students leave their mainstream classroom to spend a period of time each day (ideally) with the ESL teacher in small groups or individually (Ramirez 1985; Snow 1986). Recently, pull-in, or "in-class" (Jenkins and Heinen 1989; McDonald 1987) models have emerged and are receiving increasing attention. The concept behind the pull-in model extends beyond the domain of LEP students and incorporates all support services for students with special needs (e.g., Chapter I programs, special education). In a pull-in program, support-service professionals (in this case, ESL teachers) work with the children in regular classrooms with the regular classroom teachers. The theory behind this model is that all students have the opportunity to benefit socially and intellectually from the diversity in the classroom.

As is evident from our description of language programs serving our young people in U.S. schools, they are varied, complex, and representative of many constituents and traditions. In the areas of both study and practice, second language education for majority-language students and that for minority-language students seems to have evolved on two tracks. Rarely are they examined together, with an eye to the fundamental similarities, common goals, or glaring inequities that may exist. In the next section, we conduct such an examination.

The Sociopolitical and Curricular Context of Second Language Education

The sociopolitical and curricular context of second language education in U.S. schools is an important phenomenon to explore as we discuss both foreign language education programs serving majority-language students and second language programs serving minority-language students. Clearly there are different agenda at work concerning the development of a bilingual populace, as the following points illustrate. Our experiences as second language educators have led us to believe that the failure of second language education programs (for both majority- and minority-language children) to meet their full potential is largely due to three fundamental problems: (1) fragmentation and isolation, (2) a failure to consider the interdependence between first and second languages and cultures, and (3) the pervasive view of language as "object." We recognize that these problems are not in and of themselves the only issues facing our profession; instead, we see them as umbrella issues that encompass the vast majority of dilemmas we face. Our discussion of these problems sets the stage for what we see as the kind of growth that needs to occur so that second language education meets the needs of our changing society.

Fragmentation and Isolation

Second language programs in elementary schools, middle schools, and high schools are seen as separate entities from each other and from the larger curriculum, each planned and carried out by separate people or groups of people. Foreign language education, ESL, bilingual education, and language arts are not only represented by different programs and individuals within schools, they are often the purview of distinctly separate administrative entities within a school district. Such divisions create units that find it very difficult to talk across the perceived chasm that exists between their fields—and in the process, the development of knowledge in one area has been hard pressed to find itself examined and explored in another. This lack of cross-fertilization manifests itself in the continued isolation of language programs at the school-site level; ESL / bilingual and foreign language teachers do not see themselves as serving the same students, and thus often don't believe they have anything of interest to share with one another.

Where foreign language study is concerned, in the past two decades many school districts have independently set up study committees and ultimately chosen to offer elementary or middle-school foreign language programs (Met and Galloway 1992; Müller 1989; Rhodes and Oxford 1988). Many of the resulting programs are unrelated to other language programs in the same district, and, far from allowing students to begin a long sequence of second or foreign language study culminating in ability to use it for real communication purposes, they may actually serve to stifle motivation for further study of that language (Müller 1989). Now that immersion programs have flourished in selected elementary schools in several U.S. cities, the failure to consider secondary level options for those students poses a real problem. Students completing six years of partial- or full-immersion programs need second language study that is far beyond what is often available at the secondary level, although a few schools offer language study through special magnet programs, which do take into account language acquired in elementary settings.

A far more volatile political context occurs where the issues of school programs serving nonnative speakers of English are concerned. While students depend upon these programs for their academic survival at school, there is generally no parity with other curricular areas. Substantial concerns have been identified across both bilingual and ESL instructional settings that highlight the compensatory-remedial perception that such programs hold. Teachers with whom we have worked cite a lack of commitment to staffing, curriculum, funding, and coordination with mainstream teachers (not to mention lack of attention to research findings) that results in fragmented, often frustrating, efforts to provide meaningful learning opportunities. Teachers serving LEP populations most often work within a political reality that at best is indifferent to their knowledge of what might best serve their students, and at worst presents classic examples of institutional racism (McCollum and Walker 1990). Programs serving bilingual or ESL students are often "ghetto-ized"—isolated physically, conceptually, and intellectually from the mainstream school setting. Students find great support from the bilingual and ESL staff and limited interest from other school personnel. LEP students are seen as a special-needs, "at risk" population, whose "problem" is a need for access to English—a problem that will be remedied by the presence of language teachers who can offer the proper exposure to English grammar and structure.

The fragmentation and isolation of language education, whether it be first or second language development, foreign language or ESL, elementary or secondary, is endemic. Such fragmentation results in lack of communication, reinvention of the wheel, duplication of efforts, and, in an era of reduced funding for language education, the lack of political will and cohesiveness to lobby for change.

Interdependence between First and Second Languages and Cultures

The learning/acquisition of a second language is seen as unrelated to students' continual acquisition of their first language; this lack of links between L1 and L2 can be seen in both research and pedagogy. Historically, the failure to consider the interdependence between first and second languages has led to a bifurcation of both research efforts and pedagogy. Where the separation of the two has been most evident, however, has been in the differential manner in which second language development is viewed for U.S. students. There are different expectations for majority- and minority-language students. While native English speakers are generally encouraged to begin second language study during adolescence, students with a potential for bilingualism (who bring other language skills to the school setting) must work rapidly toward the acquisition of English language skills with no attention given to continued first language development.

This distinction, between an "additive bilingualism" and a "subtractive bilingualism" (Lambert 1975), where the first language is minimized or lost, results in differential expectations and a certain hypocrisy concerning the potential for developing bilingual language skills. Whereas second language learners of English are expected to develop native-like academic proficiency in the language (often in very limited periods of time), native English speakers are given far lower expectations for proficiency development. This distinction perpetuates a view of foreign language study for majority students as an elite endeavor with no expectation for actual practical use.

Despite what we profess about the foreign language as a vehicle for producing multicultural individuals, the twice-removed "elite" nature of foreign language education helps to maintain a distance between majority-culture students and the multicultural world in which they live. First, as evidenced by our experience with teachers and by an exploration of content in popular foreign language textbooks, within major language study, attention to culture tends to focus on the western European representations of particular cultures, i.e., "Life in France" and "A Visit to El Prado" as opposed to "Life in French-Speaking Africa" or "The Art of the Chicano Barrio of the Southwest." The limitations of such explorations of culture reinforce stereotypes, while at the same time denying students access to the diversity of language groups who share a particular language.

The elite nature of second language instruction is also evident when the lack of representation by minority students in foreign language classrooms is considered. The continued tracking away from foreign language study of African-

American and Hispanic students and those from lower socioeconomic levels effectively precludes exposure to another language for this population as well. Those Hispanic students who do have access to Spanish often find themselves studying a "foreign" language indeed, with no recognition of or attention to the richness and variety of spoken Spanishes within the United States today. The lack of interest in the language possibilities that Hispanic students bring to our culture is evidenced by the fact that even in the Southwest there are few (and inadequate) efforts to provide Spanish for Spanish speakers as a valuable endeavor. Moreover, almost no research has been done on their linguistic abilities and processes, their needs, or how they can best progress.

Language as Object

The view of language as "object" is pervasive in second language classrooms; such a perspective nullifies the essence of language as communication. We would like to argue that in most language classrooms, language is viewed as "object"— that which is acted upon, an entity to be scrutinized, analyzed, and broken down into its smallest components.[1] This view has emerged partially as a result of the historical influence that the field of linguistics has had in the field of language education and perhaps partially as a result of the long road language teachers have had to travel in order to legitimize their place in the arena of U.S. schools. Foreign language teachers in particular have traditionally needed to legitimize their place in schools and market their content area as more than a "frill." In so doing, they have needed to define a body of knowledge or content and to develop a scope and sequence for delivering that body of knowledge. They have defined the content as the lexicon, syntax, morphology, and phonology of language—or as the notions and functions. ESL teachers have followed suit, all in the name of legitimizing their place. We contend that this focus on language as object has led teachers to miss the boat. It makes language like other content areas covered in school curricula and does not set it apart as different.

The treatment of culture in classrooms is another example of the view of language as object. Culture is treated as an interesting application, or a pleasant add-on, always secondary to the more important linguistic content. Within this framework, cultures education is generally culture-specific and acontextual in nature, i.e., teaching the surface elements of culture and culture "facts" rather than critical inquiry into the personal, social, political, and economic correlates of language and culture. It is much easier to teach about a culture in a neutral and nonthreatening way.

Second language textbooks support this approach. Moore (1991), in her study of culture instruction in Spanish language texts, found that noncontroversial culture facts were emphasized, surface cultural elements about which there was a consensus. Students were not expected or given opportunities to interact substantively with the culture. And there was little if any discussion about the controversial issues. In other words, the cultural world being presented is a rather static and sanitized one. Cultural artifacts—the visible products of the people—dominate the presentation. The deeper cultural questions of values, beliefs, attitudes, and the contradictions and conflicts associated with them are left unexplored. The political economy of language and culture is not addressed at all (Apple 1986; Bourdieu and Passeron 1977).

Another symptom of the propensity to view language as object is that the study of second languages is largely decontextualized, unrelated to students' real life within their school, community, family, and peer groups. A curriculum is largely nonexistent; the major focus of too many programs is an adopted textbook with accoutrements. When this is the case, the teacher's role is to help students learn what is in the textbook. (See Church 1986; Walz 1986.) In only a few programs has the major focus shifted to student goals for language study, with a curriculum designed to help students meet those goals. Since creation of a more student-centered curriculum (i.e., geared toward student needs and interests) is an individualized, time-consuming process, it seems easier to continue to use foreign language textbooks as they come from publishers than to create new ones for each of the five different levels many teachers prepare daily in a typical program.

Until modular, flexible materials that are usable in many ways begin to arrive from publishers, this situation is not likely to change. Textbooks are still, despite changes in outward appearance over the years, grammar- and teacher-driven. It is instructive to examine several editions of any major text and note that commonly grammatical issues follow the same order of presentation from edition to edition. ESL texts give recent evidence of much more progressive interpretations of curriculum for language study, partly due to the influence of adult-education programs utilizing authentic materials necessary for real use of the language, and partly due to the influence of European English language teaching. Fortunately, some foreign language programs are incorporating the use of authentic materials and are beginning to de-emphasize the text as curriculum.

The teacher-centered classroom presents problems in both foreign language and ESL settings. Continued low academic achievement of minority-language students and limited second language skills on the part of our native English speakers should cause us to examine carefully the actual classroom strategies we employ for the purpose of language teaching and learning. We have learned much about the validity of small-group and cooperatively structured classrooms for language acquisition, but we are sometimes slow to make use of that knowledge. And we are even slower to accept the fact that maybe our students should have major responsibility for developing a curriculum to which they are committed and that makes sense to them (Enright and McCloskey 1988; Goldstein 1986; Macian 1986).

Yet another symptom of the pervasive view of language as object resides in the fact that use of the English language is still the norm in far too many foreign language classes. Even when teachers are very competent in their second language, they tend to use English as the major vehicle for actual instruction, thus devaluing the second language as a legitimate means of communication. Students may in fact feel insulted by the lack of confidence their teachers place in their ability to comprehend the target language. ESL teachers, who do not know how to use all the native languages of children in their classes, and who therefore teach entirely in the English language, could be legitimate models in this regard. Teachers in immersion programs are also notable exemplars of the idea that when we assume students will understand the target language, they will realize it is expected of them and do so—and they will be proud of their ability to do so (Cook 1991; Duff and Polio 1990). We are not arguing here for the complete exclusion of English within a second language class, for it may be preferable when discussing, for example, complex cultural issues on an abstract level. We do, however, highlight the pervasive overuse of English as an all-too-common characteristic of secondary-level classrooms.

We have discussed our perceptions of the major problems facing second language education and find that resolution of them is indeed a formidable task. We need to embrace a broad cultural *context* for language and culture learning that assumes that all students can develop both linguistic and cultural literacy beyond that of their first language and primary culture. The potential for the development of multicultural literacy may well be aided by two forces in U.S. education: efforts at educational reform, and changing theoretical perspectives related to teaching and learning.

School Reform and Governance as They Affect Second Language Education

The projection of second language and cultures education into broader contexts is necessary to bring comprehension of major educational events to this field of practice, inquiry, and scholarship. While specific decisions about the organization and delivery of school subjects are made on the local level, such as those for the organization of curriculum, instruction, assessment, and relationships between school subjects, the more global, national issues of education tend to be disregarded locally, and this prevents the evolution of a more expansive vision of the educational world. The influences on education in the last decade of the twentieth century require our careful and critical attention. Because of a decade of heavily focused criticism of education in this country, forces are now poised to create significant change in our educational culture, including second languages and cultures education.

Current efforts at educational reform can be seen in three general areas: curriculum, teacher development, and school restructuring.

Curriculum

The first responses to this reform agenda are wide and varied; they vacillate among conservative and progressive voices on curricular issues. Even before the *Nation at Risk* document was generated, Adler (1982) had developed "The Paideia Proposal," which stated a similar agenda for all children, based on the conservation of Western tradition and thought through a liberal arts agenda. Another example of curricular reform in schools is found in the need for children and youth to be culturally literate. Hirsch (1987) proposed a curricular agenda that, like that of Adler, approaches knowledge through the lens of the Western world and U.S. culture, leaving aside the contributions of other societies and places to a broader world culture. These examples focus on one of the major themes in school reform, knowledge of underlying cultural traditions and excellence or "higher standards," words that served as metaphors for tougher requirements, elimination of elective courses, focus on mathematics and sciences, more homework and testing, longer school days, and consideration of year-round school (Passow 1987).

The more progressive agenda in school reform recognizes schooling or the curriculum as a constant struggle for values and forms of knowledge. Based to some degree on the works of Dewey (1944), Freire (1973), and others, this pedagogical agenda (commonly referred to as "Critical Pedagogy") directs curriculum toward democratic principles and emancipation. Its mandate is found in the unity of reflection and action within a social, economic, and political context. It allows individuals and groups to contemplate and act upon society for purposes of responding to societal inequities; it works for fairness, justice, and emancipation for all persons regardless of race, creed, age, sex and sexual preference, and social class. The intent is the development of a truly democratic society and the betterment of the human condition (Freire 1970, 1973, 1985; Freire and Faundez 1989; Giroux 1988; McLaren 1989; Pennycook 1990— among many others). This agenda is hardly known and even less discussed because of its liberal political overtones and presentation of ideas.

Implications for Second Language Education.   The two examples, one conservative and one liberal, suggest the kind of curricular debate that is occurring within the many reform efforts. There are direct implications for second language education in this debate. The discussion of curriculum continues to focus on language as object, however, and this is one of the fundamental problems facing language education as we see it. Lange (1990, 1992) portrays second language education as based on a scientific-technical orientation to language in continuing to focus on phonology, morphology, syntax, lexicon, and discourse rules. While building a bridge to communication through an emphasis on proficiency, the field is scattered, seemingly not wanting to know that communication in a second language accords learners an important tool for uncovering other cultures, including the relationship of the individual learner to individuals in the other culture(s). We continue to focus our attention largely on the structure of language and more recently the structure of communication (Bachman 1990: 81–110) because we have not progressed beyond a scientific, positivistic approach to learning, teaching, and assessment.

Teacher Development

A second major area of the school reform movement converges on the development of teachers. There are statements from a variety of higher education coalitions (e.g., Holmes Group 1986; Murray and Fallon 1989; and the Renaissance Group 1992), as well as from the Carnegie Forum (1986) and the National Board for Professional Teaching Standards (1991), on the crucial importance of teachers in the learning and achievement of children and youth in schools. It is important to recognize that, in the milieu of educational renewal in this country, teacher-preparation programs in colleges and universities have been considered part of "the educational problem." In spite of the negative attitude toward teacher development, colleges and universities have organized around confederations of ideas that represent different constituencies in teacher preparation (large research universities, state universities, and programs with a strong interest in the liberal arts), but which have a similar, singular goal, that of the preparation of quality teachers for schools in the United States. The following brief descriptions provide a flavor of these efforts.

The Holmes Group (1986) agenda for teacher development addresses five basic points: an intellectually solid program; awareness of differences and rewards for teachers' knowledge, skills, and dispositions; appropriate standards for entry to the profession; connections to schools; and a work climate that befits professionals. In addition, the Holmes Group (1990) has indicated the importance of the association of teacher development with professional development schools, which bring initial and continuing teacher development together in schools where professorial staff and local school staff work together with recognized professional inservice and university faculty to meet the needs of those preparing to teach. Thus, the restructured school is a joint effort of the faculties of the public school and the university school of education based on their collaboration on initial teacher preparation and their joint research efforts in answering particular curricular and instructional questions.

With a different agenda, the Renaissance Group (1992) operates on twelve principles that direct teacher development as an all-campus, shared, and integrated responsibility throughout the students' course of study. It is associated with appropriate state standards and rigorous learning opportunities in general, subject-matter, and professional preparation. Diversity, extensive clinical experiences, quality faculty, continuing professional development, and adequate support round out the statement of principles.

The Project 30 Alliance (Murray and Fallon 1989) represent another teacher-education reform effort, bringing together faculty in arts and sciences with faculty in education to improve teacher education. Five fundamental themes constitute the heart of this intellectual agenda for reform and provide the framework for the projects that are created by faculty in the Alliance, for seminars at the national meetings of the organization, and for forums and research endeavors connected to the Alliance. The first, *subject-matter under-standing,* goes beyond a superficial statement of the importance of subject-matter knowledge and emphasizes the way in which subject matter coheres conceptually. The second, *general and liberal education,* addresses what teachers need to know to be entitled to be called professionals in society. *Pedagogical content knowledge,* the third theme, represents the fusion between deep concep-tual understanding of subject matter and an equally rich knowledge of pedagogy in all its complexity. The final themes, *international, cultural, and other human perspectives,* and *recruitment of underrepresented groups in teaching,* are more programmatic in nature and address issues related to the general college curriculum and recruitment.

Another influence on teacher development has been the Carnegie Forum report (1986), which resulted in the development of standards for advanced voluntary certification and assessment through the National Board for Profes-sional Teaching Standards. The work of this board (National Board 1991) is based on the propositions that teachers are committed to student learning, know the content to be taught and how to teach, are responsible for managing learning, learn systematically from experience, and are members of learning communities. It is upon these propositions that an assessment system is currently being built by the Board. This evaluation system is expected to be multifaceted to include both objective and subjective measures (e.g., multiple-choice tests and portfolios, respectively). It will be designed to evaluate general pedagogical content and specific pedagogical competence in a subject field.

Another player in the assessment of teachers is the Educational Testing Service (ETS). ETS is in the process of revising the National Teachers Examinations in foreign languages. In its present form, the assumptions about language and about testing are not too far removed from those used to develop the MLA Foreign Language Proficiency Tests for Teachers and Advanced Students in the 1960s. Any system of assessments, whether for general pedagogy, content knowledge, or specific field pedagogy, will become the standard toward which teacher development programs will strive. We must all watch these developments with great care, concern, and active participation, because teacher-development pro-grams can be determined and driven by such systems.

A final factor in teacher development is the creation of state licensure boards, such as the Minnesota Board of Teaching, which was created in the early 1970s. Constituted mainly of practicing teachers, this board is responsible for the rule making associated with teacher development and the approval of all higher-education-generated programs for teacher development. Its influence is enor-mous. For example, it has recently been successful in recommending legislation toward the establishment of year-long teaching internships as part of any program for teacher development in Minnesota (Education Funding 1992). Although modified somewhat by the legislature to study pilot programs before full implementation, it is clear that such an internship will have a major impact on teacher development in terms of cost and funding of programs, number of teacher candidates, and relationship of colleges and universities to schools. When implemented fully in the year 2000, this legislation will dramatically alter teacher education in Minnesota. Teacher licensure boards in other states are considering similar approaches.

In all these developments, there remains a question about the ability of colleges and universities to become "part of the solution" to educational problems in the United States. Will these coalitions and their goals make a difference? Or, will teacher development come under the direction of agencies other than colleges and universities, such as the public schools, testing corporations such as ETS, or other agencies such as the National Board for Professional Teaching Standards? Or, will colleges and universities really take leadership in teacher development by responding to the urban crisis in schools, the lack of teachers of color, and the need for knowledge and ability to teach content responsively (Bowers and Flinders 1990)?

Implications for Second Language Education.   How will second language education professionals respond to the challenges posed for the redevelopment of teacher preparation? There are several matters from the reform of teacher preparation that we must address in second language education (Lange 1991). In collaboration with departments of foreign languages, ESL, and bilingual programs for the preparation of teachers, we must all be concerned about the language competence of those who teach in the public schools. The focus in that preparation needs to be largely on the teachers who are able to use all aspects of language, who are experienced in the culture(s) associated with the language, who have second language pedagogical knowledge, and whose view is on second language education within a broader context. As second language educators, we can accomplish these goals *if* we put aside turf issues and work across the institution toward a common goal, the quality development of teachers. In this regard, we need to work together on the development of standards for both students and teachers. Currently, uniform standards for students have yet to be developed, although ACTFL is in the process of working on such standards. A recent meeting of representatives from ACTFL and the AATs brought about an awareness of the necessity for collaborative action on this matter. ACTFL and the American Associations of Teachers of French, German, and Spanish and Portuguese are working on guidelines for teacher-education programs, standards for both teachers and students, and assessment procedures. This kind of collaboration is imperative if our field is to be taken seriously by the National Board for Professional Teaching Standards (NBPTS) or the National Council for the Accreditation of Teacher Education (NCATE).

Second language educators have also been relatively silent on the issue of members of minorities as teachers. We need to begin to participate in a number of recruiting strategies, such as alternative licensure programs, connections with historically African-American, Hispanic, and Native American colleges and universities, and special recruitment projects supported by foundations and local communities. Clearly, socioeconomic class is an issue in second language teacher preparation. If we are also to recruit students from lower socioeconomic classes, we will need to find ways to subsidize experiences abroad for those students interested in becoming foreign language teachers. Otherwise, the language and cultural proficiency we need to demand will not likely be achieved.

Finally, one important implication stands out clearly. We, as professionals in teacher-development programs, need to be connected to schools in order to make the kind of changes we have discussed and to make language learning meaningful for students.

School Restructuring

A third major area seen in education reform efforts is the refashioning of schools themselves. Certainly, *Nation at Risk* (National Commission 1983) jolted U.S. educators into looking at schools and what they were and were not accomplishing. Some different visions, structures, and relationships began to emerge, which we will sample here.

One vision involves a network of schools that transforms itself from a set of principles. In *Horace's Compromise,* Sizer (1984) explored the need for school transformation as a result of a significant study of schools in the United States. The exploration uncovered five imperatives for better schools, which Sizer has incorporated into a growing network of Essential Schools. Those imperatives involve flexibility for teachers and students to teach and to learn, student exhibition of mastery of their work, appropriate incentives for teachers and learners, focused learning, and a simple structure. It is upon this set of principles or others like them that many schools across the country are being reformulated.

Another vision of school reformulation is more specifically based on "what students know and can do," more conceptually known as Outcome Based Education (OBE). This direction asks that students demonstrate their ability in knowing by applying their knowledge, rather than focusing on the amount of time spent in a classroom. Many states have OBE projects well under way.[2] Such projects emphasize that in the future achievement will be based on knowledge and abilities that will not be assessed by time in place, but by a set of interdisciplinary tasks. This idea is closest to the very controversial concept of proficiency in second language education. In the future, graduation from secondary school could be based on a demonstration of competence in listening, reading, writing, speaking, and cultural awareness and understanding rather than having completed French One through Four.

There are issues with respect to OBE that raise questions on both a theoretical and a practical level, however. For purposes of this discussion, we question the ways in which OBE might perpetuate more traditional forms of instruction in second language classrooms, for attempts to codify assessment may well produce a strong tendency to view language as object in the classroom, particularly if teachers implement OBE as mastery learning.

A third vision of reform involves the changing nature of our population and the requirements for desegregation. Magnet schools (Estes et al. 1990) and their offshoots have become important in restructuring schools and balancing school populations. In concept, magnet schools are schools that are open to any student within a district. They are usually organized around subject-matter themes such as mathematics and sciences, foreign languages, the arts, careers, or technology, for elementary as well as secondary school students. These schools may be nonselective in that students choose to attend from their own interest and motivation. One of their major features is the focus on curriculum and instructional innovation.

A second kind of magnet school is the International Baccalaureate (IB) (1986), a school within a school. It is a curriculum for second language learning that is based on the experience of European international schools. In this program, intended largely for college-bound students at the secondary level, the study of language focuses significantly on the high culture, literature mostly, whereas most secondary school programs are currently oriented toward communication. Many IB programs attract students who have had experience with partial immersion or early foreign language instruction.

A fourth prescient position on restructuring is taken by those who advocate school reform through the application of a business disposition to it, namely a competitive one. Those schools that become competitive will survive and continue to exist. Those that lose are not competitive, cannot become so, and thus fail. One aspect of this movement started in Minnesota with the Post-Secondary Options Act (1992). The legislation gave secondary school students the option to attend and receive credit for courses given by local institutions of higher education. School funds are transferred to the college if a course is actually taken. Another form of competitive restructuring is the Open Enrollment Act (Enrollment Options 1990), also in Minnesota, which theoretically allows students to choose whichever school they desire to attend. Again, the monetary support follows the student. The theory behind these movements is that the resulting competition among schools to keep their own students through restructuring will help these schools to provide a higher-quality curriculum, resulting in higher student achievement.

Finally, in our display of school reform undertakings, the federal government, through combined governmental and private business support, has established the New American Schools Development Corporation (1991), which intends to bring innovation into U.S. education through the creation of "new" schools for the second millennium. These schools will result from a variety of synergies among divergent partners or consortia (city governments, universities, school districts, private corporations, businesses). Although at the point of our writing this piece no proposals have been funded, it is important to watch developments in New American Schools because they could say much about future directions.

Implications for Second Language Education.   It appears that the most important connection to school restructuring for second languages comes through elementary magnet immersion schools. This structure has the potential to bring majority- and minority-language students together in developing language competence. Since most magnet immersion schools are relatively new, the acceptance of these programs as the basis for regular second language programs in junior and senior high schools has yet to be experienced on a large scale, although some models are in place across the country. There is as yet little carefully planned, quality research to document the real benefits of immersion programs in the United States beyond that which reports standardized test scores demonstrating that the acquisition of English and learning of math and science are not being compromised.

International baccalaureate (IB) programs seem to be popular among foreign language teachers, probably because they match the kind of literary orientation in their preparation that comes from language departments and because they respond to concerns about "quality" in education. Since we view the IB curriculum to be developed completely outside the decision-making process of the local school context, we wonder if foreign language teachers are choosing this alternative for appropriate reasons. Is this another means of excluding less capable students and persons of color?

There is little published discussion in the second language literature about other forms of school restructuring, such as Sizer's (1984) Essential School movement or the several other approaches to restructuring. Although projects are being implemented in various locations, the second language literature is basically silent on school restructuring. It will be important for the profession to follow any such developments with a critical eye.

Looking to the Future

Substantial and important changes are occurring in how we perceive the nature of language, the art and science of teaching, and the complexity of learning. One phrase can describe the fundamental restructuring of several schools of thought in language education: social context. The consideration of the social context in which language is learned and the contextual nature of effective teaching and learning provide the key for fascinating new directions in schools of the future. Why do these new directions and perspectives mesh so well with what we know to be true about effective language learning, both for minority-language and majority-language students? How might these inform us so that we can prepare teachers to provide effective second language and culture learning?

Working toward Continuity and Integration

A first step toward continuity and integration is for foreign language, ESL, and bilingual teachers to begin collaborating with one another and with mainstream and other content-area teachers within and across schools and districts. National organizations for language teachers, such as ACTFL, TESOL (Teachers of

English to Speakers of Other Languages), and NABE (National Association for Bilingual Education), and their respective state affiliates, have historically provided network possibilities for teachers. We believe that there should be more communication and collaboration among such organizations. In addition, at the local level, teachers need to develop networks so that they can plan curricula, discuss student progress, and lobby for change at the local and state levels.

In moving away from fragmentation of the curriculum, the trend is toward content-based and interdisciplinary instruction. Literacy programs in elementary schools integrate curriculum and provide for the interaction of reading and writing in content areas: social studies, mathematics, science, and so on. Some middle schools and junior high schools are developing a structure that allows for content-based instruction as well, as groups of teachers work with the same group of students throughout their secondary study. Certainly foreign language skills can be used for content other than literary study, and students will see the relevance of their language study when they can use the foreign language for work in any content area. (See, for example, Brinton et al. 1989; Met 1989; and Mohan 1986 for discussions of content-based language instruction.)

Language professionals are not the only ones who need to collaborate and communicate more than they have in the past. We believe that minority- and majority-language students have much to offer one another. Peer tutoring programs (where majority-language students provide academic tutoring for ESL and bilingual students) have begun in a number of high schools. In addition, language students in secondary schools provide instruction for elementary school students. More foreign language programs should be encouraged to follow such examples. Hispanic students, for instance, could be recruited to work and converse in Spanish with Anglo students of Spanish. These kinds of collaborative efforts are inspiring and should continue to be developed.

Capitalizing on the Interdependence
between First and Second Languages and Cultures

Changing conceptualizations of teaching and learning in school reform movements neatly dovetail with what we now know about effective second language acquisition / learning. These conceptualizations focus on learning within a total social framework and on subject content, including foreign languages, as part of the entire context of developing students' cultural perspectives rather than as peripheral to their real world.

Content needs to reflect the present situation of language and culture in student life. Course boundaries shift and strain as we revise our conceptualization of the world. It is possible that a school might offer many foreign languages; a language could form the focal point of integrated units of study that include all subject areas and are cooperatively planned by a group of teachers and a group of students, working together to extract and meet real-world student goals.

Spanish provides a clear example. Social issues dividing groups of people (in this case, Spanish-speaking and Anglo) in a town or city can be the focal points for social studies, language arts, second language, and other fields. As students try to address the problems they identify, the use of the Spanish language becomes central to their solutions. Such study could include and involve the entire community—school-aged, preschool, and adult—as well as other institutions in society (Cummins 1986). The effects of such study on current and future students would enrich and inform possible community action, and in effect, the target culture and its relationship to students' own culture would become the focus of the language classroom (Crawford-Lange and Lange 1984; Kramsch 1991).

Increasing use of cooperative group structure and cooperative orientations in business and the workplace, as opposed to competitive and individualistic orientations, will also support the interdependence of first and second languages and cultures. Much of the research on the use of cooperative groups has taken place in school settings (Johnson and Johnson 1974, 1987). And what we have learned about the use of groups in language learning validates the use of groups in second language classrooms (Archer 1988). We should be encouraged to explore cooperative orientations beyond the classroom walls as well; for example, teachers can work together to organize cooperative group activities with majority-language students in foreign language classrooms and minority-language students in ESL or bilingual classrooms.

Meeting the Challenge of Viewing Language as "Subject"

Viewing language as "subject" (that which *acts*) emphasizes its communicative nature and the fact that language exists and contains meaning when embedded within a social context. In essence, an understanding of language as subject leads one to approach language instruction in ways described above—in ways that reflect the social nature of language, that capitalize on interaction, and that emphasize contextualization of language learning. Such approaches would not be grammatically based and sequenced. Instead, they would focus, for example, on building language teaching around themes/topics/issues that are relevant to students and from which grammatical instruction *naturally* emerges.

Working across disciplinary boundaries, considering interdependent language development as a holistic enterprise, and changing our views of language in a way that affects instruction and assessment, all support what we believe to be both necessary for student learning and an imperative for the development of multicultural literacy. The three primary areas of concern in the field of second language education that we have discussed, and the ways in which radical changes can be made relevant to those areas underlie a most critical goal for U.S. education: the work toward the development of a multicultural citizenry.

A Multicultural Approach to Second Language Education in Tomorrow's Schools ⎯⎯⎯⎯⎯⎯⎯⎯

> Multicultural education is an idea stating that all students, regardless of the groups to which they belong, such as those related to gender, ethnicity, race, culture, social class, religion, or exceptionality, should experience educational equality in the schools. (Banks 1989: 23)

Multicultural education is a proactive reform movement with an extensive agenda (Sleeter and Grant 1988). It is intended to combat racism, sexism, and other forms of discrimination. It attempts to promote equity by means of a far more inclusive curriculum, one that more accurately presents the experiences and accomplishments of ethnic and racial minorities and women in this country (Banks and Banks 1989). It attempts to forge a new sense of national unity in the decades ahead, based on a multicultural vision of the United States. It is a celebration of diversity, rather than one based exclusively on white European cultural norms, a negation of diversity. At its most ambitious, it seeks to reconstruct U.S. society; Sleeter and Grant (1988) refer to this as "multicultural education for social reconstruction." It certainly attempts to transform the structures of schooling that are discriminatory. It is, in Banks's view, education for all, not just education for the minority.

Few settings offer a more important opportunity for promoting multicultural literacy than the second language classroom. Attention has long been given by foreign language educators to the teaching of culture, and it is the case that second language pedagogy today is much more culture-education-oriented than in past decades. In theory, the possibility exists for students to acquire an in-depth understanding of the political, economic, and social contexts of the language and culture, all fundamental components of multicultural education. We would submit, however, that this is rarely done. In our view, few second language educators have made explicit the multicultural dimension of second language instruction. With the exception of some ESL and bilingual educators, most language educators have tended to shy away from these issues because of their politically explosive nature.

A multicultural education approach to second languages views the content and process of education far differently. It stresses the acquisition of inter-cultural communication skills; knowledge about second language/culture communities; the reduction of prejudice, racism, and sexism; transformation of the structures of schooling to promote greater equality of opportunity; and social reconstruction. If the foreign language classroom were to become an educational setting for "social reconstruction" per Grant and Sleeter (1989), the role of the teacher would be significantly altered, the goals and objectives of foreign language and ESL instruction dramatically expanded. In addition, teaching that promotes language acquisition and culture-specific knowledge would address concrete social, economic, and political issues associated with those who speak the language in the United States and elsewhere.

A multicultural approach does not consider languages and cultures to be divorced from their political milieu. Languages confer upon their speakers socioeconomic status, advantage or disadvantage in economic mobility, greater or lesser educational access and opportunity. *Second languages and cultures education in the twenty-first century will be faced with the question of whether it will contribute to the development of a multicultural society.* We submit that a multicultural education approach to the teaching of second languages and cultures is an imperative. Teaching in this manner is controversial. As students learn the language and the culture(s) of the language, they begin to ask penetrating questions about the society. The study of the language for communicative purposes promotes both English language acquisition and critical inquiry into the status of their home languages and cultures in U.S. society; personal values are challenged; and preparation for participation in the majority culture is integrated with support for cultural diversity.

If schools are to prepare our youth adequately for adult life in a multicultural society, they must promote new communication and interaction skills, second language and culture skills, more positive attitudes toward those who are culturally different, and significantly more knowledge of the cultural communities that make up the United States. In other words, our students must become *multiculturally literate,* a term we use to refer to the skills, patterns of behavior, attitudes, and values that characterize a citizenry knowledgeable about and supportive of its diversity. A large portion of our population—the minority-language groups—have tremendous experience with language and culture learning that is not academic in nature. We must begin to tap into these rich linguistic and cultural resources that already exist in our society and no longer treat cultural and linguistic diversity as a problem.

The changing demographics of U.S. society and the patterns of global commerce are bringing all Americans into greater contact with culturally different populations than ever, at home and abroad. Schools, communities, and workplaces are becoming far more culturally heterogeneous. In their adult lives, Americans can anticipate that they will be working side by side with people from other cultures and countries. As more and more women enter the work force at all levels and in all occupations, men and women will find themselves working together in nontraditional arrangements. The diversity we will all experience can be the source of conflict and strife or cooperation and creativity. The multicultural literacy imperative for education is to help Americans manage diversity in positive, constructive ways.

We end this chapter with a series of questions. We recognize that these are generally not the kinds of questions posed to second language professionals; they are difficult questions and reflect the learning of language as a more critical, analytical experience. We submit these as challenges to the profession for approaching the difficult road ahead for second language education in tomorrow's schools.

- What considerations will bring together the varied second language curricula described in this chapter to produce a cross-disciplinary focus that will help students prepare for the multicultural society of the twenty-first century?

- Since language programs at the present moment concentrate heavily on language as the object of study, which attitudes of teachers and learners need to be addressed to lead them to treat language as subject—to turn language and culture study toward language use as a means of uncovering the personal, familial, social, political, and economic contexts in which both the native and second language are utilized? If we consider language as subject and owned by individuals, how can we help learners use their individual differences to maximize the acquisition of a second language in the classroom?

- Is it possible to agree on standards of language competence for students to reach in our programs? On what can those standards be based? multicultural competence? language proficiency? What is the process to be used to arrive at such standards? Who contributes?

- From social, economic, cultural, and political perspectives, what are the purposes of teaching various languages as second or foreign languages in the United States? In the bilingual education context, what is the role of second language instruction for minority-language communities and for the European-American majority?

- In what ways are future educational and economic opportunities associated with language (specifically, English language proficiency) and with culture (specifically, familiarity with white European cultural norms, standards, beliefs, and values)?

- How do we value the languages of the peoples who have arrived in this country in the past couple of decades? In what ways does second language education help preserve this heritage and contribute to a multicultural and multilingual society?

- As professionals, are we willing to continue to accept the pervasive underachievement of minority-language students while continuing to view language and culture as the culprits of that underachievement?

- Are we capable of making curricular decisions that fit the culture of education in the United States? When we look outside our system, do we accept critically what others have accomplished and adapt possibilities to our own system?

- Can reform movements that tend to stress assessment and accountability be compatible with goals for the development of a multicultural citizenry?

- How does a reflective orientation by teachers contribute to more appropriate learning of second languages for students in the next decade and beyond? What difference can such an orientation make to the development of students to communicate with language and understand themselves and their own culture and those of others?

- Since school reform has not really affected second language education dramatically, except for immersion magnet schools, what aspects of second language education could be important to school reform? Is it a multicultural orientation? Is it the importance of language as a reflection of person, society, culture? Where do we fit?

- Since the development of teachers of second languages in the reform context seems to have been somewhat ignored, who or what entity brings the disparate elements of the profession together to establish and help implement standards for teacher development in foreign language, ESL, and bilingual education areas?

- By what means are already licensed teachers socialized into and helped to understand and implement a multicultural approach to teaching so that experienced teachers contribute to the changes in our schools?

- What dispositions need to be addressed and what program characteristics need attention to attract, retain, and graduate more racial- and language-minority students in second language teacher development programs as our society becomes more diverse?

- Do foreign language, bilingual education, and ESL professionals recognize and accept the future of second languages and cultures education as residing in a multicultural orientation? How can we begin to work together toward this future?

Notes

1. The "subject" and "object" distinction is referred to frequently in texts that focus on critical theory and critical pedagogy, usually in relation to the situatedness of humans in their worlds. Freire, in *Pedagogy of the Oppressed* (1970: 20), defines the terms: "'Subjects' denotes those who know and act, in contrast to 'objects,' which are known and acted upon." In this chapter, we apply the subject/object distinction to language education, arguing that language has historically been viewed as "object" (that which is acted upon), and that instruction has reflected this view (see, for example, Pennycook 1990, for a discussion of language as an objective system). We argue for a movement toward viewing language as "subject," (that which acts); this view emphasizes the communicative, dynamic, and social nature of language as well as the power of language. A more detailed description of this distinction and its manifestations appears in Tedick (1992).

2. Minnesota is just one example of states having OBE mandates. See Success (Minnesota Department of Education 1992) for a detailed description of the OBE mandate in that state.

References, Second Language Education in Tomorrow's Schools

Adler, Mortimer J. 1982. *The Paideia Proposal: An Educational Manifesto.* New York: Collier.

Apple, Michael. 1986. "Ideology, Reproduction, and Educational Reform," pp. 51–71 in P. G. Altbach and G. P. Kelley, eds. *New Approaches to Comparative Education.* Chicago: Univ. of Chicago Press.

Archer, Julie Ann. 1988. "Feedback Effects on Achievement, Attitude, and Group Dynamics of Adolescents in Interdependent Cooperative Groups for Beginning Second Language and Culture Study." Ph.D. diss., Univ. of Minnesota.

Bachman, Lyle F. 1990. *Fundamental Considerations in Language Testing.* New York: Oxford Univ. Press.

Banks, James A. 1989. "Multicultural Education: Characteristics and Goals," pp. 2–26 in James A. Banks and Cherry A. McGee Banks, eds., *Multicultural Education: Issues and Perspectives.* Needham Heights, MA: Allyn and Bacon.

_____, and Cherry A. McGee Banks, eds. 1989. *Multicultural Education: Issues and Perspectives.* Needham Heights, MA: Allyn and Bacon.

Bourdieu, Pierre, and Jean-Claude Passeron. 1977. *Reproduction in Education, Society, and Culture.* London, Eng.: Sage.

Bowers, C. A., and David J. Flinders. 1990. *Responsive Teaching: An Ecological Approach to Classroom Patterns of Language, Culture, and Thought.* New York: Teachers College Press.

Brinton, Donna M., Marguerite Ann Snow, and Marjorie Bingham Wesche. 1989. *Content-Based Second Language Instruction.* Boston: Newbury House (Heinle and Heinle).

Burstein, Nancy, and Beverly Cabello. 1989. "Preparing Teachers to Work with Culturally Diverse Students: A Teacher Education Model." *Journal of Teacher Education* 40: 9–16.

Carnegie Task Force on Teaching as a Profession. 1986. *A Nation Prepared: Teachers for the 21st Century.* Rochester, NY: National Center on Education.

Church, D. M. 1986. "Textbook Specific Computer Exercises for Elementary French Students." *Modern Language Journal* 70: 251–57.

Coleman, James S., E. G. Campbell, C. J. Hobson, A. M. Mood, F. B. Weinfeld, and R. L. York. 1966. *Equality of Educational Opportunity.* Washington, DC: U.S. Dept. of Health, Education, and Welfare.

Collier, Virginia P. 1987. "Age and Rate of Acquisition of Second Language for Academic Purposes." *TESOL Quarterly* 21: 617–41.

_____. 1989. "How Long? A Synthesis of Research on Academic Achievement in a Second Language." *TESOL Quarterly* 23: 509–31.

Cook, Vivian. 1991. *Second Language Learning and Language Teaching.* New York: Edward Arnold.

Cortes, Carlos E. 1986. "The Education of Language Minority Students: A Contextual Interaction Model," pp. 3–33 in *Beyond Language: Social and Cultural Factors in Schooling Language Minority Students.* Sacramento, CA: Bilingual Education Office.

Crawford-Lange, Linda M., and Dale L. Lange. 1984. "Doing the Unthinkable in the Second-Language Classroom: A Process for the Integration of Language and Culture," pp. 139–77 in Theodore V. Higgs, ed., *Teaching for Proficiency, the Organizing Principle.* ACTFL Foreign Language Education Series, vol. 15. Lincolnwood, IL: National Textbook.

Cummins, Jim. 1981. "The Role of Primary Language Development in Promoting Educational Success for Language Minority Students, " pp. 3–49 in California State Department of Education, ed., *Schooling and Language Minority Students: A Theoretical Framework.* Los Angeles, CA: Evaluation, Dissemination and Assessment Center, California State Univ.

_____. 1984. *Bilingualism and Special Education: Issues in Assessment and Pedagogy.* San Diego, CA: College Hill Press.

_____. 1986. "Empowering Minority Students: A Framework for Intervention." *Harvard Educational Review* 56: 18–36.

Curtain, Helena A., and Carol Ann Pesola. 1988. *Language and Children—Making the Match: Foreign Language Instruction in the Elementary School.* Reading, MA: Addison-Wesley.

Cziko, Gary A. 1992. "The Evaluation of Bilingual Education: From Necessity and Probability to Possibility." *Educational Researcher* 21,2: 10–15.

Dandonoli, Patricia. 1987. "Report on Foreign Language Enrollment in Public Secondary Schools, Fall 1985." *Foreign Language Annals* 20: 457–70.

Dewey, John. 1944. *Democracy and Education.* New York: Free Press.

Duff, Patricia A., and Charlene G. Polio. 1990. "How Much Foreign Language Is There in the Foreign Language Classroom?" *Modern Language Journal* 74: 154–66.

Education Funding Conference Committee. 1992. *Bill Summary, H.F. 2121 and S.F. 2326.* St. Paul: Minnesota House and Senate Education Staff.

Enright, D. Scott, and Mary Lou McCloskey. 1988. *Integrating English: Developing English Language and Literacy in the Multilingual Classroom.* Reading, MA: Addison-Wesley.

Enrollment Options Program. 1990. Minnesota Statutes, Chapter 120, subdivision .j062, vol. 3, section "Definition, Attendance, Special Education, and Fees." St. Paul, MN: Revisor of Statutes.

Estes, Nolan, Daniel U. Levine, and Donald R. Waldrip, eds. 1990. *Magnet Schools: Recent Developments and Perspectives.* Austin, TX: Morgan.

Fishman, Joshua. 1966. *Language Loyalty in the United States.* The Hague, Neth.: Mouton.

Freire, Paulo. 1970. *Pedagogy of the Oppressed.* New York: Continuum.

_____. 1973. *Education for Critical Consciousness.* New York: Seabury.

_____. 1985. *The Politics of Education: Culture, Power, and Liberation.* South Hadley, MA: Bergin and Garvey.

_____, and Antonio Faundez. 1989. *Learning to Question: A Pedagogy of Liberation.* New York: Continuum.

Gil, William. 1989. "Who Will Teach Minority Youth?" *Educational Leadership* 46,8: 83.

Giroux, Henry A. 1988. *Schooling and the Struggle for Public Life: Critical Pedagogy in the Modern Age.* Minneapolis: Univ. of Minnesota Press.

Goldstein, Nina White. 1986. "Vamos al Barrio: Presenting Spanish in Its Primary Context through Field Trips." *Foreign Language Annals* 19: 209–17.

Grant, Carl A., and Christine E. Sleeter. 1989. "Race, Class, Gender, Exceptionality, and Educational Reform," pp. 49–65 in James A. Banks and Cherry A. McGee Banks, eds., *Multicultural Education: Issues and Perspectives.* Needham Heights, MA: Allyn and Bacon.

"Here They Come, Ready or Not: An Education Week Special Report on the Ways in Which America's 'Population in Motion' Is Changing the Outlook for Schools and Society." 1986. *Education Week,* May 14, pp. 13–37.

Hirsch, E. D., Jr. 1987. *Cultural Literacy: What Every American Needs to Know.* Boston: Houghton Mifflin.

Holmes Group. 1986. "Tomorrow's Teachers: A Report of the Holmes Group." East Lansing, MI: Holmes Group.

_____. 1990. *Tomorrow's Schools: Principles for the Design of Professional Development Schools.* East Lansing, MI: Holmes Group.

Hornberger, Nancy H. 1990. "Bilingual Education and English-Only: A Language-Planning Framework." *Annals of the American Academy of Political and Social Science* 508: 12–26.

International Baccalaureate North America. 1986. *International Baccalaureate.* New York: International Baccalaureate North America.

Jenkins, Joseph R., and Amy Heinen. 1989. "Students' Preferences for Service Delivery: Pull-Out, In-Class, or Integrated Models." *Exceptional Children* 55: 516–23.

Johnson, David W., and Roger T. Johnson. 1974. "Instructional Goal Structure: Cooperative, Competitive, or Individualistic." *Review of Educational Research* 44: 213–44.

_____. 1987. *Learning Together and Alone: Cooperation, Competition, and Individualization.* Rev. ed. New York: Prentice Hall.

Kjolseth, Richard. 1976. "Bilingual Education Programs in the United States: For Assimilation or Pluralism?" pp. 122–40 in F. Cordasco, ed., *Bilingual Schooling in the United States: A Sourcebook for Educational Personnel.* New York: McGraw-Hill.

Kramsch, Claire. 1991. "Toward a Pedagogy of Cross-Cultural Competence." Paper presented at Interdisciplinary Perspectives on Culture Learning in the Second Language Curriculum, Univ. of Minnesota, Minneapolis, May.

Lambert, William E. 1975. "Culture and Language as Factors in Learning and Education," pp. 55–83 in Aaron Wolfgang, ed., *Education of Immigrant Students.* Toronto: Ontario Institute for Studies in Education.

Lange, Dale L. 1990. "Sketching the Crisis and Exploring Different Perspectives in Foreign Language Curriculum," pp. 77–109 in Diane W. Birckbichler, ed., *New*

Perspectives and New Directions in Foreign Language Education. ACTFL Foreign Language Education Series, vol. 20. Lincolnwood, IL: National Textbook.

_____. 1991. "Implication of Recent Reports on Teacher Education Reform for Departments of Foreign Languages and Literatures." *ADFL Bulletin* 23,1: 28–34.

_____. 1992. "Foreign Language Education," in Marvin Alkin, ed., *Research.* Vol. 2. 6th ed. New York: Macmillan. [In press]

Lau v. *Nichols.* 1974. United States Supreme Court. No. 72-6520.

Legarreta, Dorothy. 1977. "Language Choice in the Bilingual Classroom." *TESOL Quarterly* 11: 9–16.

Leibowitz, Arnold H. 1982. *Federal Recognition of the Rights of Minority Language Groups.* Rosslyn, VA: National Clearinghouse for Bilingual Education.

Macian, Janice L. 1986. "An Analysis of State Adopted Foreign Language Textbooks Used in First- and Third-Year High School Spanish Classes." *Foreign Language Annals* 19: 103–18.

Mackey, William F. 1970. "A Typology of Bilingual Education." *Foreign Language Annals* 3: 596–608.

Manuel, Herschel T. 1930. *The Education of Mexican and Spanish-Speaking Children in Texas.* Austin: Univ. of Texas Press.

_____. 1965. *Spanish Speaking Children of the Southwest.* Austin: Univ. of Texas Press.

McCollum, Pamela A., and Constance L. Walker. 1990. "The Assessment of Bilingual Students: A Sorting Mechanism," pp. 293–314 in Steven Goldberg, ed., *Readings in Equal Education.* New York: AMS.

McDonald, Michael. 1987. "Project Merge: Maximizing Educational Remediation within General Education." *Counterpoint* 7,3: 17.

McLaren, Peter. 1989. *Life in Schools: An Introduction to Critical Pedagogy in the Foundations of Education.* White Plains, NY: Longman.

Met, Myriam. 1989. "Learning Language through Content: Learning Content through Language," pp. 43–64 in Kurt E. Müller, ed., *Languages in Elementary Schools.* New York: The American Forum, National Council on Foreign Languages and International Studies.

_____, and Vicki Galloway. 1992. "Research in Foreign Language Curriculum," pp. 852–90 in Philip W. Jackson, ed., *Handbook of Research on Curriculum: A Project of the American Educational Research Association.* New York: Macmillan.

Minnesota Department of Education. 1992. *Success for Every Learner: Outcome-Based Education in Minnesota.* St. Paul: Minnesota Dept. of Education.

Mohan, Bernard A. 1986. *Language and Content.* Reading, MA: Addison-Wesley.

Moore, Jean Marie. 1991. "An Analysis of the Cultural Content of Post-Secondary Textbooks for Spanish: Evidence of Information Processing Strategies and Types of Learning in Reading Selections and Post-Reading Adjunct Questions." Ph.D. diss., Univ. of Minnesota.

Müller, Kurt E. 1989. "Policy and Curricular Implications of Expanding Language Education in Elementary Schools," pp. 204–32 in Kurt E. Müller, ed., *Languages in Elementary Schools.* New York: The American Forum, National Council on Foreign Language and International Studies.

Murray, Frank B., and Daniel Fallon. 1989. *The Reform of Teacher Education for the Twenty-First Century: Project 30 Year One Report.* Newark, DE: Project 30.

National Board for Professional Teaching Standards. 1991. *Toward High and Rigorous Standards for the Teaching Profession: Initial Policies and Perspectives of the National Board for Professional Teaching Standards.* 3d ed. Detroit: NBPTS.

National Commission on Excellence in Education. 1983. *A Nation at Risk: The Imperative for Educational Reform.* Washington, DC: U.S. Dept. of Education.

New American Schools Development Corporation. 1991. *Designs for a New Generation of American Schools: A Request for Proposal.* Arlington, VA: New American Schools Development Corp.

Nieto, Sonia. 1992. *Affirming Diversity: The Sociopolitical Context of Multicultural Education*. White Plains, NY: Longman.

Oakes, Jeannie. 1988. "Tracking in Mathematics and Science Education: A Structural Contribution to Unequal Schooling," pp. 106–12 in Lois Weis, ed., *Class, Race, and Gender in American Education*. Albany: State Univ. of New York Press.

Ogbu, John. 1978. *Minority Education and Caste: The American System in Cross-Cultural Perspective*. San Diego, CA: Academic Press. [out of print]

Otheguy, Ricardo. 1982. "Thinking about Bilingual Education: A Critical Appraisal." *Harvard Educational Review* 52: 301–14.

Passow, Harry A. 1987. "Present and Future Directions in School Reform," pp. 13–39 in Thomas J. Sergiovanni and John H. Moore, eds., *Schooling for Tomorrow: Directing Reforms to Issues That Count*. Needham Heights, MA: Allyn and Bacon.

Pennycook, Alastair. 1990. "Critical Pedagogy and Second Language Education." *System* 18: 303–14.

Placer-Barber, Venus. 1981. "Starting an English as a Second Language Program." *Bilingual Education Resource Series*. Washington, DC: U.S. Dept. of Health, Education, and Welfare. [ED 302 090]

Post-Secondary Options Act. 1992. Minnesota Statutes, vol. 10, sections 120–23, "School Districts, Powers and Duties," St. Paul, MN: West.

President's Commission on Foreign Languages and International Studies. 1980. "Strength through Wisdom: A Critique of U.S. Capability." *Modern Language Journal* 64: 9–57.

Ramirez, Arnulfo G. 1985. *Bilingualism through Schooling: Cross Cultural Education for Minority and Majority Students*. Albany: State Univ. of New York Press.

Renaissance Group. 1989. *Teachers for the New World: A Statement of Principles*. Cedar Falls: Univ. of Northern Iowa.

Rhodes, Nancy C., and Rebecca L. Oxford. 1988. *A National Profile of Foreign Language Instruction at the Elementary and Secondary School Levels*. Technical Report #6. Los Angeles: Center for Language Education and Research.

Sizer, Theodore R. 1984. *Horace's Compromise: The Dilemma of the American High School*. Boston: Houghton Mifflin.

Skutnabb-Kangas, Tove. 1984. *Bilingualism or Not: The Education of Minorities*. Avon, Eng.: Multilingual Matters.

Sleeter, Christine, and Carl A. Grant. 1988. *Making Choices for Multicultural Education: Five Approaches to Race, Class, and Gender*. New York: Merrill.

Snow, Catherine. 1992. "Perspectives on Second-Language Development: Implications for Bilingual Education." *Educational Researcher* 21,2: 16–19.

Snow, Marguerite A. 1986. "Common Terms in Second Language Education." Los Angeles: Center for Language Education and Research. [ED 278 259]

Tedick, Diane J. 1992. "Reconceptualizing Language in Second Languages and Cultures Teacher Education." Unpublished manuscript, Univ. of Minnesota.

Walker, Constance L. 1987. "Hispanic Achievement: Old Views and New Perspectives. Success or Failure?" pp. 15–32 in Henry T. Trueba, ed., *Learning and the Language Minority Student*. Boston: Newbury House (Heinle and Heinle).

Walz, Joel. 1986. "Is Oral Proficiency Possible with Today's French Textbooks?" *Modern Language Journal* 70: 13–20.

4

Inquiry in Language Teacher Education

JoAnn Hammadou

University of Rhode Island

Background

The Need for Research

There is much evidence of serious dissatisfaction with the outcomes of U.S. education. Students are reported to lack various skills and facts that we wish them to have (National Commission 1983). One suggested remedy to this deplorable situation is better teachers based on better teacher education (Carnegie Forum 1983; Holmes Group 1986; National Commission 1985). This recommendation assumes that better-educated teachers will be able to bring about the kinds and amounts of learning that we desire but do not yet see, an assumption that raises complex issues, worthy of serious study on if, how, when, and where such change for the better can be effected.

Foreign language education's success rate has not been immune to the criticisms leveled at U.S. education in general. (See Lange 1987 for an overview.) Although we have some helpful ideas about what general principles work in generic teacher education (Brophy and Good 1986), we have much less information on how to develop teachers that produce language learners with open-minded curiosity about other cultures, languages, and literatures who make steady gains in language proficiency and steady losses in ethnocentrism. Nevertheless, the mandate to do so is in all the reform literature, and the goal is certainly a laudable one. If we truly have the desire to improve foreign language

JoAnn Hammadou (Ph.D., The Ohio State University) is Assistant Professor of French in the Department of Modern and Classical Languages and Literatures at the University of Rhode Island, where she teaches preservice and inservice courses on foreign language education and second language acquisition. Author of several articles on language teaching and research in such journals as *The Modern Language Journal, Foreign Language Annals,* and the *French Review,* she is a member of ACTFL, AERA, AATF, and RIFLA (Rhode Island Foreign Language Association).

education, we must also have the will to improve foreign language *teacher* education. Unfortunately, the study of foreign language teacher education is very much in its infancy. The prerequisites for improvement seem threefold: (1) study what we currently do to identify its strengths and weaknesses; (2) study what is done in all other areas of teacher education in order to learn from others, avoid reinventing the wheel, and situate foreign language teachers' development in the larger context of all teacher education; and (3) study proposed changes and reforms to decide their worth or merit.

In 1987, a review of the previous ten years of research in foreign language teacher education found 75 articles on the topic, but only 8 that were teacher-education research reports (Bernhardt and Hammadou 1987). A quick review of the research listed in the ERIC data base produces 7 new studies since then, including 3 surveys and 2 program evaluations. Given the growing expectations and hopes being placed in teachers and in teacher educators' abilities to influence teachers, serious inquiry is long overdue.

The first step that we may need to take is to look closely at what research on teacher education is. It makes good sense to study foreign language teacher education if so many hopes and expectations are tied to it. What will it mean to conduct such research? The responses will be numerous and diverse. Many different styles of research are possible, all giving different perspectives on similar questions. Language educators must become more familiar and more comfortable with the conventions of educational research if we are ever going to find answers to key questions plaguing the profession. Certainly, in order to fulfill prerequisites (1) and (3) above we must conduct our own original research; no one is going to do it for us, nor should we want them to if we want to shape and control meaningful improvement in the development of foreign language teachers.

Parameters of Teacher-Education Research

One difficult challenge is to pin down what educators mean by the term "teacher-education research." Most globally, if one plans to study areas that affect teachers and what teachers do, then any and all educational research becomes teacher-education research. More narrowly, one might restrict the definition to the study of the university curricula for the training of preservice teachers. The solution for how to delineate teacher-education research seems somewhere in between with much gray area around the edges.

Cruickshank (1990) reviewed several models for defining the variables of the teacher-education field. One model (Cruickshank 1984) uses six variables: (1) *teacher educators* (which includes the cooperating teachers as well as all professors of the teacher candidate), (2) *preservice teacher-education students,* (3) *contexts* where teacher preparation takes place (usually campuses and K–12 schools), (4) *content* of the teacher-education curriculum (general education, professional and specialty studies, clinical and laboratory experiences),

(5) *instruction* (real, vicarious, or abstract), and (6) *outcomes* (the preparation of capable teachers).

The contexts and content of teacher development lead us quickly back to the larger domain of teaching/learning research. For foreign language teachers this includes studies on second language acquisition, language learners, and the language classroom. Research conducted by foreign language educators in recent years has emphasized these areas rather than the process of preparing teachers to teach.

The Teacher-Education Researcher

It is not entirely clear who will conduct teacher-education research for foreign-language-specific pedagogy. Traditionally the educators who identify themselves as *teacher* educators are located in diverse settings. The membership of the Association of Teacher Educators (ATE), for example, is composed of university faculty and administrators, teachers and administrators of precollegiate schools both public and private, and professionals in state departments, federal governmental agencies, and private practice (Buttery et al. 1990). Foreign language educators are also spread among all these settings, and any one of them could be a site for research. Nevertheless, it is usually expected that the bulk of educational research will fall to university faculties. Among foreign language faculties, however, those who are most active in teacher development often have little or no training in educational research methods. As we decry the lack of teacher-education research in foreign languages, we have met the enemy and he is us. Can we wait until new faculty trained in research methods takes over the majority of teacher preparation in the United States (which may never happen)? Or should we encourage, support, train, and assist those who are trained in literary analysis, linguistic analysis, or teaching methods to retool themselves to do teacher-education research? If so, how can this be done in a way to assure quality research results?

The answer to these questions is not clear, but at the least, we need to recognize that one of the largest constraints on research is the lack of research training of those who are most active in preparing future language teachers. It seems appropriate that those professionals who are doing teacher education are the ones who will have the pertinent questions that need answering. Support should be provided to turn those questions into research studies to inform the profession. Language educators with research training should volunteer to work collaboratively with others, and/or teacher educators without such training should seek support from researchers from other disciplines or from colleagues around the country. Indeed, the value of collaboration goes beyond the ability to offset one individual's deficits and, as discussed later under the rubric of Action Research, may be a powerful research tool. The purpose of this chapter is to demystify the research process for novices and act as catalyst for teacher-education research for novice and expert alike.

The following review is not intended as a critique of earlier research studies or a complete review of foreign language teacher-education literature, but rather as an overview of the kinds of inquiry that are being or can be conducted in the field. It is hoped that this overview will inspire foreign language education researchers to expand their horizons by trying other research methods. Also, teacher educators who have not yet taken the plunge into any research projects can be inspired to delve into the study of research methodology in order to help increase the research knowledge base. Finally, interested consumers of teacher-education research can take a peek backstage at some of the considerations that accompany such research. Stimulating interest in research and increasing the number of participants in different styles of inquiry should permit an expansion of the quantity and quality of foreign language teacher-education research.

Inquiry Paradigms

Research, defined as systematic inquiry in a field of study, is guided by an agreed-upon set of concepts, procedures, and standards of judgments (Soltis forthcoming), or *paradigms* (Kuhn 1970). In plant science, for example, concepts such as *fungi, parasite,* and *symbiosis* aid researchers in understanding and explaining what they are studying, and rigorous experimental testing with experimental and control groups is both the procedure required for discovery and the standard used for judgment of the merit of the discovery. The two major paradigms that have been used in educational research, including teacher-education research, traditionally have been labeled the *quantitative* and *qualitative* paradigms.[1]

The quantitative paradigm is also often called the positivist approach by its critics or scientific or experimental research by its practitioners, who stress the need for tight controls on all variables in order to be able to demonstrate clearly that any results obtained are due to specified factors rather than to intervening extraneous variables or to chance. The second major paradigm, qualitative research, was so labeled to underscore its concern for investigating the quality of human existence. Sometimes it is called constructionist to emphasize the study of people's construction of social life and institutions. Others refer to it as "naturalistic" to emphasize the study of a naturally occurring social setting. Rather than attempting to exclude extraneous variables, these researchers examine all relevant variables and their interactions.

No single paradigm could possibly fit all inquiries in education, and no single paradigm is monolithic; each subsumes a range of inquiry styles. Moreover, individual research projects often overlap both research paradigms. Still, the traditional distinctions are useful starting points for understanding what teacher-education research is and how it is conducted.

Each broad category of research approach is summarized below with illustrative examples from teacher-education research and with possible research questions for the future. Those interested in collaborative research and /

or answering questions of local concern may find the last paradigms of greatest interest. First, however, the principles of quantitative research provide an important introduction to the notion of investigative rigor that should be kept in mind regardless of the techniques of inquiry that one chooses.

Quantitative Methods

Experimental Studies

Underlying Principles.   Experimental studies using the quantitative paradigm have their roots in natural science methodology. Their primary objective is to find causal relationships. The researcher designs a study to investigate a *research question,* such as "What is the relationship between the number of months spent in a Spanish-speaking country and Spanish listening ability?" or "What is the relationship between participation in an early field experience and teaching evaluations during student teaching?" Each of these studies contains two *variables* that can be represented numerically, either as a score or as a numbered category. In the first study, the number of months can be counted and listening ability measured as a test score. The researcher must be able to demonstrate, with a specified degree of certainty, that changes in listening scores are due to study abroad rather than to some other factor. In the second study, preservice teachers can be categorized as participants (1) or nonparticipants (0) in an early field experience and earn scores based on evaluations of teaching criteria. Again, careful design of the study is paramount in obtaining results that are *generalizable* to other similar groups and situations.

At the heart of quantitative research is the rigorous testing of research *hypotheses,* such as: "There will be no significant differences attributable to months of stay in the foreign country on the measure of listening comprehension." Statistical analyses are used to test the accuracy of research hypotheses. Within given limits of certainty the hypothesis is found to be probably true and "accepted" or unproven and "rejected."

These analyses serve as an important check or balance to the fallible use of human observation of phenomena. Sports fans around the world tend to believe, for example, in some version of what basketball fans call the "hot hand," that is, that a player who has scored points will tend to continue to do so. Statistical analysis using the laws of probability have proven this concept to be false. Players overall have not been found to follow a successful shot with a series of successful shots beyond what the laws of probability would predict for them. Nevertheless, observers of the game remain convinced of what they see. It is not difficult to think of similar common beliefs about language learning and teaching that still require experimental research to investigate their validity.

One of the great strengths of quantitative experimental research is the ability, through statistical analysis, to make inferences. For example, we may need to know why students who begin a teacher-education program in a foreign language do not complete the program, but we are unlikely to be able to survey every foreign language preservice teacher. With a well-designed research project, we can generalize from a *sample* of that population. Nevertheless, most educational research involves some compromise of the ideal of fully *random sampling* from the intended population. Even much medical research must be conducted on animals rather than humans with resulting problems of generalizability of their findings. Researchers and consumers of research need to be alert to the fact that the farther away the sample is from a truly random sample of the intended population, the greater the violation of a major assumption of inferential statistics.

Finally, the terms of the research question must be *operationally defined.* That is, the variables to be studied must be defined in terms of the operations or processes that create them. For example, native language may be defined as the language spoken with one's primary caregiver while a child. If the researcher is unable to identify reliably events that lead to a variable, it is operationally identified by its dynamic properties. For example, the variable "teacher praise" must be defined by the comments and behaviors that will "count" as a teacher's praise of students. Intelligence might be the symbolic ability to solve logic problems, and a bilingual may be a person who is judged to be a native speaker among unilingual speakers of each of two languages.

Usually, the more unique an operational definition is, the more useful it is for research purposes. An anxious language learner may be someone who forgets words or phrases just learned, but many other reasons might also explain why a student cannot remember. If we say that an anxious student is one who forgets words just learned, stammers as he talks, and suffers a nervous stomach or sweaty palms during class, we have added a more unique set of criteria associated with language-learning anxiety. Researchers must consider how clearly the criteria distinguish the concept from everything else (Tuckman 1978).

Examples of the Paradigm in Practice.   A classic example of quantitative research in foreign language was the Pennsylvania Foreign Language Project of 1970. In this study three teaching methods ("traditional," "functional skills," and a combined method) were compared (Smith 1970). A large number of students and their teachers were randomly assigned to a teaching method, and their language skills were thoroughly tested. The project, although a skillful application of experimental research design, suffered from inconsistencies within a given "method" as practiced by individual teachers. No procedures were the same in all separate classrooms. Random assignment of teachers and students to each method could not overcome that flaw.

Since the Pennsylvania Project left many unanswered questions despite accurate use of random assignment and statistical analyses, the quantitative research paradigm has been used more profitably for much more narrowly focused research questions. These studies have examined individual learning questions as narrow as language learners' acquisition of a single morpheme and have not often dealt directly with foreign language teacher education. (See Kasper and Dahl 1991 for several examples.) The paradigm has been used extensively and profitably in areas such as elementary math and reading education and science education. The probable differences between foreign language classes and others make the applicability of the findings of this research to foreign language teacher education problematic.

An interesting example of the paradigm in practice is the body of research on "wait time" (pauses between teachers' questions and students' responses in classrooms). Early studies in this area, primarily in science classrooms, revealed significant positive effects on cognitive and affective outcomes for students when teachers paused longer than usual after asking a question and after a student answered a question. The dependent variables studied include length of student responses, number of unsolicited responses, failures to respond, inflected responses, speculative responses, student-to-student comparisons of data, evidence-inference statements, incidence of student questions, incidence of responses from slower learners, variety in verbal behavior, teacher-response flexibility, teacher expectations, and number and type of questions asked by the teacher (Gooding et al. 1984). Positive changes in teachers' questioning level and in student achievement have been the two factors that seem to have generated the most interest in this research area. By adhering to the principles of the quantitative research paradigm, a cause-and-effect relationship has been determined between the independent variable of wait time and many of the above dependent variables.

Evidence was also generated that the teaching skill of using wait time profitably can be taught. Researchers have shown that it is possible to train teachers to use wait time in order to allow more time for students to initiate and complete their own statements in classroom dialogue. (Rowe 1974; Swift and Gooding 1983). From this research it was discovered that teachers need to modify their uses of wait time because classes working on memory level drill do not benefit from extended times, although classes working on higher-level thinking skills do.

Through the use of the quantitative research paradigm, researchers in this area have been able not only to make inferences to other similar students and teachers, but to build on each others' work, thanks to the paradigm's required operational definitions of terms. Definitions of which classroom pauses constitute wait time and which ones do not have been refined, and accurate measurement of wait time has been increasingly improved.[2]

Responding, in part, to research on teacher questioning such as wait-time research, Brock (1986) tested the ability of teachers of English as a Second Language to increase the number of "referential questions" (that is, questions that "request information not known by the questioner," p. 48). Furthermore, she described the different characteristics of students' answers to such questions versus answers to "display questions," for which there is only one right answer already known by the questioner.

In an attempt to adhere to the requirements of experimental research design, Brock randomly assigned students to one of four groups and then two of the four groups to treatment and two to the control. One of four teachers was randomly assigned to each student group.[3] This procedure is preferable to the use of intact classes and their teachers as a unit, because it is likely, for example, that factors other than chance may influence the formation of classes and make them different in ways that will ultimately change the result of the study.

Brock concluded that teachers could be trained to ask considerably more referential questions and that answers to such questions were notably different from those to display questions. No attempt was made to measure whether such differences ultimately led to improved language learning.

The distinction between referential questions and display questions may suffer, at times, from a less-than-crystal-clear operational definition. Tollefson (1988: 39) offers as an example of a display question "Where are you from?" The answer to this question may or may not be known already to the questioner and probably is only known, at best, in part. Tollefson states that display questions are rarely asked in natural interaction, but this example seems to be a common one in natural interactions. A common agreement among researchers and readers of research on the operational definition of variables is an important first step to allow for the sharing and expanding of research results.

Examples for the Future.   Researchers have been fascinated in the recent past by the development of the language learner. Lines of research have investigated such phenomena as interlanguage and fossilization, among many others. Now, new research tracks must be opened to study the development of the language teacher. Experimental trials can be used to test the efficacy of most that we do to assist the development of teachers. Trials of the effects of different clinical settings and of different entry routes into teaching are needed. The effects of what we are currently doing should be examined for various populations of preservice and novice teachers. Do current training practices affect minority candidates differently from others? Which interventions with novice teachers have the greatest impacts on their decision making? Are some teaching practices, such as microteaching, most appreciated by novice teachers early or late in their preservice development? When is the use of case-study analysis most salient for novice teachers? Are principles from case writing remembered better than those from case analysis?

Finally, the knowledge base about language learners that is slowly growing should be put to the test. Which elements of the research base on language learning are most useful for novice teachers? Using the experimental research paradigm, we would ask if there are any measurable improvements in the teaching of those who could demonstrate understanding of those concepts. Almost any intervention that we use to influence the professional lives of teachers is potentially subject to experimental inquiry when comparisons of two or more options can be made.

Statistics.   There are numerous inferential statistical procedures available for use in quantitative studies. Extensive course work is needed to learn to design and apply them appropriately. If the reader is interested primarily in becoming a more knowledgeable consumer of quantitative research, a review of only the most commonly used procedures would probably suffice. Kennedy (1988) surveyed sixty-seven educational research journals to identify the most commonly reported statistical procedures. In order of frequency they were: analysis of variance, correlation, t-test, multiple analysis of variance, multiple regression, and chi-square.[4]

Quasi-Experimental Studies

When random assignment of subjects to experimental groups does not or cannot happen, the experimental design is labeled *quasi*-experimental. If other important features of experimental design are respected (such as clear, operationally defined variables and the use of nontreatment or "control" groups for comparison purposes), much useful information can still come from the manipulation of variables and the statistical analysis of results from these studies. The procedures for conducting the studies are otherwise the same as those for experimental studies.

Example for the Future.   Common sense would suggest that if all foreign language teacher educators that a group of students encountered believed equally strongly about a given teaching principle, the students would be more likely to modify their own beliefs accordingly. A study could be conducted in which all faculty were inventoried for their agreement with such statements as "Every foreign language class should include personalized questions for students to answer." Their students could be similarly polled. The variability within student groups could be compared in relation to the variability within their respective faculty groups at the beginning and at the end of the students' formal training. The size of the differences over time would help to reveal the ability of faculty consensus to produce change in preservice teachers.

Correlational Studies

Correlation coefficients are statistical tools that are used to compare measurements on two or more variables to determine the degree of relationship among these variables. Studies that use correlation are used to uncover relationships, often to understand better what factors make up a complex unit. They are frequently expressed from –1.00 to +1.00 with a value +1.00 meaning that as one variable increases the other increases in exactly the same ratio. A value of –1.00 means that as one increases the other decreases in exactly the same ratio. The closer the correlation is to .00, the less relationship there is between the variables.

For example, Politzer (1983) studied the relationship between course grades and learner strategies such as correcting other students' language mistakes to oneself. A positive correlation was found between frequency of use of such a strategy and the teacher's evaluation of a student's proficiency. Sometimes correlations are used as predictors of some future event. Postlethwaite and Denton (1978) sought the relationship between placement in homogeneous ability groups and achievement gains in French, math, English, and social studies. No relationship could be found. In other words, students of comparable ability made comparable gains regardless of the grouping.

Other Examples of the Paradigm in Practice. Loadman and Deville (1990) analyzed the correlation between scores on the National Teacher Examination (NTE), the American College Test (ACT), and the GPAs of students in teacher education. The ACT (the ability that students bring to the program) proved to be a better predictor of final success on the NTE than did GPA (what is learned during the program). The outcome of this general education correlational study is an example of research results that seem most likely to have implications for any area of teacher education, including foreign language. The statistical procedure of correlation can only indicate a relationship, of course. In this example, it is still up to the teacher educators to decide how to use the predictive value of the ACT variable, the appropriateness of the NTE cutoff score, or the merit of the use of the NTE. The predictive power of the variable does not help identify the validity of the overall procedure.

Welch (1988) correlated final scores in an intensive Spanish course with various student behaviors and found volunteering in class to have an especially significant relationship. Volunteering had a .65 correlation with final course grade. This correlation is quite high for classroom research. When squared, the correlation coefficient represents a percentage of the shared attributes of the two variables. This means that 42 percent of whatever goes into the final course grade is shared by whatever goes into the behavior of volunteering. This leaves 58 percent of the elements in each not in common and shows that even the best correlations in classroom research leave many things unexplained.

In addition, one must remember that correlation cannot identify cause and effect. Therefore, volunteering may have caused higher final scores, or both variables may have been influenced by some additional, unexamined variable. Correlation coefficients can measure the strength of the relationship but not its cause.

Correlation coefficients are affected by the range of the scores being studied. In other words, correlations will be lower if the range is narrow and will increase when the range is widened.[5] The more homogeneous the group being studied, the smaller the correlations will be. Correlation is most helpful, therefore, with a sizeable random sample with an interesting amount of variability within the variables being studied.

Examples for the Future. An advantage of correlational research is that a wide variety of different variables can be studied at once. Novice teachers' satisfaction with their collegiate program and/or their first teaching assignment can be measured and then correlated with numerous features of the teacher-development process. A goodness of fit can be identified for the aspects of the program that correlate most highly with teacher satisfaction and, equally important, those features of the teacher-preparation program that correlate with teacher dissatisfaction can be noted.

University faculties make selection choices and administrators allocate resources for preparing future Japanese, Spanish, or ESL teachers or for preparing secondary teachers versus FLES teachers. Do we make those choices, which have important consequences, based on sound evidence? Correlational studies of perceived needs among different components of the community, retention rates, and willingness of advanced language learners to pursue teaching are some of the factors that should influence universities when they make these important allocations rather than the ability of one campus interest group to lobby harder than another. In a similar vein, the selection of individuals for teacher-development programs has important long-lasting results. What factors lead to the choice of a foreign language teaching career? What are the common causes for abandoning foreign language teacher training? What are the consequences of the teacher selection process and how do these features correlate with both teacher satisfaction and productivity? The correlations or relationships among many of these variables would, especially on a large scale, give us an interesting portrait of beginning teachers and the system that encourages or discourages them.

Descriptive Studies

Descriptive research is also used to test research hypotheses or answer research questions, but unlike experimental researchers, descriptive researchers exercise no control over the variables being investigated. There is more to it, nevertheless, than simply asking questions and reporting the results. Appropriate sampling techniques are crucial, and data collection is an issue that comes into sharp focus as well in such studies.

Quantitative descriptive studies involve the use of a data collection instrument of some kind in order to record the frequencies or durations of the variables of interest. The challenge in classrooms is obviously great to divide the infinitely varied elements of human behavior into categories that others can recognize and understand, and that will lead to further understandings. Several instruments have been adapted for use in foreign language classrooms (e.g., Flanders 1960; Hough 1980; Jarvis 1968; Moskowitz 1970; Wragg 1970), and others have been devised specifically for categorizing foreign language learning behaviors (e.g., Fanselow 1987). The researcher must grapple with the validity (reality) of such categories as "initiating information" versus "soliciting clarification" and the reliability with which different observers can agree upon instances of each category. Once such categories are identified, much useful descriptive information can be gathered about their frequency, their sequencing, etc.

One of the important functions that descriptive studies serve is to provide a baseline of information about the status quo of an area of research. This baseline then becomes a clear starting point for other research efforts to influence and improve education in that area. For example, before the science education findings about changes in wait time could be applied to foreign language classrooms, foreign language educators needed to know what wait times were currently being used in the foreign language setting. Shrum (1985a, 1985b) measured wait times over a four-week period in first-year Spanish and French classes. Her descriptive study showed that wait time was longer in second language classes than in the science classes (as reported by Rowe 1974). She also found that both high and low performers had significantly longer wait time than average performers (unlike the science studies, which showed only high performers being afforded longer thinking time).

Nyikos (1992a) found that inservice teachers who did not incorporate learning strategy instruction into their lesson plans after a teacher-education course on learning strategies were also teachers who used the transmission model of education (e.g., lectures) with their own students. Only one-third of the 47 subjects included in their plans all aspects of learning strategy instruction as presented in the course and these were teachers who also averaged the greatest number of interactive activities per lesson. She concludes that the change in teaching behavior was accomplished only for those teachers who needed to make the smallest changes in their teaching routines. The remaining teachers summarized strategy use for their students rather than embedding it into student work or seemed to believe that assigned tasks would automatically produce task-appropriate strategies from students.

For further research Nyikos suggests that teacher-education research has much to gain from building on learning research. The self-monitoring ability of the teacher as learner should be described more fully as well as the difficulties of transfer of skills and metacognitive control for the teacher as learner in general. Much useful descriptive research can be done to chart the change process in the teacher as learner.

Foreign language teacher education has been a field in which numerous reports have been published about what should be changed before methodical study has been made of what *is* (Bernhardt and Hammadou 1987). Descriptive studies are a necessary first step in the process of learning what is being done in the development of new teachers, before we can move to the next step of how we can improve on the status quo.

Survey Studies

A common category of descriptive study, the survey, is sometimes viewed with a certain disdain because many people have been the victim of poorly planned or poorly written questionnaires. This is unfortunate, because survey research, when conducted thoroughly, can provide very valuable data. In a sample or cross-sectional survey the researcher is able to infer information about a larger population as in other quantitative research.

Surveys can be used to explore relationships between variables as well as to determine the distribution of individual variables.[6] An appreciation of the potential pitfalls of survey research will help to improve their overall quality.

First, a reasonable goal must be established. If, for example, the question of interest is whether foreign language students are more interested in study abroad than other students, not just foreign language students should be surveyed. If 75 percent of foreign language students respond that they are interested in study abroad, that fact alone could not be used to proclaim them more or less interested than anyone else; it may be that the figure reflects the student body as a whole. It may or may not be a precondition to language study; it may or may not be a result of language study. The limitations on conclusions that can be drawn from certain questions and what questions are needed to attain the researcher's goal must be adequately identified. Finally, the design of the individual questions will restrict the type of statistical analysis that can be performed; the severity and the kind of restriction will depend on the form of the data collected.

Examples of the Paradigm in Practice.   Surveys have been used successfully in foreign language education to provide useful demographics about several of the variables in the teacher-education field as described earlier by Cruickshank. A complete survey of the nature of the school sites in which foreign language teacher training (e.g., student teaching) is taking place has not occurred recently. In 1988, however, Rhodes and Oxford provided a national picture of foreign language teaching sites that reveals that 22 percent of elementary schools and 87 percent of secondary schools offer foreign languages. They also discovered that a shortage of foreign language teachers and inadequate inservice training were listed among the six major problems facing these schools.

Schrier (1989) investigated the location of foreign language preservice teachers' field experiences and found that a majority (55 percent) were in private and public secondary schools and that only 29 percent of foreign language teacher-education programs provided preservice teachers with a comprehensive set of experiences in urban, suburban, and rural schools. In this survey of 500 four-year institutions, Schrier also investigated the variables of the teacher educator and the content of the foreign language teacher-preparation curriculum. Of those institutions that had a foreign language teacher educator (only 43.48 percent), most were found in a foreign language department. The majority of these teacher educators (85 percent) had a doctorate in literature; only one of the institutions reported having a specialist with a doctorate in foreign language education. Examples of some of the findings about the teacher-preparation curriculum include: 41 percent report that instruction in computer-assisted instruction in foreign languages is unavailable and 74 percent report that the principal source of learning about curricular design is during student teaching under the direction of the cooperating teacher.

Hammadou and Schrier (1988) went beyond the counting of frequencies to explore the relationships between administrators' foreign language backgrounds and their perceptions of their roles as supervisors of foreign language instruction. A chi-square analysis revealed very few relationships between language ability and items of difficulty in supervising foreign language teachers. Administrators were evenly split over whether their generally limited foreign language ability plays a role in their effectiveness as supervisors of foreign language instruction.

Numerous factors can influence the success rate with questionnaire responses. Hammadou and Schrier received responses from 46 percent of those surveyed. Rhodes and Oxford received 52 percent of the responses from over 2,000 questionnaires after sending a small incentive (a button) and, when necessary, a second questionnaire and follow-up phone call. Schrier received 70 percent after sending a small incentive that referred to the need for the data to complete her dissertation and the importance of the topic to foreign language teacher education. Forty-five to 55 percent is considered excellent, and more than 56 percent is considered an exceptional response for survey research.

Examples for the Future.   There is still much to be known about the status of all variables of teacher education. Who are the novice teachers? Are a disproportionate number of foreign language teachers teaching outside of their area of expertise? It appears that most foreign language teacher-education faculty came to teacher education from "somewhere else." Why do they choose to make such changes? What are the factors that influence such career moves? Does the different preceding work experience influence the supervisory style, for example, of teacher educators in any consistently different ways?

Qualitative Methods

Naturalistic studies using qualitative methods have their roots in both anthropology and sociology. Both areas focus on the social nature of human behavior. Within this general research paradigm one finds numerous research techniques, such as ethnography, case studies, diary studies, life histories, in-depth interviews, work portfolios, and semiotics.

Bogdan and Biklen (1982: 27–30) outline five general characteristics of the paradigm:

1. Qualitative research has the natural setting as the direct source of data, and the researcher is the key instrument.
2. Qualitative research is descriptive.
3. Qualitative researchers are concerned with process rather than simply with outcomes or products.
4. Qualitative researchers tend to analyze their data inductively.
5. "Meaning" is of essential concern to the qualitative approach.

It seems natural that foreign language researchers would be leaders in the field of qualitative research, given that there is such an obvious link between an interest in language and an interest in human interaction. Although some of the seminal classroom work in ethnography has been done by language educators (e.g., Cazden et al. 1975; Heath 1983; Welch 1988), many questions about the culture of the foreign language classroom and language learning remain uninvestigated. The use of the paradigm has long historical roots but has gained widespread interest in teacher education or in foreign language education only in recent years.[7]

The naturalistic paradigm frames generalizability differently from the experimental paradigm. Rather than highlighting sampling procedures, this paradigm relies on the depth of understanding of a single case to provide relevance to others, although a large and diverse sample of cases, together with description of ever larger cultural contexts, also help readers of ethnography to see implications to their own settings (Watson-Gegeo 1988: 581).

"Participant observation" in naturalistic studies means that the researcher takes an active part in the processes being observed in order to understand them better. A consensus of understanding is sought from all participants. The successful researcher must be able to generate and maintain the full trust of participants to ensure open and honest input into the research by all.

Qualitative studies seem especially well suited to describing change over time and capturing variables that emerge over time, unlike experimental research, which identifies and defines all variables before the study begins. Process discovery has been the hallmark of qualitative studies.

Ethnography

Ethnography is one subcategory of the paradigm. It has its roots in anthropology, which inspires interest in the interactions between the cultural group studied and the larger cultural group contexts in which it is found. Two major procedures distinguish ethnography from other research methods: extensive investment of time in the natural setting and the inclusion of all participants' perspectives. It is a collaborative process, and the researcher must attempt to understand the events on the participants' terms. It requires, therefore, "intensive, detailed observation of a setting over a long period of time" (Watson-Gegeo 1988).

Many ethnographers advocate the use of *triangulation*. The most common type is data triangulation, which is an attempt "to gather observations with multiple sampling strategies. Observations on time, social situations, and persons in various forms of interaction can all be gathered" (Denzin 1970: 472). The likelihood of uncovering negative cases is thereby increased. Other common versions of triangulation include multiple observers' perceptions and multiple perspectives on data analysis.

Examples of the Paradigm in Practice.   Welch (1988) investigated what students are required to know and do in a beginning Spanish course and how students influence, negotiate, and interpret language-learning tasks. She questioned the assumption that teachers are the primary determinants of classroom interactions and set out to use the methodology of "thick description" (Geertz 1973) to describe the social behavior of groups in the language classroom. Using a summer intensive Spanish course sequence, Welch observed 150 hours of beginning language classes, generated 150 hours of audiotapes, approximately 200 typed pages of field notes, and scores of hours of interviews (Welch, personal communication). She sought to ascertain the students' role in shaping the course. She discovered that students recognized and could explain the social skills needed for academic success in this particular course, such as rehearsing and appearing enthusiastic. When instructors changed, Welch found that more successful students were able to identify changes in the new teacher's focus and adjust their behaviors accordingly. Furthermore, students' behaviors thwarted the new instructor's attempts at conducting class entirely as he might have liked. Welch's research design permitted a confirmation that the (language) teacher is not the sole determinant of classroom interactions. Instead, many interactions and classroom procedures are negotiated among the students and teacher. This study illustrates the benefits of using all participants' perspectives as the locus of observation.

A much-cited example of language ethnography is Carrasco's (1981) study of second language kindergartners and teachers' awareness of students' performance level. Like Welch, Carrasco used ethnographic methods and applied them to certain elements of the social context of the classroom. He was able to make visible as a result the discrepancies between teachers' and peers' views of students' abilities.

Kleinsasser's (in Kleinsasser and Savignon 1991) version of triangulation was to combine surveys, interviews, and "micro-ethnographic observations" of teachers to describe the social organization of their school and language department in order to better understand the sources of discrepancies between theory and practice in language teaching. He describes differences among teachers' "technical culture" along such continua as teacher certainty, teacher cohesiveness, and collaboration, and believes them to be linked with different teacher behaviors in the classroom. These researchers, and most other second language classroom ethnographers, have limited the scope of their investigations more than did the anthropologists who first devised the methods being used.

Examples for the Future.   Ethnography of the foreign language classroom is not yet aimed specifically at studying foreign language teacher development, but rather is still describing the social interactions between teachers and learners or learners and learners (Carrasco 1981; Enright 1984; van Lier 1984; Welch 1988). No ethnographer has yet reported from a foreign language methods class, for example.

There is anecdotal evidence that we teach as we were taught, and this phenomenon is obviously a barrier to change. Ethnography that studies the broad teacher developmental context of novice teachers and their prior language teachers could search for the ways in which those influences are initiated. Through interviews with novices and their former teachers and using reactions to videotaped samples of each others' lessons, insights could be gained into how the years of being an observational student of language teaching shapes the beliefs, knowledge, and behaviors of novices.

The dynamics of change need to be more fully understood. Nyikos (1992b) provides examples of some belief changes in preservice foreign language teachers and raises the interesting question of why her subjects seemed unable to see the disharmony between their initial altruistic beliefs about teaching and their growing belief in a "teacher control model" of language teaching. How and why changes occur in instructional choices as well as in beliefs and attitudes are at the heart of teacher education. The strong influence that belief systems have on how teachers approach their work in classrooms needs additional clarification.

In a related area, research that describes how "expert" teachers acquire and structure their understanding of foreign language teaching is also needed. Foreign-language-specific examples are needed to show what is unique to expert teachers. Using naturalistic methods, researchers could make explicit how foreign language teachers interpret classroom scenes and bring knowledge of foreign languages, pedagogy, learners, and management to their curricular plans and teaching practices. Although the results of this mode of research would not be a list of predictors to apply to teacher evaluation, it could help teachers interpret their own situations and invent their own solutions to similar dilemmas.

Case Study

Carrasco labels his ethnography (1981) a "case study," a term that nearly everyone is familiar with but hardly anyone can define. A primary feature of a case study is that a "bounded system" has been identified as the focus of the investigation (Merriam 1988). The bounded system, or case, is an example drawn from a class of possibilities. If the researcher were interested in the process of student teaching, for example, he or she would select a particular instance of student teaching to study intensively. Such an instance might be an individual student teacher, a specific teacher-education program, or a specific school.

Unlike survey research, for example, case studies do not claim any specific data-collection methods, although certain techniques seem to be used more than others. Guba and Lincoln (1981: 371) state that the purpose of a case study is "to reveal the properties of the class to which the instance being studied belongs." Intensive description of a single case is sometimes selected when the case is especially unique, such as the case study of French immersion teachers in the U.S. inner city (Salomone 1991). The qualitative case study uses most of the research techniques described previously to attain its goals.

Case studies are often "financed by people who have, directly or indirectly, power over those studied and portrayed." Sometimes "what people *think* they're doing, what they *say* they are doing, what they *appear* to others to be doing, and what in fact they are doing, may be sources of considerable discrepancy. . . . Any research which threatens to reveal these discrepancies threatens to create dissonance, both personal and political" (MacDonald and Walker 1977). All this creates an important ethical responsibility on the part of the researcher as well as demands on his or her powers of observation and interviewing and interpersonal skills. The researcher is, after all, the primary instrument of data collection in a case study.

Examples for the Future.   One useful line of inquiry could be to describe fully the changes (or lack thereof) in a small group of novice teachers during their professional university course work. Another interesting case study would be to examine a program in flux, such as a middle school program or a program just being considered, such as a FLEX program, and provide the "rich description" over time and / or from multiple perspectives that could be a helpful catalyst for others' introspection. Other case studies might examine the broad assumptions about language teacher education held by teacher educators, as begun by Freeman (1991). Fears of hindering teacher-education graduates in their attempts to get jobs or of damaging a floundering program may have held us back from probing too deeply in the past or encouraged us to preserve illusions. Complex problems demand such complete descriptions and will require complex solutions in the future, however.

Research Integration: Meta-Analyses

Very often the findings of educational research are many and conflicting. Synthesis of the findings of diverse studies is certainly desirable in order to reach some sort of coherent and understandable conclusion. Although many educators see the need for principled methods of integrating findings from qualitative studies, to date only methods for integrating quantitative studies have been substantially agreed upon in the profession. The procedure was named meta-analysis by Glass (1976).

There are numerous examples of meta-analysis in the educational research literature. Glass (forthcoming) estimates the number of published educational studies using the method to be in the thousands. It was devised as a reaction to earlier synthesizing techniques that lumped all original data for many studies into one and found significant results almost every time as a result of large groups. Meta-analysis does not eliminate completely that problem but reduces it by addressing additional questions such as the distributions among variables.

The four-step procedure is as follows: (1) collect all research on a given topic or sample literature if the body is very large; (2) code the characteristics of the studies, e.g., how the study was performed, with what materials, in what setting, etc.; (3) translate all findings from the studies into a ratio or coefficient, such as the mean differences on the key variable between groups studied; and (4) analyze the translated data using standard statistical techniques.

Example of the Paradigm in Practice.   The only foreign language education example of meta-analysis apparent via ERIC search is the synthesis of results on suggestopedia by Moon et al. (1986). Forty studies were identified on the topic, but only 14 supplied enough quantitative information to allow meta-analysis. Among the 14 the variables coded were: type of outcome (foreign language acquisition, language retention, or affective outcome), type of treatment (explicit suggestion, de-suggestion, or implicit suggestion), and degree of control. The final measures, or dependent variables, were achievement scores of some kind. A ratio was calculated by subtracting the means of the control groups from the means of the treatment groups. The conclusions included the finding that suggestopedia does have an overall positive effect on learning and, not surprisingly, that studies with weaker experimental controls had greater variability within the effect size.

Skeptics about suggestopedia and its use of music and relaxation to improve language learning may be pointing out already that meta-analysis does not and cannot correct flaws in the original studies. A common problem is disagreement about operational definitions of variables among studies. If it is not clear in the original study what exactly suggestopedia is, or if suggestopedia has a different definition in the second study, meta-analysis will naturally suffer.

The large number of meta-analyses being conducted in other areas of educational research should not be ignored by foreign language educators. For example, Kulik et al. (1990) conducted a meta-analysis of 108 evaluations of mastery learning programs and found an unusually strong positive effect on student achievement in colleges, high schools, and the upper grades of elementary schools. The effects were strongest for the weakest students, and mastery learning also had positive effects on student attitudes toward the courses. Self-pacing (such as exists in some university foreign language programs) often reduce, however, the completion rate of the course. Although only 1 foreign language study and 2 teacher-education studies were included among the 108 studies used, the composite evidence is compelling. The positive results for mastery learning are not limited to the hard sciences and math; on the contrary, the effects were strongest in the social sciences, such as education. Other research areas that have been able to show positive effects across studies through meta-analyses include peer and cross-age tutoring and computer-assisted instruction (Kulik and Kulik 1989).

Topics in foreign language education that appear to be reaching a "critical mass" of studies that might be examined together include those on the effect of advance organizers on comprehension or studies that compare student attention to language form versus attention to language meaning. No foreign language teacher-education-specific topic seems to have reached that stage.

Slavin (1986) proposed that meta-analyses should use only the "best evidence" and before bothering to code variables across studies, criteria should be pre-established to weed out all but the best research. Glass (forthcoming) argues, however, that "studies are not clearly demarcated in the real world outside of methods textbooks as either good or bad, valid or invalid. Valid findings sometimes arise from bad studies" and therefore, rather than trying to draw imprecisely some imaginary line between good and bad studies, the researchers should code deficiencies as one more variable to study in the meta-analysis. Glass continues to make an important point that could be expanded to refer to all responses to research, not just to meta-analysis: that is, that all studies inform on each other and that it is not reasonable that the less-than-perfect study, once completed, can or even should be ignored.

Action Research

The goal of action research is to gather evidence that can help the educator make decisions related to the local setting. The practicing educator (in this case teacher educator) is not interested in generalizing the results beyond the local setting (e.g., university, school site, or single classroom). Because generalizability to other settings is not part of the research goal, the measure of success is "practical significance" rather than "statistical significance" (Borg 1981: 249). Either or both quantitative and qualitative paradigms are used during action research projects.

The features of action research include: (1) It is *situational.* Researchers are interested in the context at hand. (2) It is *collaborative* between experienced researchers and experienced practitioners working together. (3) Team members themselves implement the research, which is therefore called *participatory.* (4) It is *self-evaluative,* that is, based on ongoing evaluation of the results by the participants (Cohen and Manion 1985).

The term "action research" usually is credited to John Collier, Commissioner of Indian Affairs from 1933 to 1945 (Wann 1953), who used it to describe a collaborative research effort of administrators, scientists, and Indians to improve Indian farming. Collier stressed the collaborative effort, which he believed resulted in more learning and more practical use of what was learned. Interest in the concept waned, however, and did not return in earnest until the 1980s. When the concept did return, the focus was once again on the importance of parity among teachers and researchers (Lieberman 1986; Oja and Pine 1983; Tikunoff and Ward 1983). These efforts from the early eighties reflected a definite interest in ways to enhance and improve teacher development. No examples could be found, however, that dealt specifically with foreign language teachers' learning other than those that dealt with foreign language learning itself.

Example of the Paradigm in Practice. Huebner and Jensen (1992) provide a recent example of the practice of action research that is collaborative, participatory, and self-evaluative. They set out to study the foreign language program of San Jose, CA, high schools, in which Jensen is a teacher and foreign language coordinator. The program faculty had, since 1984, increased their emphasis on oral proficiency by stressing "language use," "communicative exercises in a situational context," and, most recently, the use of the ACTFL Oral Proficiency Interview (OPI) as a testing device (p. 107). Specifically, they investigated the relationship between performance on the OPI and on more traditional measures of foreign language achievement, i.e. the College Board Achievement Tests in French and Spanish.[8] They found that students who did better on the OPI than other students in the program also did better on the College Board tests. They also noted that they found a great deal of variability in scores within each of the language courses (levels 2–5). They concluded that students who did well on the OPI did not suffer on more traditional measures of achievement after a program emphasis on oral proficiency.

The project was clearly collaborative, as the report describes participation from several levels of the school district, San Jose State University, and the

Stanford/School Collaborative. The project was clearly participatory, since Jensen was a teacher, administrator, and researcher. The project was less clearly situational, and in fact, the authors never label the project "action research."

The situational feature becomes an unclear and critical factor in labeling this research example. If the main interest is guiding the development of the local program, the research has met the necessary and appropriate criterion of practicality. Local program decisions would be made from evidence more rigorous than is often the case (e.g., personal experience of an administrator or expert advice from outside a program). Furthermore, the study serves as an excellent example to other school districts of how action research could be used to address other local dilemmas.

If the research is to be an example of experimental research, however, the study is more troubling. It is an example of a quasi-experimental study without adequate sampling and without a control group or random assignment. These research design problems weaken its ability to be generalized to other settings. During data collection, the lack of interrater reliability measures becomes more of a problem. Finally, during the reporting of the results, the omission of statistics such as standard deviations to reveal variability among subjects makes the task of building on these findings by other researchers more difficult. This example demonstrates clearly the impact that researchers' goals have on how the work should be carried out and how its merits should be evaluated.

Examples for the Future.   In this, probably the broadest of all the paradigms, the sky is the limit. Local solutions should be sought for the myriad problems plaguing teacher education. Foreign language educators should borrow from the environmentalists to "think globally, act locally." Research does not have to restrict itself to testing the effects of the status quo before launching new innovations. The five most critical issues in teacher education according to the ATE (Buttery et al. 1990) are mentoring for first-year teachers, the poor conditions of practice in schools that defeat improvements in teacher education, multiethnic/multicultural education, evaluation of entering teacher candidates, and licensing exams for teacher education. The second concern in particular becomes the question of the chicken and the egg: which came first, ineffective teacher education or ineffective schools? Local action research that is subject-matter-specific could be the site of important breakthroughs in any of these problem areas if local talent takes the initiative to experiment and explore. Waiting for an entire state to change may mean waiting forever, but change on a more specific, local level that is exciting and encouraging should then be shared with the larger research community.

An excellent source of ideas for action research can be found throughout the text *Second Language Teacher Education,* edited by Richards and Nunan (1990). Each chapter offers suggestions for teacher-education studies of various paradigms and is followed by questions from the editors that could also help generate research questions and ideas of how to approach them.

Reflective Practitioners _____

A recent correlate of action research is more focused on the individual teacher and his or her classroom and called alternately teacher research, reflection-on-action, or the work of the reflective practitioner (Olson 1990; Rudduck 1985; Schön 1987). The importance of this line of work to teacher education has been immediately recognized. Schön (1987) describes good teaching as having a core of artistry that includes the art of problem solving, the art of implementation, and the art of improvisation. Many researchers have now turned their attention to describing teachers' ability to perform their art (Shulman 1987).

How people acquire this artistry and how they can be helped to do so are obvious teacher-education research questions. Schön calls for teacher-education programs modeled on the coaching format used in architectural design studios. Research in teacher education would then look to defining not only teaching artistry but also coaching artistry. This work in foreign language teacher education has not yet begun substantially.

A principal argument underlying research in this area is that teachers are the masters of their own destiny and need not depend on the outside researcher to inform them or their practice. Rudduck argues: "Teacher research—or the less challenging but possibly more realistic habit of reflection-on-action through classroom enquiry—is an important means of sustaining professional curiosity and focusing professional dialogue" (1985: 281). She claims that research is the best defense against possible monotony in the teaching act, and the teacher as researcher is necessary for the "democratization of the research community" (p. 282).

Stenhouse (1981) defines research as systematic inquiry made public. The preceding discussion of research paradigms has explored some of the numerous definitions of *systematic*. Work by reflective practitioners may as often as not hinge on the decision whether to make the work public or in which forum to make the work public. It is impossible to measure the scope of reflection-on-action in foreign languages or in any other domain because much of it is not shared publicly. Van Lier (1991) describes his own attempts at "self-monitoring" (p. 59), and Gebhard (1989) describes examples of inquiry conducted by his students while they were inservice second language teachers. Other examples of reflection-on-action shared publicly can be found in workshops and presentations at national and regional teachers' associations.

Teacher researchers or reflective practitioners may use any or all of the quantitative or qualitative paradigms to investigate the questions that interest them. This activity may not qualify as research by everyone's definition of the term and may be seen instead as a way of doing the work of teaching. Its stamp of approval and its possibility to improve teacher development came early, however, from such greats as John Dewey:

> There is no way to discover what is "more truly educational" except by the continuation of the educational act itself. The discovery is never made; it is

always making. It may conduce to immediate use or momentary efficiency to seek an answer for questions outside of education, in some material which already has scientific prestige. But such a seeking is an abdication, a surrender. In the end, it only lessens the chances that education in actual operation will provide the materials for an improved science. It arrests growth; it prevents the thinking that is the final source of all progress. (cited in Shannon 1990: 153)

Conclusion

The temptation to pronounce here the future goals for teacher-education research in foreign language is immense. One way to avoid damaging bandwagon effects, however, is consciously *not* to prioritize research goals but, rather, to encourage any and all questions to be pursued. Foreign language teacher-education research is new enough that this open-ended approach may be the most fruitful. As Shulman (1992) suggests to educational funding agencies, we should look kindly on "any proposal that has a 'quizzical look' in it, even, or maybe even especially, those that are willing to 'muck around' in unclearly defined areas of teacher development."

Teaching and learning are no longer seen as generic phenomena in educational research. The teaching/learning process is now believed to vary considerably in different contexts and with different subjects. The crux of the individual teacher's knowledge is at what Shulman calls "the intersection of content and pedagogy" (1987: 15), or pedagogical content knowledge. This belief reinforces the need for foreign-language-specific teacher-education research. If a key variable in good teaching is the ability of the teacher to portray subject knowledge in meaningful ways to reach all students, then subject-matter-specific models of the process and of ways to teach the process are needed. Within foreign language teacher education, all the variables—teacher educators, contexts, content, instruction, and preservice/inservice teachers themselves—need to be examined.

If teaching/learning is no longer viewed as a generic phenomenon, how widely should foreign language teacher-education research be defined? The preceding discussion of the research paradigms includes research from foreign language, second language, English as a Second Language, bilingual education, and immersion education indiscriminately as examples. How great are the differences among these different contexts, however? Can research from these areas be linked together to inform foreign language teacher education? Or are the differences too important to allow for this?

Bernhardt and Tedick (1991) note that four major interacting factors influence the results of second language educational research: individual differences, tasks, materials, and contexts such as program model or political climate. They caution that there are different tendencies in each of these broad categories for foreign language, second language, bilingual, or immersion education. They call for controlling for these differences whenever possible when conducting research and warn against the indiscriminate application of research findings to areas that differ considerably on these categories. Nevertheless, despite these important differences, the unavoidable similarity of the language-learning enterprise would suggest that researchers in teacher education in second language, foreign language, immersion, and bilingual language could share findings profitably and should communicate about research endeavors regularly. (Chapter 3 in this volume argues for close collaboration among these areas in other educational endeavors as well.)

The principal need seems to be an extension of the range and quality of research techniques. There needs to be proper attention to the most common (or at least the most obvious) sins in research: inadequate sampling or sampling size in experimental studies and inadequate depth of description in naturalistic studies. Professional journals in foreign language education need their manuscript reviewers to make the analysis of the appropriate use of research methodology a top priority in order to encourage top-quality studies. Journal editors may need to reexamine the length restrictions on some articles in order to do justice to the large body of data that is required to support ethnographic results. Researchers in both paradigms must guard against premature generalizations to larger or vastly different contexts when reporting their findings.

Researchers' goals will continue to be to supply educators with new knowledge from which to make better-informed educational decisions. Improvement in teacher education is an important key to improvement in all education. Teacher education alone is not the panacea for all of education's ills, of course. We still will be faced with the problems of the larger societies of school, family, community, and culture. Good teachers working under bad conditions may still fail to achieve all society's desired results. Still, might not foreign language teacher educators be the ones to find the way to make clear the message in schools that a student's cultural difference is not a deficiency, for example? Our own teacher-education research ultimately may enhance other educational fields and not just accommodate our own unique needs.

As foreign language teacher-education research gets off the ground, the operant expression will be teacher *development* rather than teacher training or even preparation. The latter two terms suggest only preservice learning, whereas the term *teacher development* reflects the awareness that the path to becoming an expert foreign language teacher is a career-long one. By encouraging healthy debate but refusing damaging battles, teacher-education researchers can use all the modes of inquiry at their disposal for the worthy goal of serving teachers better. In this way they will have done their part toward the common goal of improving foreign language education.

Notes

1. Much energy has been squandered debating whether quantitative methods are better than qualitative ones and also whether there even are such things. Since all the debates begin at these two terms, they will be the starting point for this discussion. My regrets to all those who dislike one or the other and to those who do not believe the constructs exist. For a persuasive discussion of the overlaps across both paradigms see Reichardt and Cook (1979).
2. A related area of research less widely known by teacher educators is study of "pause time" that has documented cross-cultural differences in pause durations during conversations that can be problematic when individuals from different cultures interact. (See Albas et al. 1976; LaFrance and Mayo 1976; Rosenfeld 1978.)
3. More specifically, a "block" design was used purposely to distribute teachers by gender before they were randomly assigned to either treatment or control groups. *A priori* knowledge that this variable will be significant is one reason for using this procedure, but very small numbers make the statistical analyses problematic.
4. Helpful overviews of statistical procedures for consumers of research results can be found in Borg (1981) and Huck et al. (1974).
5. Mathematical corrections for restrictions in range are possible.
6. The researcher compares the distribution of results to the typical bell curve consisting of a cluster in the middle and fewer responses at either extreme.
7. Ethnography's earliest widespread use in language education seems to have been the use of ethnographic methods to evaluate bilingual programs for young children in Project Head Start during the 1970s. The restriction to that context seems likely to be a result of limited availability of federal research funds. See, for example, Chesterfield and Goncalves (1978).
8. The project also used interview data to determine student and teacher attitudes; it is not discussed as part of the illustration here.

References, Inquiry in Language Teacher Education

Albas, Daniel C., Ken W. McCluskey, and Cheryl A. Albas. 1976. "Perception of the Emotional Content of Speech: A Comparison of Two Canadian Groups." *Journal of Cross-Cultural Psychology* 7: 481–90.

Bernhardt, Elizabeth B., and JoAnn Hammadou. 1987. "A Decade of Research in Foreign Language Teacher Education." *Modern Language Journal* 71: 289–98.

Bernhardt, Elizabeth B., and Diane J. Tedick. 1991. "On Paradoxes and Paradigms in Language Education Research," pp. 43–63 in Ellen S. Silber ed., *Critical Issues in Foreign Language Instruction.* New York: Garland.

Bogdan, Robert C., and Sari Knopp Biklen. 1982. *Qualitative Research for Education: An Introduction to Theory and Methods.* Needham Heights, MA: Allyn and Bacon.

Borg, Walter. 1981. *Applying Educational Research: A Practical Guide for Teachers.* White Plains, NY: Longman.

Brock, Cynthia A. 1986. "The Effects of Referential Questions on ESL Classroom Discourse." *TESOL Quarterly* 20: 47–60.

Brophy, Jere E., and Thomas L. Good. 1986. "Teacher Behavior and Student Achievement," pp. 328–75 in Merlin C. Wittrock, ed., *Handbook of Research on Teaching.* 3d ed. New York: Macmillan.

Buttery, Thomas J., Martin Haberman, and W. Robert Houston. 1990. "First Annual Survey of Critical Issues in Teacher Education." Unpublished manuscript. [ED 318 699]

Carnegie Task Force on Teaching as a Profession. 1983. *A Nation Prepared: Teachers for the 21st Century.* Washington, DC: U.S. Government Printing Office.

Carrasco, Robert L. 1981. "Expanded Awareness of Student Performance: A Case Study in Applied Ethnographic Monitoring in a Bilingual Classroom," pp. 153–77 in Henry

Trueba et al., eds., *Culture and the Bilingual Classroom: Studies in Classroom Ethnography.* Boston: Newbury House (Heinle and Heinle).

Cazden, Courtney B., E. Cancino, E. Rosansky, and J. Schumann. 1975. *Second Language Acquisition Sequences in Children, Adolescents and Adults.* Final report submitted to the National Institute of Education, Washington, DC.

Chesterfield, Ray, and Jose Goncalves. 1978. "An Evaluation of the Head Start Bilingual Bicultural Curriculum Development Project: Field Supervisor Observations and Quality Control of Ethnographic Data." Unpublished manuscript. [ED 190 220]

Cohen, Louis, and Lawrence Manion. 1985. *Research Methods in Education.* 2d ed. London, Eng.: Croom Helm.

Cruickshank, Donald R. 1984. "Toward a Model to Guide Inquiry in Preservice Teacher Education," *Journal of Teacher Education* 35,6: 43–48.

————. 1990. *Research That Informs Teachers and Teacher Educators.* Bloomington, IN: Phi Delta Kappa.

Denzin, Norman K., ed. 1970. *Sociological Methods: A Source Book.* Chicago: Aldine.

Enright, D. Scott. 1984. "The Organization of Interaction in Elementary Classrooms," pp. 23–38 in Jean Handscombe, Richard A. Orem, and Barry P. Taylor, eds., *On TESOL '83: The Question of Control.* Washington, DC: TESOL.

Fanselow, John F. 1987. *Breaking Rules: Alternatives for Language Teachers.* White Plains, NY: Longman.

Flanders, Ned A. 1960. *Interaction Analysis in the Classroom: A Manual for Observers.* Ann Arbor: Univ. of Michigan Press.

Freeman, Donald. 1991. " 'Mistaken Constructs': Re-Examining the Nature and Assumptions of Language Teacher Education," pp. 25–39 in James E. Alatis, ed., *Linguistics and Language Pedagogy: The State of the Art.* Georgetown University Round Table on Languages and Linguistics. Washington, DC: Georgetown Univ. Press.

Gebhard, Jerry G. 1989. "The Teacher as Investigator of Classroom Processes: Procedures and Benefits." Unpublished manuscript. [ED 304 877]

Geertz, Clifford. 1973. *The Interpretation of Culture.* New York: Basic Books.

Glass, Gene V. 1976. "Primary, Secondary and Meta-Analysis of Research." *Educational Researcher* 5,10: 3–8.

————. Forthcoming. "Research Integration," in Marvin C. Alkin, ed., *Encyclopedia of Educational Research.* 6th ed. New York: Macmillan.

Gooding, C. Thomas, Patricia R. Swift, and J. Nathan Swift. 1984. "The Identification, Definition, and Measurement of Key Variables in Wait Time Research." Unpublished manuscript. [ED 260 087]

Guba, Egon G., and Yvonna S. Lincoln. 1981. *Effective Evaluation.* San Francisco: Jossey-Bass.

Hammadou, JoAnn, and Leslie Schrier. 1988. "A Four-State Survey of Secondary Administrators' Perceptions of Foreign Language Supervision." *Foreign Language Annals* 21: 259–67.

Heath, Shirley Brice. 1983. *Ways with Words: Language, Life, and Work in Communities and Classrooms.* New York: Cambridge Univ. Press.

Holmes Group. 1986. "The Holmes Group Report: Tomorrow's Teachers." *Teachers College Record* 88: 314–25.

Hough, John B., ed. 1980. *Concepts and Categories for the Study of Instruction: The Observational System for Instructional Analysis.* Columbus: The Ohio State Univ.

Huck, Schuyler W., William H. Cormier, and William G. Bounds, Jr. 1974. *Reading Statistics and Research.* New York: HarperCollins.

Huebner, Thom, and Anne Jensen. 1992. "A Study of Foreign Language Proficiency-Based Testing in Secondary Schools." *Foreign Language Annals* 25: 105–15.

Jarvis, Gilbert A. 1968. "A Behavioral Observation System for Classroom Foreign Language Skill Acquisition Activities." *Modern Language Journal* 52: 335–41.

Kasper, Gabriele, and Meret Dahl. 1991. "Research Methods in Interlanguage Pragmatics." *Studies in Second Language Acquisition* 13: 215–48.

Kennedy, Robert L. 1988. "Statistical Methodology Content Analysis of Selected Educational Research Journals." Unpublished manuscript. [ED 298 138]

Kleinsasser, Robert C., and Sandra J. Savignon. 1991. "Linguistics, Language Pedagogy, and Teachers' Technical Cultures," pp. 289–301 in James E. Alatis, ed., *Linguistics and Language Pedagogy: The State of the Art.* Georgetown University Round Table on Languages and Linguistics. Washington, DC: Georgetown Univ. Press.

Kuhn, Thomas. 1970. *The Structure of Scientific Revolutions.* Chicago: Univ. of Chicago Press.

Kulik, Chen-Lin C., James A. Kulik, and Robert L. Bangert-Drowns. 1990. "Effectiveness of Mastery Learning Programs: A Meta-Analysis." *Review of Educational Research* 60: 265–99.

Kulik, James A., and Chen-Lin C. Kulik. 1989. "Meta-Analysis in Education." *International Journal of Educational Research* 13: 221–340.

LaFrance, Marianne, and Clara Mayo. 1976. "Racial Differences in Gaze Behavior during Conversation." *Journal of Personality and Social Psychology* 33: 547–52.

Lange, Dale L. 1987. "The Nature and Direction of Recent Proposals and Recommendations for Foreign Language Education: A Response." *Modern Language Journal* 71: 240–49.

Lieberman, Ann. 1986. "Collaborative Research: Working with, Not Working on . . ." *Educational Leadership* 43: 28–32.

Loadman, William E., and Craig W. Deville. 1990. "The NTE as a Measure of General Academic Ability: Implications for Teacher Education." Unpublished manuscript. [ED 330 667]

MacDonald, B., and R. Walker. 1977. "Case Study and the Social Philosophy of Educational Research," in David Hamilton et al., eds., *Beyond the Numbers Game.* London, Eng.: Macmillan.

Merriam, Sharan B. 1988. *Case Study Research in Education: A Qualitative Approach.* San Francisco: Jossey-Bass.

Moon, Charles E., Gary F. Render, and Deborah R. Dillow. 1986. "A Meta-Analysis of Suggestopedia, Suggestology, Suggestive-Accelerative Learning and Teaching (SALT), and Super-Learning." Unpublished manuscript. [ED 271 503]

Moskowitz, Gertrude. 1970. *The Foreign Language Teacher Interacts.* Minneapolis: Association for Productive Teaching.

National Commission for Excellence in Teacher Education. 1985. *A Call for Change in Teacher Education.* Washington, DC: American Association of Colleges for Teacher Education.

National Commission on Excellence in Education. 1983. *A Nation at Risk: The Imperative for Educational Reform.* Washington, DC: U.S. Dept. of Education.

Nyikos, Martha. 1992a. "Making the Conceptual Shift to Learner-Centered Classrooms." Unpublished manuscript.

_____. 1992b. "Toward Pedagogical Knowledge: Belief Systems of Foreign Language Teacher Candidates." Unpublished manuscript.

Oja, Sharon N., and Gerald J. Pine. 1983. *A Two-Year Study of Teacher Stage of Development in Relation to Collaborative Action Research in Schools.* Durham: Univ. of New Hampshire, Collaborative Action Research Project Office.

Olson, Mary W. 1990. "The Teacher as Researcher: A Historical Perspective," pp. 1–20 in Mary W. Olson, ed., *Opening the Door to Classroom Research.* Newark, DE: International Reading Association.

Politzer, Robert L. 1983. "An Exploratory Study of Self-Reported Language Learning Behaviors and Their Relation to Achievement." *Studies in Second Language Acquisition* 6: 54–68.

Postlethwaite, Keith, and Cliff Denton. 1978. *Streams for the Future?* Slough, Eng.: National Foundation for Educational Research.

Reichardt, Charles S., and Thomas D. Cook. 1979. "Beyond Qualitative *versus* Quantitative Methods," pp. 7–32 in Thomas D. Cook and Charles S. Reichardt, eds., *Qualitative and Quantitative Methods in Evaluation Research.* London, Eng.: Sage.

Rhodes, Nancy C., and Rebecca L. Oxford. 1988. "Foreign Languages in Elementary and Secondary Schools: Results of a National Survey." *Foreign Language Annals* 21,1: 51–61.

Richards, Jack C., and David Nunan. 1990. *Second Language Teacher Education.* New York: Cambridge Univ. Press.

Rosenfeld, H. M. 1978. "Conversational Control Functions of Nonverbal Behavior," pp. 291–328 in Aron W. Siegman and Stanley Feldstein, eds., *Nonverbal Behavior and Communication.* Hillsdale, NJ: Erlbaum.

Rowe, Mary Budd. 1974. "Wait-Time and Rewards as Instructional Variables, Their Influence on Language, Logic and Rate Control." *Journal of Research in Science Teaching* 11: 81–94.

Rudduck, Jean. 1985. "Teacher Research and Research-Based Teacher Education." *Journal of Education for Teaching* 11: 281–89.

Salomone, Ann. 1991. "Immersion Teachers: What Can We Learn from Them?" *Foreign Language Annals* 24: 57–64.

Schön, Donald A. 1987. *Educating the Reflective Practitioner: Toward a New Design for Teaching and Learning in the Professions.* San Francisco: Jossey-Bass.

Schrier, Leslie. 1989. "A Survey of Foreign Language Teacher Preparation Patterns and Procedures in Small, Private Colleges and Universities in the United States." Ph.D. diss., The Ohio State Univ.

Shannon, Patrick. 1990. "Commentary: Teachers Are Researchers," pp. 141–54 in Mary W. Olson, ed., *Opening the Door to Classroom Research.* Newark, DE: International Reading Association.

Shrum, Judith. 1985a. "Wait-Time and Student Performance Level in Second Language Classrooms." *Journal of Classroom Interaction* 20: 29–33.

————. 1985b. "Wait-Time and the Use of Target or Native Language." *Foreign Language Annals* 18: 305–13.

Shulman, Lee S. 1987. "Knowledge and Teaching: Foundations of the New Reform." *Harvard Educational Review* 57: 1–22.

————. 1992. "Pedagogical Content Knowledge: Usefully Wrong?" Comments presented at symposium conducted at the meeting of the American Educational Research Association, San Francisco, April.

Slavin, Robert E. 1986. "Best-Evidence Synthesis: An Alternative to Meta-Analytic and Traditional Reviews." *Educational Researcher* 15,9: 5–11.

Smith, Philip D., Jr. 1970. *A Comparison of the Cognitive and Audiolingual Approaches to Foreign Language Instruction: The Pennsylvania Foreign Language Project.* Philadelphia: Center for Curriculum Development.

Soltis, Jonas F. Forthcoming. "Inquiry Paradigms," in Marvin C. Alkin, ed., *Encyclopedia of Educational Research.* 6th ed. New York: Macmillan.

Stenhouse, Lawrence A. 1981. "What Counts as Research?" *British Journal of Educational Studies* 29: 103–14.

Swift, J. Nathan, and C. Thomas Gooding. 1983. "Interaction of Wait Time Feedback and Questioning Instruction on Middle School Science Teaching." *Journal of Research in Science Teaching* 20: 721–30.

Tikunoff, William J., and Beatrice A. Ward. 1983. "Collaborative Research on Teaching." *Elementary School Journal* 83: 453–68.

Tollefson, James W. 1988. "Measuring Communication in ESL/EFL Classes." *Cross Currents* 15: 37–46.

Tuckman, Bruce. 1978. *Conducting Educational Research.* 2d ed. New York: Harcourt, Brace.

van Lier, Leo. 1984. "Discourse Analysis and Classroom Research: A Methodological Perspective." *International Journal of the Sociology of Language* 19: 111–33.

_____. 1991. "Inside the Classroom: Learning Processes and Teaching Procedures."
    Applied Language Learning 2,1: 29–70.
Wann, Ken D. 1953. "Action Research in Schools." *Review of Educational Research* 23:
    337–45.
Watson-Gegeo, Karen Ann. 1988. "Ethnography in ESL: Defining the Essentials." *TESOL
    Quarterly* 22: 575–92.
Welch, Jill K. 1988. "Student Participation and Achievement in an Intensive Spanish
    Class: An Interactive Sociolinguistic Perspective." Ph.D. diss., The Ohio State Univ.
Wragg, E. C. 1970. "Interaction Analysis in the Foreign Language Classroom." *Modern
    Language Journal* 54: 116–20.

5

Prospects for the Professionalization of Foreign Language Teaching

Leslie L. Schrier
University of Iowa

The sociopolitical events of the recent past have shown us that there is no guarantee that the future will bear any resemblance to the present. When the future is not predictable, there is a tendency to control factors that have been known to influence events, and in the education profession, the most controllable element has been its teachers. Indeed, reviews of current literature on teacher-education reform (e.g., Devaney 1992; Kennedy 1990; Reynolds 1992) have a common thread—the regulation of professional licensure standards. Yet regulation of licensure standards is just one major issue in the struggle toward professionalizing teaching. This chapter focuses on the interactive elements that contribute to shaping the career of teaching and hence the practitioner. Since many of these factors are embedded in past practices as well as current research, it is appropriate to review both before developing a profile of the profession as it will look, ideally, in future decades.

Past and Present Efforts at Professionalization of Foreign Language Teaching

Professionalization is not a separate event or a state of grace into which an occupation clearly falls; it is a historical process. Professionalization describes points along a continuum representing the extent to which members of an

Leslie L. Schrier (Ph.D., The Ohio State University) is an Assistant Professor of Curriculum and Instruction/Spanish and Portuguese at the University of Iowa, where she is Chair of the Foreign Language Education Program and Teacher-Education Director of the Iowa Critical Languages Program. She researches and writes on a variety of issues related to teacher-education programs, and she is Chair of the ACTFL SIG on Teacher Development, member of the Executive Board of the AERA SIG on Second Language Acquisition, and member of the MLA, TESOL, and the FLES Committee of the AATSP.

occupation *share a common body of knowledge and use shared standards of practice in exercising that knowledge on behalf of a defined clientele.* For the purposes of this chapter, a distinction is made between teaching as an *occupation,* a means of employment, and teaching as a *profession,* a vocation that involves a codification of advanced learning (Sykes 1990).

Presented in this section are issues affecting our shared knowledge, our efforts to set guidelines and standards, and the compromises that have resulted in our loss of influence in the important area of teacher licensure, threatening the professionalization of the occupation as well as the quality of instruction.

A first concern for the professionalization of language teaching is the lack of an adequate data base, as documented by Bernhardt and Hammadou (1987) and again by Hammadou in chapter 4 of this volume. With sufficient information on our shared knowledge, beliefs, and assumptions, we would be better able to inspect those assumptions, debate our proposed guidelines, and transform them into meaningful standards that both the public and the practicing teacher could share. Describing who is doing the teaching and what these teachers hold as knowledge of teaching is necessary to develop an understanding of the issues involved in making the teacher of the future a professional. What little information we have is noted in the next section of this chapter.

A second concern is the widespread practice of emergency licensure. Historically speaking, the teaching occupation has had to compromise its ideals of professionalization because of the absence of sufficient numbers of highly qualified teaching candidates. Horace Mann recognized this when he spearheaded the first U.S. reforms to professionalize teaching over a century ago with the establishment of the first state normal school for the training of teachers in 1839. Mann argued that educational improvements depended on increased public support, including state involvement, and called for the careful selection, advanced training, and improved status and authority of teachers that are clearly echoed in today's appeals for educational reform (e.g., Holmes Group 1986). Further historical examples of proposals for quality education can be found in Dewey (1968) as well as many of the progressive era reformers. Cremin (1965) notes that because of the lack of highly skilled teachers in each of these movements, attempts at reform in education gave way to standardizing influences. Examples of these influences are evident in the efficiency movement of the 1920s, the teacherproof curricular reforms of the 1950s, and the back-to-basics movement of the 1970s.

The foreign language teaching occupation has not been immune to proposing ideals for the education of its students and then succumbing to the reality of transmitting those ideals via less-than-qualified teachers. (For an excellent review of this topic, see Lange 1983.) In our most recent past, we have had to deal with both a redefinition of our teaching goals and an understanding of the foreign language teaching discipline's role within the overall education of the nation's youth. The profession has had to mesh the proposals for changes in education with the specific criticism of the language competency of its students, beginning with the presidential commission report, "Strength through Wisdom: A Critique of U.S. Capability" (President's Commission 1980). One of the report's many recommendations was the improvement of the professional development of foreign language teachers in the areas of their language and cultural competence.

The response to this criticism has taken several forms. The first involved the reassessment of the process of evaluating foreign language achievement, which culminated in the publication of a set of guidelines measuring a language learner's proficiency (ACTFL 1986). The second set of reactions was articulated in papers by Jarvis (1983) and Lange (1983), who called for particularizing the knowledge base, to make its foundation one that was unique to foreign language learning and not merely restated or generalized theories captured from other disciplines. This particularization would require interaction among second language researchers, teachers, and learners, and it was hoped that such interaction would articulate a knowledge base that eventually would affect the development of future foreign language teachers.

In yet another response in the latter part of the eighties, the profession addressed the need to form new models for the preparation of foreign language teachers with the publication of the *ACTFL Provisional Program Guidelines for Foreign Language Teacher Education* (1988). And currently, individual language groups—notably the American Associations of Teachers of French (AATF), German (AATG), and Spanish and Portuguese (AATSP)—have been working simultaneously to create language-specific guidelines and standards for teacher preparation. All these efforts could be defined as attempts at moving the foreign language teaching occupation further along the continuum of professionalization.

The Public Interest Compromised

Both the general teaching and the foreign language teaching occupation seek professionalizing policies that are intended to protect the public. These policies are based on the following premises: (1) all individuals permitted to practice in certain positions are adequately prepared to do so responsibly; (2) when certainty about practice does not exist, practitioners, individually and collectively, continually seek to discover the most responsible course of action; and (3) as the first two points suggest, practitioners pledge that their first and primary responsibility is to the welfare of the student (Darling-Hammond 1990).

The first of these premises is the key issue in the professionalization of an occupation. It is in not respecting this premise that public regulations have had their greatest effect in undermining the professionalization movement in teaching. When 46 states maintain emergency licensure procedures and 23 have recently sanctioned a double standard for entry by adopting alternative certification provisions (Darling-Hammond and Berry 1988), the public trust in a profession may be violated. These allowances are deemed necessary to ensure an adequate supply of teachers, but by failing to distinguish the roles and responsibilities that special entrants are qualified to assume, the state departments of education have fundamentally undermined the presumption that all professionals holding the same job share common knowledge and commitments. This compromising situation needs to be addressed energetically in the foreign language teaching community, for it allows states to implicitly set minimal requirements for licensure, thus rendering less effective efforts by any recognized professional organization (e.g., ACTFL) to specify professional standards.

The problem of professional standards is especially acute in at least two areas of foreign language education. The first is the lack of certification for teachers in the foreign language in the elementary school (FLES) programs. The data on the types of certification held by active teachers in FLES programs are provided by Rhodes and Oxford (1988) in their statistical report on the status of foreign language instruction in the nation. In the FLES programs they surveyed, 46 percent of the respondents stated that their current teachers were not certified to teach languages at the elementary school level. Furthermore, in 1989 less than half of the institutions that offered secondary certification in foreign languages also offered FLES certification (Schrier 1989). As evidenced by the failure of the FLES programs of the 1960s (Andersson 1969), poorly prepared instructors can contribute greatly to the failure of a curriculum.

The second area of concern is the emergency licensing of teachers in the less commonly taught languages (LCTs).[1] The need for instruction in these languages has been brought to the public attention both in the popular press and in the profession (e.g., Walker 1989; Jorden and Walton 1987). Means for the professional development of teachers in the LCTs have been fostered by programs such as the Iowa Critical Languages Program (ICLP), which is a two-part collaborative effort among the Ford Foundation, the University of Iowa, and school districts to develop and place outstanding teachers of Chinese, Japanese, and Russian languages in the Iowa public school systems. In the first, university-based part of the program, participants are provided with intensive language preparation, one year of study in the target language country, and specialized pedagogical preparation for the preservice teachers. The second part of the ICLP has provided financial assistance to school districts that hire these teachers and provided funds for computers, specialized software, and other teaching materials to enrich the LCT curriculum. It also has offered language-specific in-services for the ICLP program districts (Parrott et al. 1991).

This effort to develop professionally prepared teachers of Chinese, Japanese, and Russian is admirable, but programs like the ICLP require time. In the usual haste to expose secondary students to a current and popular subject, public pressure has caused some states to issue temporary certification to native speakers of these languages solely on the basis of language ability, with minimal concern for their language-teaching preparation and knowledge of U.S. students and cultures. In the state of Iowa alone, between 1988 and 1990, over 23 emergency certificates were issued for the teaching of Japanese and Russian (Lepley 1991). This need for immediate exposure to the LCTs may have similar results to that of immediate and intense exposure to the sun, in that temporarily certified teachers may peel away students' interest in continued study of these noncognate languages. Indeed, interest in studying the second year of Japanese dropped 30 percent in the districts using temporarily certified Japanese language teachers compared with a drop of 2 percent in districts using certified personnel (Schrier forthcoming). Yet we know from experience that the LCTs require as much as three times the length of instruction to achieve similar proficiency as with the commonly taught languages (Walker 1989). The professionalization of language teaching, then, requires a united effort to set standards of preparation and insist that they be consistently applied. Unfortunately, reactions to public regulation of teaching licensure have as yet had very little publicized response in foreign language teaching circles.

The tremendous efforts involved in professionalization must be shared by the researcher, educator, and teacher alike. Having shared knowledge and shared commitments to extend that knowledge depends in large part on shared membership in a group that articulates and supports its policies in one voice.

Examples of adoption by the public of standards for the mathematics discipline are presented in chapters 1 and 6 of this volume. Similar and perhaps more analogous to the foreign language discipline is the successful effort of science education to present a unified voice to the public for the professionalization of science teaching (cf. Yager and Penick 1990). The efforts by the science-education discipline should be looked at very closely because science, like foreign language, speaks in many voices (e.g., those of the chemist, the botanist, and the biologist). Science education's models began first with area-specific inquiries into teacher preparation. The National Association of Chemistry Teachers, for example, met and created chemistry-specific standards, and then with a compilation from each association, the Association for the Education of Teachers of Science presented guidelines and models for science teacher preparation and licensure to public regulating bodies in a unified voice (Yager and Penick 1990: 667–69). Legislating bodies respect the unified voice, because here the structure of the profession is visible. The foreign language teaching occupation has thus far suffered from the lack of such a unified professional effort.

Characteristics of the Foreign Language Teaching Occupation

Identifying the characteristics of foreign language teachers can help define the occupation and isolate the factors that affect who may be attracted to teaching foreign languages in the future. Using descriptions of the current practitioners and their introspections on teacher-preparation practices, it is possible to project a profile for the future practitioner that will subsume preparation characteristics and professional development issues. Presented in this section are the summaries of research studies of both generic and foreign-language-specific teacher characteristics, categorized by demographics, shared knowledge base, and the curricular practices that influence the hiring of teachers.

Research literature on generic practicing teachers is twofold. The first area of research, demographics, is plentiful (e.g., Brookhart and Freeman 1992). The second area, research on effective teachers' knowledge base, is just beginning to unfold (e.g., Carter 1990; Reynolds 1992). Within the foreign language profession, research on its practitioners is limited in both areas, demographics and the knowledge base, yet there is sufficient information to provide a partial profile of foreign language teachers in relationship with their colleagues in other disciplines.

Demographics.   In 1984, the average U.S. teacher was 39 years old, had 4.9 years of college education, worked 42.9 hours per week, and earned $20,649 per year. Compared with the general population of college-educated workers, teachers were older, had completed more years of college, earned less, and were more likely to be female or to be a member of a minority group (U.S. Bureau of the Census 1984).

In 1987 the majority of teachers in the United States had over 15 years of teaching experience, and more than one-quarter had over 20 years of experience (NEA 1987). This high experience level has been associated with an increase in the average age of teachers, whose median age increased from 35 in 1971 to 41 in 1986 (NEA 1987). Over 11 percent of U.S. elementary and secondary school teachers were age 55 or older, and another 22 percent were between 45 and 54 years of age. Given that average ages at retirement have been declining, and assuming the continuation of that trend, we may expect that one-third of all current teachers will be retiring by the turn of the century (NEA 1987).

Many of today's teachers entered the profession during the period of rapid expansion of the teaching force to accommodate the baby boom. This expansion, which began in the mid-1950s and lasted through the early 1970s, was followed by significant teaching staff reductions during the late 1970s and early 1980s, which fell disproportionately on younger teachers (NEA 1987). Thus, a high percentage of current teachers are now reaching retirement age. At the same time that demand for teachers is increasing once again, we can expect to see more hiring of younger teachers to replace those who will be retiring throughout the 1990s. This means that at the turn of the century foreign language teachers will not only be in demand, but the new teachers, because of their numbers, will have the ability to influence generations of language learners as no other cohort of teachers has done before them.

Within the foreign language research literature, the reports compiled by Brickell and Paul (1981) and by Wolf and Riordan (1991) are of interest in creating a demographic profile of the current foreign language teacher. In 1979, ACTFL commissioned Brickell and Paul to conduct a national survey of foreign language teaching in secondary schools. The survey provided results from 80 school districts in 10 states and from 20 teacher-training institutions on teacher characteristics, teacher preparation, the supply and demand for foreign language teachers in the late 1970s, patterns of preservice and inservice training, the teaching load of foreign language teachers, and current and anticipated language teaching trends. Wolf and Riordan (1991) compiled data from a survey of teachers who were associated with a state foreign language organization. This descriptive information offers frequencies, percentages, and modal data

Table 5-1
Characteristics of
Current Foreign Language Teachers
and Their Colleagues

Characteristics	Foreign Language		Others
	1980	1991	1987
Gender	75% female	78% female	69% female
Ages	25–35 (50%)	41–50 (44%)	35–44 (44%)
Race	85% white	N/A	90% white 7% black 3% other
Experience	10 yrs. (60%)	21 yrs. (35%)	15 yrs.
Degree	N/A	M.A. (57%)	48% B.A. 50% M.A.

Compiled from Brickell and Paul (1981), NEA (1987), and Wolf and Riordan (1991).

intended to profile teacher characteristics and attitudes toward foreign language instruction in one state.

Table 5-1 compares the known data on foreign language teacher characteristics with that compiled by the NEA (1987) on the characteristics of U.S. public school teachers. Even though the data base is very limited, it appears that the profile of the current foreign language teacher does not differ greatly from that of his or her colleagues in the general teaching population.

The current language teacher is a white, middle-aged woman who has taught for over twenty years and holds both bachelor's and master's degrees. Foreign languages do not appear to attract significantly more or fewer minority teachers than other disciplines. In the general teaching public, the breakdown between women and men is at roughly two-thirds and one-third respectively, and in foreign languages the breakdown holds at about three-fourths to one-fourth. Nationally, the proportion of black teachers decreased steadily from over 8 percent in 1971 to under 7 percent in 1986. The proportion of other nonwhite teachers dipped sharply from 3.6 percent in 1971 to 0.7 percent in 1981, increasing again to over 3 percent by 1986 (NEA 1987). The decrease in the numbers of minority teachers could have been caused partly by attrition, but these statistics certainly reflect the dramatically reduced numbers of minority college graduates entering teaching since the early 1970s (Center for Education Statistics 1986). There is no reason to believe that this trend is not reflected in the minority population teaching foreign languages, although there are no specific data on black and other minority foreign language teachers in the occupation.

The demographic profile presented here of the current teaching population should not be continued in the future, considering the richness that a diverse teaching force brings to the classroom and the need for the teaching force to mirror more accurately the makeup of the general population of students. The socioeconomic elements that have created this unidimensional teaching force will be touched on later in this chapter.

Knowledge Base.   It is widely accepted that the process of professionalization of an occupation is in part determined by both its members' shared knowledge and their shared commitment to extend that knowledge. The general research on the character and substance of teachers' knowledge is emerging through new conceptual and methodological tools of cognitive science and interpretive research. This type of research is clearly in its infancy, and this line of inquiry is generating lively discussions about theory, research methodology, and teacher-education practices. It also seems to be a promising framework, establishing focus and coherence in research on how teachers learn to teach.

Teachers' knowledge is usually placed in three categories: (1) teachers' information processing, including decision making and expert-novice studies; (2) teachers' practical knowledge, including personal knowledge and classroom knowledge; and (3) pedagogical knowledge, that is, the ways teachers understand and represent subject matters to their students (Carter 1990). Even though the research base on this foundation in teaching is in its infancy, there have been over 175 studies conducted by researchers in teacher education in the decade of the eighties alone that were deemed worthy of comment by the teacher-education profession (Houston 1990). Unfortunately, as was stated earlier, the foreign language teaching profession is still very limited in its evidence of inquiry in this domain.

Central to developing the knowledge base in foreign language education is understanding what the teachers have received in their content area preparation, how they perceive this preparation to be reflected in their teaching assignments, and what they believe is needed for their own professional growth. It is possible to extract some of this information from the data provided by Brickell and Paul (1981), Schrier (1989), and Wolf and Riordan (1991).

Of greatest interest in the study by Brickell and Paul (1981) are the findings they present on the content area preparation of their respondents as it relates to their current teaching situation. Among the practicing foreign language teachers studied, 90 percent of the French teachers majored in French, 60 percent of the Spanish teachers majored in Spanish, and 50 percent of the practicing German teachers majored in German (p. 173). Of the actual practicing foreign language teachers, the French teachers appear to be the best prepared because so many of them majored in French. The German teachers seem the least prepared because half of them did not major in German. No further information is given, however, on the nature of their language preparation.

When describing their foreign language major, the teachers in this study stated that they spent roughly 50 percent or more of their time in college foreign language courses studying the literature of the language (p. 173), an area of concentration in college that was not reflected in their teaching assignments. The majority of the teachers surveyed taught levels I and II, where language and culture are emphasized.

Among the teachers surveyed, only 50 percent had ever studied in a foreign country, although they also listed maintaining their competency in the spoken foreign language as their main preparation concern. Furthermore, within their professional education course work, they reported that only 35 percent of their professional training was foreign-language-specific, even though foreign language methods and student teaching were included as part of this component. Interestingly enough, when asked to state what they missed most in preparation, they cited more foreign language pedagogical preparation second after conversational practice.

In the data provided from her study of foreign language teacher-preparation programs in four-year colleges and universities, Schrier (1989) discovered that the preparation patterns for preservice teachers had not altered greatly. In the content-area course work, the future foreign language teacher in 56 percent of the 500 responding institutions still had a heavy emphasis on the study of literature (p. 110). In their professional education course work, a pattern of foreign-language-specific methods followed by student teaching was in place in the majority of the responding institutions (pp. 110–12). Within the foreign language pedagogical course work, however, only 23 percent of the future foreign language teachers were presented with instructional techniques involving modern technology, e.g., interactive video or CALI (p. 93). The inservice teachers in the findings by Brickell and Paul (1981) had complained about preparation because its focus was not reflected in the typical language teaching assignments; the Schrier study shows that preparation has changed very little.

These studies found that the future foreign language teacher could select from nine foreign languages in which to major. Preparation for secondary teaching certification was also available in five of these languages: French, German, Japanese, Russian, and Spanish (p. 73). Seventy-five percent of the teaching candidates, however, selected Spanish as their major, this again reflecting the current teaching population, of which 70 percent teach Spanish (Wolf and Riordan 1991).

Besides the demographic information it provided, another purpose of the study conducted by Wolf and Riordan (1991) was an attempt to gain a picture of what practicing teachers believe about processes involved in foreign language instruction and where the information about those processes was obtained. Although some interesting points are made in this study, caution must be used in any attempt to generalize the results because the respondents represent one state only (p. 472). Several elements of classroom practices were described in the study, from beliefs about assessment of reading comprehension to techniques to promote oral proficiency. One of the more interesting findings was that there seemed to be an inverse relationship between the respondents' exposure to teaching for proficiency and their preference for using these concepts as classroom techniques (p. 477).

The answers to the questions in this study, of course, are not convincing evidence of a shared knowledge base, but they are the beginnings of a data base. Sadly, the findings of the study by Schrier (1989) and those of Wolf and Riordan (1991) reinforced those in Brickell and Paul (1981), especially in that needs and desires of practicing teachers for meaningful preservice course work and in-service activities had not been met.

Curricular Policies. As Nunan (1990) implies, effective second language curricular innovation is dependent on having the appropriately prepared teaching personnel to implement the curriculum. Curricular policies and hence staffing policies can very well determine the nature of teacher demand as well as affect teaching as an occupation. The study by Feistritzer (1984) describing subject-matter hiring demands, and the foreign-language-specific study of Rhodes and Oxford (1988) predict that by the completion of the nineties, 32 out of the 50 states will have shortages of both elementary and secondary foreign language teachers (Feistritzer 1984: 48–49; Rhodes and Oxford 1988: 62–63).

The Rhodes and Oxford study is a survey of foreign language instruction in 2,765 public and private elementary and secondary schools in the United States. Of interest to this chapter are the data presented on the qualifications of current and future foreign language teachers. In 81 percent of the secondary schools, all their foreign language teachers were certified to teach the language at the secondary level, while only 26 percent of the elementary schools with foreign language programs reported that all their teachers were certified for foreign language teaching at the elementary level (pp. 42–43). The authors felt these results reflected the lack of available teacher training and certification programs directed toward the elementary foreign language teacher (p. 62). This concern about the questionable qualifications of both FLES teachers and teacher-education practices has been echoed by Met (1989), who relates the success and staying power of solid programs to the quality and qualifications of their teachers.

Implications. Societal changes have always been reflected in the academic curriculum in the public schools. This reflection can currently be found with the increased interest in the teaching of languages at the elementary school level and in the interest in learning less commonly taught languages. For the first time, however, sociopolitical changes are affecting teachers. Changes in life-styles and changes in career opportunities of college graduates, especially women and minorities, have combined to alter the traditional patterns of supply and demand in the teaching world. What was once sufficient to attract new entrants looks less appealing in comparison with other alternatives now available.

The composition of the foreign language teaching force and the nature of teaching work that result from the replenishment of this force have important implications for the future of foreign language teaching and learning. For example, from the information gathered in this section, it is easy to assume that if a school district wished to replace a retiring high school Spanish language teacher, there should be an adequately qualified secondary Spanish language teacher to replace her. But if the school district wished to augment its Spanish language instruction by developing an articulated K–12 curriculum, finding staffing to meet this curricular innovation could be difficult. Moreover, if a district wished to meet the needs of the Asian members of its community by offering Chinese language instruction in the secondary school, finding an appropriately prepared and licensed teacher could be possible. After a few years of successful program growth, however, attracting another Chinese language teacher to help out a growing program or even just replacing a teacher may be very difficult. These examples may be the reality of the future with a teaching force heavily weighted toward very old or very young teachers.

Moving the foreign language teaching occupation toward becoming a highly selective and attractive professional career should be the goal of the foreign language community. Concerns about recruiting into teaching talented candidates, especially minorities, are valid; however, we must look closely at why specialized recruitment is now necessary, whereas in previous decades this effort was not needed.

There are two socioeconomic changes that interact to make teaching a less attractive career goal. The first is basic and fundamentally understandable: for the preparation and effort involved in teaching, it is financially unattractive. For those teachers who leave for other occupations, the most prevalent single reason is financial; 60 percent of recent former teachers surveyed in 1985 said they left due to teaching's low salaries. The same answer was given by over 60 percent of preservice and inservice teachers considering not finishing their teaching preparation or leaving their current positions (Metropolitan Life 1985). Interacting with the unattractive financial aspect of the teaching occupation is the fact that the pool of talented women and minorities that were once automatically interested in teaching have found careers in professions that previously were not options. The energy and funds directed toward specialized recruiting efforts may be better spent in working toward those professionalization efforts that might make teaching a more attractive career for all.

Profiles for the Future

Although people have speculated about the future since the dawn of civilization, long-range thinking has not been a major activity in teacher education (Dede 1990). The reason for this is the dependency on the sociopolitical structures linked to financing every aspect involved with education from the faculty hired to prepare teachers to the very space used in public school classrooms. But a positive profile of foreign language teaching can be drawn if the following assumptions are understood.

First, the picture of the future presented here is based on a holistic approach to the study of teaching and teacher development as defined by Richards (1990). He classifies two approaches to teacher-education research: the micro approach, which looks at teaching in terms of its directly observable characteristics; and the macro approach, which is holistic in intent and used to make generalizations and inferences that go beyond what can be observed directly (p. 4). The professional profile presented here flows in part from the micro research base presented in the previous section.

Second, the concept of a profile as used in this section is an outline that draws only the essential features of teachers and their professional environment. In outlining these teacher characteristics and support structures, no attempt is made to suggest that one element precedes the other or that the elements and structures are in any way hierarchically arranged.

Because they will be replacing a disproportionate number of retiring teachers, the new foreign language teachers of the twenty-first century will have the chance to make perhaps the greatest impact on foreign language learning of any other cohort in foreign language teaching history. The actualization of this opportunity will depend upon the interactions of many factors related to the teachers themselves and the kinds of preparation and support that they receive throughout their professional lives. Described below and in figure 5-1 are the interrelated, interacting elements that will be necessary to make foreign language teaching an attractive, meaningful profession.

The Career of Teaching

From the criticisms of teaching and learning in the United States and the recommendations expressed in various papers and reports (e.g., Carnegie 1986; Holmes Group 1986), it is apparent that the following conditions must occur before a positive environment for the future professional teacher can be realized:

1. Salary scales and career structures must be sufficiently competitive with most alternative occupations open to college graduates.
2. Teaching must include and reward high levels of autonomy and decision-making responsibility with opportunity for advancement or variability in job functions. These are important to professionals who value opportunities for growth, challenge, and change in their work.
3. There must be increased community regard for the occupation of teaching.
4. Attractive working conditions with respect to physical facilities, access to office space and equipment, and opportunity for collegial exchange must be created.

The Foreign Language Teacher

The profile of the future foreign language teacher is largely dependent on defining the characteristics of language learning and meshing those learning processes with unique classroom teaching environments. The decade of the eighties provided the foreign language community with an expanding body of research on language learning and teaching. Converting that research into holistic practices is in its infancy. Problematic to this conversion is the ever-

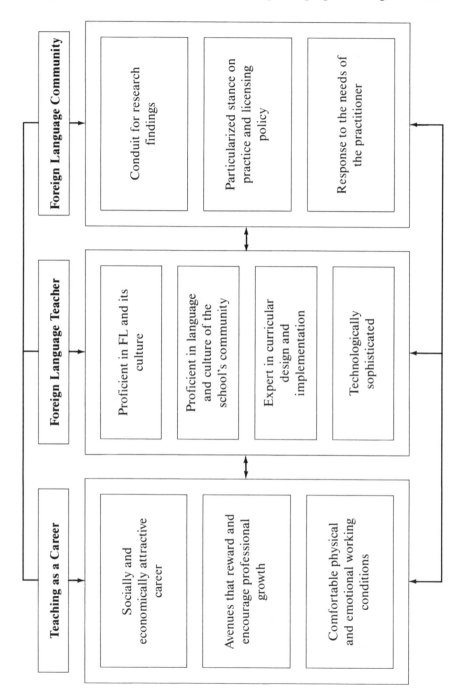

Figure 5-1. Prerequisites for professionalization

changing nature of the public school classroom and the society it mirrors. This outline does not attempt to map out the entire process of language teaching, but at best it presents a sketch of the salient qualities that will be necessary in a future professional. Chapters 6 and 7 of this volume treat individual aspects of teacher development in detail.

Proficient in a World Language and Culture.   Within the language-teaching community this requirement might seem obvious; unfortunately, it must be made to reinforce professionalization efforts within teaching and for the public regulating bodies. Many practicing teachers have anecdotal evidence to confirm the misassignment of colleagues because they had a few course hours in a language, and hence, it was assumed they could teach that language. Because this assumption is not self-evident, several states and over 45 percent of foreign language teacher-education programs in the United States (Schrier 1989: 115) have moved to assure proficiency with licensure standards that either use a recognized instrument to assess the language proficiency of their teachers (e.g., the ACTFL Oral Proficiency Interview) or have created their own metrics for assuring this qualification. ACTFL itself has included this professional quality within its published guidelines (ACTFL 1988: 75).

Chapter 6 deals exclusively with the details of the specialized knowledge of language and culture and the integration of the two, including discussion of the Specialist Development section of the ACTFL guidelines.

Proficient in the Language and Culture of the School and the Community They Serve.   Recent teacher education has pointed out that the more effective novice teachers are those that have taken the time to be informed about the ways the school and the community value and interpret the roles and responsibilities of the teacher (e.g., Copa 1991; Ryan 1992). This attribute for the foreign language teacher is a quality that is usually implicit; however, it is necessary to make it explicit. With the increased use of native speakers to seed or augment language curricula and the placement of novice teachers in schools of which they have had little personal experience, knowledge in the ways of the school and its community is an enabling feature that would allow the teachers' work to be biased for success. Teachers that are proficient in the native language and culture of their students and are familiar with the community within which they work should be more effective in creating and implementing a curriculum for their students.

Experts in Curricular Design and Implementation.   This feature is all-subsuming. It implies a degree of sophistication in the knowledge base of foreign language pedagogy that is both theoretical and clinical. With the variety of language teaching environments emerging (e.g., FLES, immersion, and literacy), the teacher who is expert in analyzing the learners' needs and developing a curriculum to meet those needs will be invaluable. Competent curricular development requires the teachers to be able to select and implement a language learning/ teaching approach, methods, and techniques appropriate for their unique instructional environment. The ACTFL guidelines (1988: 74–79) allude to this preparation, and concrete efforts are appearing in teacher-education programs.

The pedagogical content knowledge that will be required of future language teachers is developed more fully in chapter 7 of this volume.

Technologically Sophisticated. A future foreign language teacher needs to be able to understand the power that technology can have in a fully articulated language curriculum. An element in its power lies in its ability to enhance creative development in the language learner and not merely the mechanical, uncontextualized acquisition of facts. Furthermore, capturing this creative development must be linked to the furthering of communicative skills of the language learner, and technology must be used to provide the learner with positive links back to traditional sources of information and knowledge (viz., books and human interaction). The ACTFL guidelines (1988: 73) touch on the need for this quality. Sadly, Schrier (1989: 93) discovered that only 41 percent of the preservice teachers had any foreign-language-specific exposure to using technology as a technique in foreign language teaching.

Thoroughly Grounded in a Solid General Education. The teaching qualifications described above are dependent upon a strong basis in personal qualities and a liberal arts education. The Personal Development section of the ACTFL Guidelines details the ability to communicate effectively, both orally and in writing; the ability to seek, analyze, and synthesize information and apply it to problem solving and decision making; strong leadership qualities; and skills in organizing, taking action voluntarily, and working independently. The professional literature calls for reflective teachers who generate and test hypotheses, conduct action research in their classrooms, and use new information as a basis for further professional development. It is evident that in order to be an effective teacher and to invite the kinds of material, moral, and professional support described here and depicted in figure 5-1, the ideal teachers of tomorrow need to embody qualities that raise them above the average. A great many teachers already fit this description; these are the leaders who should serve as mentors for the newer generation of teachers and colleagues for university teacher educators, so that all three can work together to raise teaching to a higher professional level.

The Foreign Language Professional Community

The overall foreign language professional community subsumes classroom teachers, teacher-education researchers, second language researchers, and public foreign language advocates (e.g., state consultants, special interest groups, and lobbyists). Responsive to the needs articulated by and for its teachers and learners, and speaking in one united and informed voice, this community should provide the leadership necessary to articulate and advocate the goals of the professionalization movement.

Conduit for Research on Foreign-Language-Specific Demographics and Knowledge Base. Compiling an accurate picture of the current and preservice foreign language teaching occupation is a difficult task given the few studies generated by foreign language education researchers. The need for this information is central to movement along the professionalization continuum. It should be possible to draw decisions on curriculum changes and licensure policies from documented records of current practices and profiles. Efforts should be made not only to seed these descriptive studies but to ensure widespread dissemination of the data to the public.

Particularized Stance on Licensure and Practice Policies.   A unified and informed voice that represents policy on licensure and practice is a mark of a profession. Teaching in general and foreign language teaching specifically need to take the responsibility for stating what its professional's qualities are, developing these qualities within its novice practitioners, and then monitoring their practice. This is an enormous effort, but other recognized and esteemed professions have these licensure regulating bodies and recognized schools of expertise (e.g., medicine, law, pharmacology, and architecture).

Responsive to the Needs of the Practitioner.   The voice that teaches world languages should be the voice that is most listened to and esteemed. Unfortunately, in many aspects of the language teaching community, the practitioner has not been listened to. For example, language teachers have expressed the need for accessible and meaningful inservices for at least a decade, but there has been little response to this need. Furthermore, the teacher-preparation curriculum still needs to be augmented to prepare the preservice teacher better for his or her environment. The language teaching community needs to facilitate teachers' efforts in becoming professionals by creating avenues for professional improvement that respond to their articulated needs.

Conclusion

The processes involved in the professionalization of the foreign language teaching occupation were dynamic during the decade of the eighties. Developing evaluation metrics to determine language-learning outcomes, setting standards for appropriate teacher development, and providing avenues for dialogue about teaching are all important factors that moved teaching along the professionalization continuum. Furthermore, we have become aware of the need for amassing sophisticated data and research that will further define our practitioners and particularize what are held to be common foreign language pedagogical beliefs and practices. The unfolding of these shared beliefs will further define the practice of teaching foreign languages, and it will help us fill in the fine features needed to complete the profile of the future professional.

The future of teaching foreign languages, however, may not be what we envision it to be because of the composition of the teaching force. The efforts the foreign language community puts out in defining and refining the practice of teaching will be compromised if teaching does not become more attractive to bright, talented people seeking a meaningful profession. But compromising with the future should not have to be a constant in the profession if we could develop resources to help influence the preparation opportunities of the future teachers of world languages and above all make the practice of teaching more enriching for its teachers.

Note

1. At least 91 percent of the academic study of foreign languages is directed toward languages used by 12 to 13 percent of humanity. The languages of the remaining 87 to 88 percent comprise the category of less commonly taught languages, a term that is routinely shortened to less-commonly-taughts or more simply LCTs (Walker 1989: 111).

References, Prospects for the Professionalization of Foreign Language Teaching

American Council on the Teaching of Foreign Languages. 1986. *Proficiency Guidelines.* Yonkers, NY: ACTFL.

_____. 1988. *Provisional Program Guidelines for Foreign Language Teacher Education.* Yonkers, NY: ACTFL.

Andersson, Theodore. 1969. *Foreign Languages in the Elementary School: A Struggle against Mediocrity.* Austin: Univ. of Texas Press.

Bernhardt, Elizabeth B., and JoAnn Hammadou. 1987. "A Decade of Research in Foreign Language Teacher Education." *Modern Language Journal* 71: 289–98.

Brickell, Henry M., and Regina H. Paul. 1981. *Ready for the '80's? A Look at Foreign Language Teachers and Teaching at the Start of the Decade.* New York: Policy Studies in Education.

Brookhart, Susan M., and Donald J. Freeman. 1992. "Characteristics of Entering Teacher Candidates." *Review of Educational Research* 62: 37–60.

Carnegie Task Force on Teaching as a Profession. 1986. *A Nation Prepared: Teachers for the 21st Century.* Rochester, NY: National Center on Education.

Carter, Kathy. 1990. "Teachers' Knowledge and Learning to Teach," pp. 291–310 in W. Robert Houston, ed., *Handbook of Research on Teacher Education.* New York: Macmillan.

Center for Education Statistics. 1986. *Racial/Ethnic Data for 1984 Fall Enrollment and Earned Degree Recipients for Academic Year 1984–85.* Washington, DC: U.S. Dept. of Education.

Copa, Patricia M. 1991. "The Beginning Teacher as Theory Maker: Meanings for Teacher Education," pp. 105–36 in Lilian G. Katz and James D. Raths, eds., *Advances in Teacher Education.* Vol. 4. Norwood, NJ: Ablex.

Cremin, Lawrence. 1965. *The Genius of American Education.* New York: Vintage.

Darling-Hammond, Linda. 1990. "Teachers and Teaching: Signs of a Changing Profession," pp. 267–90 in W. Robert Houston, ed., *Handbook of Research on Teacher Education.* New York: Macmillan.

_____, and B. Berry. 1988. *The Evolution of Teacher Policy.* Santa Monica, CA: RAND Corporation.

Dede, Christopher. 1990. "Futures Research and Strategic Planning on Teacher Education," pp. 83–97 in W. Robert Houston, ed., *Handbook of Research on Teacher Education.* New York: Macmillan.

Devaney, Kathleen, ed. 1992. "Sanibel Voices Sing 5 'C's.' " *The Holmes Group Forum* 6,2: 1, 24–25.

Dewey, John. 1968. *The School and Society.* Chicago: Univ. of Chicago Press. (Original work published in 1900).

Feistritzer, C. E. 1984. "The Making of a Teacher: A Report on Teacher Education and Certification." Washington, DC: National Center for Education Information.

Holmes Group. 1986. "Tomorrow's Teachers: A Report of the Holmes Group." East Lansing, MI: Holmes Group.

Houston, W. Robert, ed. 1990. *Handbook of Research on Teacher Education.* New York: Macmillan.

Jarvis, Gilbert A. 1983. "Pedagogical Knowledge for the Second Language Teacher," pp. 234–41 in James E. Alatis, H. H. Stern, and Peter Strevens, eds., *Applied Linguistics and the Preparation of Second Language Teachers: Toward a Rationale.* Georgetown University Round Table on Languages and Linguistics. Washington, DC: Georgetown Univ. Press.

Jorden, Eleanor H., and A. Ronald Walton. 1987. "Truly Foreign Languages: Instructional Challenges." *Annals of the American Academy of Political Sciences* 490: 110–24.

Kennedy, Mary M. 1990. *A Survey of Recent Literature on Teachers' Subject Matter Knowledge.* Research Report No. 90-3. East Lansing, MI: Michigan State Univ., National Center for Research on Teacher Education.

Lange, Dale L. 1983. "Teacher Development and Certification in Foreign Languages: Where Is the Future?" *Modern Language Journal* 67: 374–81.

Lepley, William. 1991. "Schools Must Meet Challenges of Change." *Dispatch* 21: 2–7.

Met, Miriam. 1989. "Walking on Water and Other Characteristics of Effective Elementary School Teachers." *Foreign Language Annals* 22: 175–81.

Metropolitan Life Insurance Co. 1985. *Former Teachers in America.* New York: Metropolitan Life.

National Education Association. 1987. *Status of the American Public School Teacher, 1985–1986.* Washington, DC: NEA.

Nunan, David. 1990. "Action Research in the Language Classroom," pp. 62–81 in Jack C. Richards and David Nunan, eds., *Second Language Teacher Education.* New York: Cambridge Univ. Press.

Parrott, Ray, Leslie L. Schrier, Donna Grundstad, and John Wazke. 1991. "The Iowa Critical Languages Program: Priming the Pump." Presentation at ACTFL Conference, Washington, DC.

President's Commission on Foreign Languages and International Studies. 1980. "Strength through Wisdom: A Critique of U.S. Capability." *Modern Language Journal* 64: 9–57.

Reynolds, Anne. 1992. "What Is Competent Beginning Teaching? A Review of the Literature." *Review of Educational Research* 62: 1–35.

Rhodes, Nancy C., and Rebecca L. Oxford. 1988. *A National Profile of Foreign Language Instruction at the Elementary and Secondary School Levels.* Technical Report #6. Los Angeles: Center for Language Education and Research.

Richards, Jack C. 1990. "The Dilemma of Teacher Education in Second Language Teaching," pp. 3–15 in Jack C. Richards and David Nunan, eds., *Second Language Teacher Education.* New York: Cambridge Univ. Press.

Ryan, Kevin. 1992. "Conclusion: Rules for Riding the Roller Coaster," pp. 247–59 in Kevin Ryan, ed., *The Roller Coaster Year: Essays by and for Beginning Teachers.* New York: HarperCollins.

Schrier, Leslie L. 1989. "A Survey of Foreign Language Teacher Preparation Patterns and Procedures in Small, Private Colleges and Universities in the United States." Ph.D. diss., The Ohio State Univ.

————. Forthcoming. "Preparing Teachers of Critical Languages for the 21st Century," in Keiko Samimy, ed., *Foreign Language Education: Teaching Critical Languages in the American Schools.* Theory into Practice. Columbus, OH: The Ohio State Univ. College of Education.

Sykes, J. B., ed. 1990. *The Concise Oxford Dictionary of Current English.* New York: Oxford Univ. Press.

U.S. Bureau of the Census. 1984. *1984 Current Population Survey.* Washington, DC: U.S. Bureau of the Census.

Walker, Galal. 1989. "The Less Commonly Taught Languages in the Context of American Pedagogy," pp. 111–37 in Helen S. Lepke, ed., *Shaping the Future: Challenges and*

Opportunities. Report of the Northeast Conference on the Teaching of Foreign Languages. Middlebury, VT: Northeast Conference.

Wolf, W. C., and Kathleen M. Riordan. 1991. "Foreign Language Teachers' Demographic Characteristics, In-Service Training Needs, and Attitudes toward Teaching." *Foreign Language Annals* 24: 471–78.

Yager, Robert E., and John E. Penick. 1990. "Science Teacher Education," pp. 657–73 in W. Robert Houston, ed., *Handbook of Research on Teacher Education*. New York: Macmillan.

Subject-Matter Content: What Every Foreign Language Teacher Needs to Know

Robert C. Lafayette
Louisiana State University

Teacher-education programs are traditionally divided into three areas: general education, specialist education, and professional education. This chapter is devoted exclusively to the specialist component, which in the field of foreign languages consists of proficiency in and knowledge about the language and culture to be taught. In order to present a broad overview of specialist education, the chapter will first examine various generic reports and opinions on the importance of subject-matter knowledge for teachers. This will be followed by an analysis of the subject-matter recommendations as found in the teacher-education guidelines published by selected national organizations in other fields such as the National Council of Teachers of English and the National Council of Teachers of Mathematics. The major portion of the chapter will be devoted to a critical discussion of the primary areas of foreign language subject-matter content: culture, language, linguistics, and literature. This will include an exam-ination of the official teacher-education recommendations proposed by national foreign language organizations, as well as a discussion concerning the means of reaching and evaluating the outcomes. The chapter will conclude with a series of recommendations for continued development of the specialist component of teacher education.

Robert C. Lafayette (Ph.D., The Ohio State University) is Professor of Curriculum and Instruction and of French at Louisiana State University, where he also serves as Director of the French Education Project, the pedagogical arm of the Center for French and Francophone Studies. He has authored and edited several books and textbooks and numerous monographs and articles published in foreign language professional journals. His areas of expertise include the teaching of culture and the use of video in the classroom, and he has been active in state, regional, and national associations, serving as Chairman of the Central States Conference Board of Directors and member of the ACTFL Executive Council. He has received numerous awards for his work.

Subject-Matter Content Knowledge: An Overview ——————

What knowledge is essential for teaching a language? More specifically, to what degree must the teacher master the language being taught? What must the teacher know about the language? What must the teacher know about the culture(s) and literature(s)? At first sight, these questions appear to be obviously critical to the act of teaching, but unfortunately, in discussions of teacher education, content is often the component that receives the least attention. For example, among the forty-eight chapters in the *Handbook of Research on Teacher Education* (Houston 1990), only one specifically addresses the subject-matter preparation of teachers. No doubt this lack of attention stems from the fact that the need for content knowledge appears to be so obvious that there is little urgency to justify it. As Petrie (1987) says:

> The relevance of disciplinary content areas for secondary teachers is obvious and, as far as I am concerned, non controversial. Every secondary school teacher should major in the discipline he or she is going to teach. (p. 37)

The College Major

The solution to what every teacher, especially every foreign language teacher, needs to know unfortunately is more complicated than completing an undergraduate major, and completing a major does not necessarily achieve the needed expertise. It is not obvious that the knowledge taught in academic disciplines at the college level is necessarily relevant to the content covered in the schools. It is also not obvious that the decision of what might constitute the knowledge or proficiency needed to teach a specific subject matter should be in the hands of the experts in that discipline. The integrity and value of existing academic majors was questioned in the report of the Association of American Colleges (1985) during its project on redefining the meaning and purpose of baccalaureate degrees:

> The undergraduate major—the subject, academic discipline, or vocational specialty in which a student concentrates—everywhere dominates, but . . . the major in most colleges is little more than a gathering of courses taken in one department, lacking structure and depth, as is often the case in the humanities and social sciences, or emphasizing content to the neglect of the essential style of inquiry on which the content is based, as is too frequently true in the natural and physical sciences. (p. 2)

Some of the important changes in teacher education proposed by the Holmes Group (1986) and currently being effected in numerous major universities involve the elimination of undergraduate education degrees and majors in favor of undergraduate concentrations in the arts and sciences. In fact, in many secondary and K–12 subject-matter-specific programs, this means abandoning significant control over the content of the major, since these fifth-year students may arrive in the teacher-development program with bachelor's degrees from a variety of four-year institutions. In its report, however, the Holmes Group argues that the elimination of education majors must be accompanied by dramatic improvement in academic subjects.

we urge that our universities take three steps to strengthen education in the academic subjects, as accompaniments to the elimination of undergraduate education majors. One is to sharply revise the undergraduate curriculum, so that future teachers can study the subjects they will teach with instructors who model fine teaching and who understand the pedagogy of their material. A second step is to organize academic course requirements and courses so that undergraduate students can gain a sense of the intellectual structure and boundaries of their disciplines, rather than taking a series of disjointed, prematurely specialized fragments. . . . The third major change must be in schools and departments of education. Instead of our present sprawling and often scattered courses of study, we need to devise coherent programs that will support the advanced studies in pedagogy required for solid professional education. (pp. 16–17)

Teacher Knowledge of Content and Student Learning

In general, the relationship between teacher knowledge of subject matter and student achievement has not been firmly established. Grannis (1970) found that at the elementary school level, there is little relationship between the two, and that at the secondary school level, the only relationship between teachers' knowledge and students' achievement is one for bright students in advanced mathematics, chemistry, and physics. In the field of foreign language, Smith (1970) found no significant relationship between scores of 89 French and German teachers on all seven parts of the *MLA Proficiency Tests for Teachers and Advanced Students* and the achievement scores, both gross and gain, of their classes in foreign language skills. Teacher factors were not major contributors to final class variance (p. 166). Does this lack of relationship emanate from an inadequate content knowledge, or might it be due to a deficiency in a certain type of content knowledge? In his comprehensive study of 29 universities involved in teacher education, Goodlad (1990) found that prospective high school teachers were usually unable "to make connections between their undergraduate subject matter education and the high school curriculum they were required to teach" (p. 242). He speculated that this problem was due especially to a lack of understanding of the structure of the discipline.

Recent research (Wilson et al. 1987) also suggests that there are at least two dimensions of subject-matter knowledge necessary for teaching: (1) the subject content, that is, the facts, the organizing principles, and the basic concepts, and (2) the subject method of inquiry, that is, how we know the things we know or, as concerns teachers, how academic disciplines can be transformed into teachable subjects for the diverse population of students enrolled in our classes. Shulman (1987) refers to the latter as "pedagogical content knowledge—that special amalgam of content and pedagogy that is uniquely the province of teachers, their own special form of professional understanding" (p. 4). If teachers understand what they know, their subject-matter preparation will have a strong influence on the way they conceptualize, select, organize, and deliver what they teach.

Impact of Content Knowledge on the Teaching Act

Buchmann (1984) claims that knowledge is what teaching is all about, that it gives the teacher epistemic control as well as social control of the learning environment. Content knowledge helps the teacher view the learning process from the perspective of the learner and subsequently to recognize the logic of student questions and answers. This is especially important in the foreign language classroom when the teaching act leaves the confines of textbook exercises and embarks onto authentic and personal topics. Buchmann (1984) further postulates that content knowledge helps eliminate control or management problems, since the well-informed teacher is always mentally organized and prepared to teach. Conversely, lack of content knowledge, which in turn causes lack of teacher self-assurance, can be a powerful factor in predisposing teachers toward a management view of the classroom, where attention is focused primarily on social control and on maintenance of teacher authority.

In the foreign language classroom, lack of proficiency often signals the use of English as the vehicle of instruction, with practice in the foreign language limited to textbook exercises. French, or any other foreign language, becomes a subject that exists between the covers of a textbook, with the teacher's objective being the completion of so many lessons in an academic year or semester. Unfortunately, these values are often transferred to the students, who also eventually view the learning of a foreign language as the completion of textbook activities rather than the ability to use the language for purposes of communication. On the other hand, the proficient teacher, who has command of the subject matter and who uses the target language as the vehicle of instruction, is an obvious reminder to the students of the power of learning another language.

Finally, Buchmann (1984) maintains that teachers need a thorough knowledge of the subject matter because they must display a high degree of clarity in their efforts to increase knowledge and understanding in students. Teachers need to focus not so much on what they know, but rather on what the students do not know. Using a wide and theoretically differentiated knowledge of subject matter, they must put themselves inside the students' minds and explain what they need to learn.

Sources of Content Knowledge

The primary source of subject-matter content knowledge for future foreign language teachers is no doubt the offerings found in foreign language departments. Ball and McDiarmid (1990) identify two other important sources of subject-matter learning, however: the precollege curriculum, and learning subject matter from teaching it. It would not be unusual for a college foreign language major to have had three or four years of high school instruction and, given today's increase in elementary school foreign language programs, four or five years of elementary school instruction as well. The impact of this instruction on future teachers should not be minimized, since they will also ultimately draw on what they were taught while in elementary and secondary school when they themselves become teachers at those same levels. Thus, new teachers who experienced three or four years of strong communicative instruction in high school are more likely to replicate those efforts simply because they think that that is what the subject matter represents at the secondary level. The other potential source of subject-matter knowledge is the experience of teaching it. Many teachers, new or old, acquire new knowledge simply because it appears in a lesson to be taught. This is especially evident when dealing with the teaching of culture, since it is impossible to be familiar with the plethora of cultural information available. Teachers' subject-matter knowledge may also be affected by the kinds of questions that students ask and in general by their attitudes and expectations. For example, teachers who lack a certain degree of oral communicative prowess will have to improve that area of subject-matter knowledge if they expect to teach a continuing-education "Spanish for Travel" course.

In addition to its basic sources, subject-matter content knowledge is also indirectly influenced by two other elements. The first concerns the hidden curriculum present in all subject-matter classes. After spending at least 500 hours in foreign language classes, a major develops certain views about what constitutes a foreign language. Just as important, however, is the fact that this same major develops ideas about teaching and learning a foreign language. Ball and McDiarmid (1990) express it as follows:

> Watching their teachers, they [prospective teachers] acquire specific scripts
> for teaching particular topics and develop views about what teachers
> should and should not do, beliefs about what contributes to academic
> success, and notions about what makes a good class. (p. 446)

Lastly, it is important to note that the sources of content knowledge extend far beyond the four walls of the classroom. In fact, a large segment of today's foreign language teachers will readily attribute their oral proficiency and their cultural content knowledge to travel or study abroad.

Content Knowledge Recommendations of Non-Foreign Language Associations

Foreign languages have yet to attain parity with the "basics." They are not included among the basics in *America 2000* (1991), President Bush's education program; the *Handbook of Research on Teacher Education* (Houston 1990) does not include foreign languages among the eleven specific curricular areas that it treats; the National Board for Professional Teaching Standards includes individuals in the area of bilingual/ESL on its Board of Directors, but none from foreign languages; the Carnegie Project 30's colleges and universities, all involved in long-term teacher-education reform, have not identified foreign languages as a priority. Probably the most glaring omission is in the *NCATE Approved Curriculum Guidelines* (NCATE 1991) for use by institutions seeking NCATE (National Council for Accreditation of Teacher Education) accreditation in fall 1993 and spring 1994. This document is a compilation of the curriculum guidelines of national specialty organizations that have been approved by NCATE. They serve to guide department heads and professors who are directly responsible for specific programs in preparing folios that are then evaluated by the national specialty organization as a mandatory precondition to the accreditation process. Curriculum guidelines submitted by specialty organizations such as the National Council of Teachers of English and the National Council of Teachers of Mathematics and approved by the NCATE exist in fifteen areas of the school curriculum.

ACTFL is fully aware of its absence in this important body and has attempted to remedy the situation. Unfortunately, due to proposed changes in NCATE policies and procedures, the latter has informed ACTFL that they will not consider new members until after these changes have been finalized. If foreign languages are to be considered among the basics of education, ACTFL must have official ties with the nation's most important and prestigious teacher-preparation accrediting body.

National Board for Professional Teaching Standards

The National Board for Professional Teaching Standards (NBPTS) was established in 1987 to set new standards of accomplishment for the teaching profession and to improve the quality of education available to all children in the United States. In its publication, *Toward High and Rigorous Standards for the Teaching Profession* (NBPTS 1991), the group claims that lack of attention to the act of teaching at the college and university level reinforces a cavalier attitude toward teaching in general, and consequently, that too many Americans believe that any modestly educated person with some instinct for nurturing has the requisite qualifications to teach (p. 6). The NBPTS proposes to establish high and rigorous standards for what teachers should know and be able to do and to certify teachers who meet those standards. Within the board's five core propositions, there is a clear commitment to subject matter. The board views nationally certified teachers as individuals dedicated to exposing students to the social, cultural, ethical, and physical worlds in which they live, and who use the subjects they teach as entrees into those worlds. Teachers appreciate how knowledge in their subjects is created, organized and linked to other disciplines. This knowledge also includes the forms of creative investigation that characterize the work of scholars and artists (p. 19).

National Council of Teachers of English

The *Guidelines for the Preparation of Teachers of English Language Arts* (NCTE 1986) are divided into two major sections. The first specifies the traditional qualifications for teachers under the rubrics knowledge, pedagogy, and attitudes. The second includes the three components that the NCTE considers as essential to the success of a teacher-development program: (1) providing prospective teachers with models of effective teaching by means of the instruction they receive, (2) encouraging prospective teachers to analyze the nature of effective teaching, and (3) placing prospective teachers in schools where they can again observe and practice various aspects of effective teaching. The 1986 Guidelines present the content-knowledge recommendations for English and language arts under four categories: language development, composing and analyzing language, reading and literature, and nonprint media. Upon examining the above recommended "knowledge," it is important to note that it includes process as well as content. It is not only the rules of grammar but also how and when language is used; it includes not only knowledge of literature but also how students read it and react to it; it includes both the practice and the understanding of oral and written discourse.

National Council of Teachers of Mathematics

The *Professional Standards for Teaching Mathematics* (NCTM 1991) and its companion volume, the *Curriculum and Evaluation Standards for School Mathematics* (NCTM 1989), represent by far the most impressive, forward-looking, and thorough documents available from a subject-matter-specific association. These documents are designed to establish a broad framework to guide reform in school mathematics in the next decade. Most important is the fact that the first document, the curriculum and evaluation standards, defines what school mathematics should be all about while the second document, the professional standards, presents a vision of what teaching should entail to support the changes in curriculum.

The *Professional Standards for Teaching Mathematics* (NCTM 1991) consists of four major components: (1) standards for teaching mathematics, (2) standards for the evaluation of the teaching of mathematics, (3) standards for the professional development of teachers of mathematics, and (4) standards for the support and development of mathematics teachers and teaching. The third set of standards, of interest to us here, expresses NCTM's vision for well-prepared teachers from the time they take their first courses in collegiate mathematics and throughout their career-long development.

Among the six standards that address the professional development of teachers (both the preservice and inservice phases), only the first two are concerned with content. It is interesting to note that the first standard is entitled "Experiencing Good Mathematics Teaching" and addresses the teaching models that the prospective teacher experiences throughout his or her professional development. In fact, it almost resembles a methods course for university faculty in that it specifies how university professors should model good mathematics teaching.

The second standard delineates what every teacher should know not only about mathematics but school mathematics as well. As was the case in English language arts, the specifics speak both to content and process. They include, among others, mathematical concepts and procedures, ways to reason mathematically, the nature of mathematics, and the impact of technology on the nature of mathematics. A discussion of course titles such as algebra and calculus appear only later as illustrations of content needed at various grade levels.

Foreign Language Subject-Matter Content

Historical Perspective

In order to place the subject-matter expertise of foreign language teachers in proper perspective, I have gone back more than fifty years to an article by Stephen A. Freeman (1941) in the twenty-fifth anniversary issue of the *Modern Language Journal*. Unfortunately, his complaints concerning the foreign language major differ little from those expressed by contemporary critics of teacher-development programs:

> Even at best, a requirement of semester hours is inconclusive. We all know that a student can sit through fifteen semester hours of lectures in English on the history of French literature, and come out as poorly prepared in the French language as when he went in. Even a Bachelor's degree with a major in the foreign language is not sufficient guarantee that the student possesses the skills which will make him a successful teacher. There is a vast amount of downright *bad* teaching going on nowadays right before our eyes; and those teachers are theoretically innocent because they comply with all requirements. (p. 295)

Eight years later, Freeman (1949) complained again that little attention was paid to the teacher and took the opportunity to restate the subject-matter essentials one more time.

In 1955, the National Association of Secondary School Principals published the "Qualifications for Secondary School Teachers of Modern Foreign Languages." It included three levels of preparation (minimal, good, superior) and testing suggestions in seven categories including the four skills, language analysis, culture, and professional preparation. Subsequently, in 1966 the Modern Foreign Language Teacher Preparation Study of the Modern Language Association, in cooperation with the National Association of State Directors of Teacher Education and Certification, published the well-known "Guidelines for Teacher Education Programs in Modern Foreign Languages." This document addressed the academic specialization and the professional education of prospective teachers. Similar to the *Professional Standards for Teaching Mathematics* (NCTM 1991), it included (1) what a modern foreign language teacher is expected to do in U.S. schools, (2) the minimum language, culture, and pedagogical objectives to be achieved by the beginning teacher, and (3) the features of a teacher-education program capable of providing its students with the opportunities to achieve the stated minimum objectives.

Current Guidelines and Standards

Between 1966 and 1987, there were no national documents issued dealing with the development or education of teachers. In the mid-eighties, however, foreign language associations were some of the first professional groups to react to criticism of teacher-education programs in the United States. In 1988 there appeared the "Provisional Program Guidelines for Foreign Language Teacher Education" (ACTFL 1988), and a year later, the American Association of Teachers of French (AATF) published its definitive version of "The Teaching of French: A Syllabus of Competence" (AATF 1989), which had been available in provisional form since 1987. In September of 1990 the American Association of Teachers of Spanish and Portuguese (AATSP 1990) published its "Program Guidelines for the Education and Training of Teachers of Spanish and Portuguese," while in 1991 the American Philological Association introduced *Latin in American Schools* (Davis 1991), which includes significant recommendations for Latin teacher development. The American Association of Teachers of German (AATG 1992) plans to publish its "Professional Standards for Teachers of German" in late 1992.

These documents have much in common in that they all address what makes a good foreign language teacher. The ACTFL and AATSP guidelines do not represent a statement of minimal thresholds to be used either as accreditation or certification instruments. Rather, they "are intended to serve a program development function; that is, to represent a forward-looking view as to what knowledge, skills and experiences are deemed by the profession as holding the most promise for the preparedness of foreign language teacher candidates" (ACTFL 1988: 71). They focus on the three areas traditionally found in university foreign language teacher-preparation programs: personal development (general education), professional development (pedagogy), and specialist development (major field), and specify the opportunities that teacher-education programs should provide prospective teachers. Phillips (1989) tells us that the state of Tennessee made excellent use of the ACTFL document when translating its new policy for teacher-education reform into more specific rules of implementation.

The AATF and AATG documents differ in that they constitute standards as opposed to guidelines. ACTFL chose guidelines because it wanted to influence teacher-education programs but knew that it had no authority to certify such programs. AATF and AATG, on the other hand, propose to give teachers the opportunity to obtain a national license in addition to state certification. Thus, these documents bear a certain authority not found in those set forth by ACTFL and AATSP. A prepublication draft of the AATG document, for example, states that it "advances a set of standards and indicators of these standards. To implement these standards it proposes to establish a German-language specific certification board made up of members of the AATG" (p. 5). It should also be noted that the AATG standards are modeled on those of the NBPTS (1991).

As is evident in table 6-1, the amount of time and space devoted to content-area knowledge in these four official documents varies immensely. AATF devotes four of their five areas or so-called "standards" to content knowledge in the language, and AATG dedicates part of one standard to German and German studies, while AATSP and ACTFL spend one-third of their document on knowledge of the content to be taught. It should be noted that the Superior Level of the AATF document, as well as the standards proposed in the AATG document, do not address individuals exiting from preservice teacher-education programs, but rather career teachers who reach the specified levels through experience, inservice, and self-reflection.

It is indeed reassuring to know that each of the major language organizations has turned its attention to the so-often-neglected area of teacher development. On the other hand, it is somewhat distressing to imagine institutions of higher learning and state departments of education having to deal with documents addressing each of the different languages. Realistically, except for the largest institutions, it is safe to say that university teacher-education programs will pay little attention to the specific language documents, since in most cases universities deal with *foreign language* programs. Might it be the lack of a united front or a common document in foreign languages that constitutes one of the causes for NCATE not addressing this field in the *NCATE Approved Curriculum Guidelines* (1991)? Would it not be more intelligent and productive to have one document in the form of guidelines for accreditation of teacher-education programs *and* separate language-association documents used for national accreditation in

Table 6-1
Overview of Documents
from Four National Foreign Language Associations
on What a Teacher Should Know

AATF	AATG	AATSP & ACTFL
Title: The Teaching of French: A Syllabus of Competence. **Date:** 1989 **Mode:** Standards; defined in terms of the teacher; defines two levels (basic and superior); includes numerous specific examples. **Contents:** 1. Standards in 5 areas: a. language proficiency b. culture c. literature d. applied linguistics e. methodology 2. Three additional chapters: a. FLES: Teachers of French in the elementary schools (defines above standards in terms of FLES teachers) b. professional concerns (addresses such concerns as class size, teachers' load, etc.) c. curricular implications (aimed especially at university level courses needed to reach the standards)	**Title:** Professional Standards for Teachers of German. **Date:** 1992 **Mode:** Standards; defined in terms of the teacher; modeled on National Board for Professional Teaching Standards **Contents:** Background and introduction; the 5 standards, each followed by a short discussion and numerous indicators; assessment techniques. The standards are as follows: 1. German teachers are committed to the success of all students and their learning. 2. German teachers know the German language and German studies and know how to teach them. 3. German teachers manage and monitor student learning effectively. 4. German teachers reflect on their practice and learn from experience. 5. German teachers are members of teaching and learning communities.	**Titles:** ACTFL Provisional Program Guidelines for Foreign Language Teacher Education / AATSP Program Guidelines for the Education and Training of Teachers of Spanish and Portuguese. **Date:** 1988 (ACTFL); 1990 (AATSP) **Mode:** Guidelines; defined in terms of the teacher-education-program characteristics. **Contents:** Each segment includes guidelines, discussion, indicators. The major categories include 1. Personal development a. communication b. acquisition and use of knowledge and modes of thinking c. leadership 2. Professional development a. rationale for foreign language study b. theories of child development and learning c. curriculum development d. instruction e. the instructional setting f. foreign language in the elementary schools g. foreign language education faculty 3. Specialist development a. language proficiency b. culture and civilization c. language analysis

specific languages? The former would be a companion instrument to the NCATE Guidelines, while the latter a companion to the standards set forth by the National Board for Professional Teaching Standards.

At the first ACTFL Summer Seminar held in Denver during the summer of 1991 on the topic of teacher education, Clifford (1991) suggested that the foreign language profession establish an accreditation program similar to those offered by the medical professions and the National Association of Schools of Music, which accredits AA, BA, and graduate programs and non-degree-granting institutions with programs in music and music-related disciplines. According to Clifford, it is the instructional system that is not permitting the language student or major to achieve proficiency, since it has never provided the time needed to develop meaningful levels of proficiency in second languages. He suggested the creation of an accrediting commission, which could use mutually agreed-upon guidelines to help local programs address systemic deficiencies—deficiencies that have often been beyond the control of the classroom teacher.

Language Proficiency

Among the components of content knowledge, none is more important to foreign language teaching than language proficiency. Each of the four national associations that have issued statements on the level of proficiency needed for teaching have done so using the ACTFL *Proficiency Guidelines*. In all cases the recommended minimum level of proficiency is either Advanced or Advanced High. In addition to recommending a proficiency level, the AATG document states that "Teachers of German have a command of the language that allows them to conduct their classes in German with ease and confidence, regardless of level of instruction using appropriate and varied language at high levels of accuracy and fluency" (AATG 1992: 9). The AATF document (AATF 1989) makes very clear that the ability to use French effectively for both oral and written purposes is not necessarily related to knowledge about French grammar, vocabulary, and pronunciation. Knowledge that teachers have about language, literature, and culture must be used to communicate effectively. The AATF document also echoes the work of Buchmann (1984) when it describes how proficiency in the language will help individuals with every component of the teaching act:

> The ability to speak, understand, read, and write French well encourages teachers to use French in class, providing expansive and accurate models for their students. A sound command of French gives teachers the linguistic freedom necessary to personalize lessons according to their students' backgrounds and interests, thereby facilitating effective lesson planning and helping them work efficiently so as to meet the many demands on their professional time. It also allows them to maintain contact with French-speaking cultures, giving them current information to share with their students. (AATF 1989: 11)

Achieving Proficiency: The Undergraduate Major

How do prospective teachers go about achieving the levels of proficiency recommended by the various professional associations? Unfortunately, it is not necessarily acquired in institutions of higher learning, since proficiency is often the area that is given the least attention by university foreign language departments. It is primarily the responsibility of the lower-division courses plus a conversation course for oral proficiency and a composition course for proficiency in writing. Advanced grammar courses, on the other hand, usually do little to advance student proficiency. Even more serious is the fact that the need to teach language is forgotten once students arrive in literature courses. According to Kalivoda (1985), the tendency to value literature at the expense of language is reflected in

> (1) the preponderance of college literature courses and the meager offerings in language per se; (2) the teaching of literature (and other content-oriented courses) in the students' native language; (3) faculties oriented toward literature in both training and interest; and (4) faculty reward systems that favor literary research and publication. (p. 16)

A good example of this train of thought is actually found in the AATF Syllabus of Competence (AATF 1989). While discussing literature in the introductory statement, the author laments the fact that "teacher education programs are so overloaded that literature has to be compressed into survey courses" (p. 10). It is ironic that the same document does not bemoan the fact that culture is always

Table 6-2
Language Proficiency Levels
Recommended for Teacher Development
by National Associations
Using ACTFL Proficiency Guidelines

	ACTFL (guidelines)	AATF* (standards)	AATG (standards)	AATSP (guidelines)
Listening	advanced high	advanced high superior	advanced	advanced high
Speaking	advanced high	advanced superior	advanced	advanced high
Reading	advanced high	advanced high superior	advanced	advanced high
Writing	advanced	advanced superior	advanced	advanced

*The AATF syllabus of competence recognizes two levels of competence: (1) basic competence needed for teachers to function well in lower-level classrooms and (2) superior competence needed for teachers to function well in upper-level classrooms or in immersion classrooms. The first line in each box represents basic competence, while the second is for superior competence.

compressed into one or at most two survey courses. In assessing foreign language teachers' perceptions of their preprofessional preparation, Lange and Sims (1990) found that by far the least useful segment of the major area was the examination and analysis of literary texts across several centuries.

Excluding the few individuals who teach the literature-based Advanced Placement course, if one analyzes the school foreign language curriculum, it is ludicrous to maintain that a teacher needs any more literature than is found in one or two survey courses. Just as foreign language teachers have functioned for years without culture courses, future teachers could just as easily function without literature courses; in fact, given the cultural load in contemporary textbooks, advisers should almost always suggest a culture course before one in literature. Unfortunately, there is an insufficient supply!

If the recommended proficiency levels are to be achieved by prospective teachers, either emphasis in the major language area must focus on language proficiency itself, or all literature and other content-based courses must include a language component. In addition, university foreign language faculty have an obligation to model good teaching, which first and foremost implies use of the target language as the vehicle of instruction. The ACTFL and AATSP Teacher-Education Program Guidelines state that future teachers must have opportunities to hear, speak, read, and write authentic language in all foreign language courses. More important, they implore foreign language departments not to confine language and grammar study to lower-division courses. Similarly, the AATF document contends that in order to develop the recommended proficiency in French, undergraduate and graduate programs in French should be conducted nearly exclusively in the French language. Finally, it is interesting to note that the California regulations for modern foreign language teacher-education programs (Commission 1991) state that the program shall consist of a minimum of 30 semester units in upper-division courses, all of which are to be taught in the target language. In fact, the language of instruction for each course must be noted in the program.

Claiming that colleges must do a better job of teaching language, James (1989) suggests the transformation of the entire college curriculum in foreign languages, from the beginning required courses to the end of the major, into an integrated sequence of courses, grounded firmly in humanistic, literary content, but teaching linguistic skills throughout (p. 86). Foreign language programs must realize that cloning experts in literary criticism is not their sole goal. The great majority of foreign language majors eventually want to make use of their language skills doing something else. James (1989) describes the new program at Hunter College as follows:

> Instead of expecting students to bridge a formidable gap from language acquisition courses to courses in literary criticism, our goal is rather that they should perceive the college-level curriculum as a smooth passage: From knowing little of a language, they gradually work up to the point where they can begin to use the language to work in any discipline which they might choose (p. 95).

. . . in our upper level courses, literature and language, there are more than twice as many students as there were before we began our curricular reform. We do not attribute this to any particular teaching method, but rather to the fact that the curriculum has changed from being a kind of obstacle race into a working support system for the students. (p. 96)

In an article entitled "What Teachers Need to Know about English," Lloyd-Jones (1990) states that first and foremost, the teacher must use the language well in daily discourse. In fact, he says, "if I had to devise for prospective teachers a training program with but one segment, I would concentrate on enhancing each teacher's performance as a user of language" (p. 120). There is little doubt that the same is true for the foreign language teacher. For most users of native or foreign languages, the real issue is not grammar, but its use. We are concerned about what words or structures are chosen in what situations to represent what set of values.

Achieving Proficiency: Study Abroad

If prospective teachers cannot fully achieve the proficiency required to teach in the classroom from their work at the university, will it help them if they study abroad? No doubt the most significant study dealing with this question is that of Carroll (1967), who maintains that even a short period of time spent abroad has a marked impact on a student's language competence. A recent study by Brecht, Davidson, and Ginsberg (1991), using longitudinal data from U.S. students of Russian studying in various in-country programs under the auspices of the American Council of Teachers of Russian, reveals significant gains in language proficiency attained by a wide variety of university-level students of Russian as a result of their in-country immersion experience. The study also demonstrates the role played by the type and degree of close contact with native speakers.

Millman (1988) reports the pretest and posttest scores on the ACTFL Oral Proficiency Interview of 8 Alabama recipients of grants to study abroad. Three remained at the same level while the other 5 improved one step, but always within the same range, such as from Intermediate–Low to Intermediate–High.

Under similar circumstances, Lafayette (1987) reports comparable results in the final report of a grant received from the Louisiana Endowment for the Humanities to fund a six-week summer institute for Louisiana teachers of French. The institute began with one week at Louisiana State University in Baton Rouge, followed by four weeks in La Rochelle, France, and the final week back in Baton Rouge. Of the 19 individuals who underwent pretest and posttest ACTFL Oral Proficiency Interviews, 10 were ranked one step above at the end of the program. Six of the 7 teachers originally ranked at Intermediate–Mid moved to Intermediate–High. The most difficult problem was getting the individuals at Intermediate–High to move to Advanced. Only 2 of 9 actually made that jump, although according to the interviewers 2 others were very close. In all cases at Intermediate–High, each individual improved considerably in the areas of context and especially fluency, but they were not able to sustain the accuracy of Advanced level speakers. Asked how they felt about their own improvement, the participants gave a mean rating of 4.33 out of 5 in their self-evaluation of improvement of proficiency.

Milleret et al. (1991) studied the use of an ACTFL-based test to evaluate gains in oral proficiency during a six-week summer study program. The gains measured by the Portuguese Speaking Test, a simulated oral proficiency interview, were significant for the group as a whole, but when divided into Intermediate and Advanced groups, they showed significance only for the Intermediate group. This is normal considering that the ACTFL ratings demand increasingly larger gains in proficiency as one moves up the scale. Although gains were not significantly evident in the test scores, the students and instructors in the Advanced class were very satisfied with their progress.

DeKeyser (1991b), on the other hand, discovered that while students studying in Spain for a semester gained in fluency and expanded their vocabulary while abroad, they did not drastically change their monitoring behavior or their use of communication strategies. "The results of our study, then, do not suggest a strong dichotomy between learning language in the classroom and picking it up abroad or between grammar and oral proficiency" (pp. 46–47). DeKeyser concludes that communicative processes are not strongly affected by study abroad and then goes on to speculate why a stay abroad can make such a significant difference in proficiency, according to previous studies. His reasons include

(1) the sheer number of hours spent in the native-speaking environment provides a huge amount of comprehensible input and a sizable amount of speaking practice for those willing to make the effort; (2) being in an environment where one can get many things done in the foreign language that could not be accomplished in the native language is a constant motivational boost; (3) students overseas acquire at least some skill in managing truly informal interaction with multiple native speakers. (p. 47)

Finally, he adds that overseas, the many communicative scenarios that recur tend to create a natural communicative drill. There is such intense focus on meaning, and the input is so comprehensible, that it permits the student to focus on form. And when focus on form leads to the remembering of a word or phrase heard in the native-speaking environment, that memory is integrated into the memory of an event, which automatically increases its durability.

There are numerous reasons, personal, linguistic and cultural, to promote study-abroad programs, but the most important is the fact that it virtually guarantees the student exposure to actual use of the target language and culture, something that unfortunately is far from guaranteed in the classroom.

Testing Proficiency

Although the Oral Proficiency Interview (OPI) and its view of language proficiency as a unitary ability was widely criticized by those who espouse the multicomponential view of proficiency (Bachman and Savignon 1986), the impact of the ACTFL Proficiency Guidelines and the OPI has been staggering and widespread. The approach and ability levels defined by the guidelines have been widely accepted as a standard for assessing oral proficiency in foreign languages, especially in the United States, and have provided the basis for the development of simulated oral proficiency interviews. At least six states and Washington, D.C., use the OPI in some form or other for the purpose of certification (Uber Grosse and Benseler 1991). Moreover, various teacher-education programs use the instrument, often informally, as one of the criteria for either admission or exit.

A potentially easier solution to oral proficiency testing is the tape-mediated simulated oral proficiency interview (SOPI) developed by Stansfield (1989) at the Center for Applied Linguistics. Imitating as closely as possible the format of the Oral Proficiency Interview, the SOPI is a tape-recorded, semi-direct speaking test consisting of six parts. Part one corresponds to the warm-up phase of the OPI, while the remaining five segments are designed to elicit language similar to that found during the level check and probe phases. Except for the warm-up, the directions are in English to avoid testing listening or reading. Parts two, three, and four use pictures to check the ability to perform Intermediate and Advanced functions such as giving directions to someone using a map, describing a person or place using a drawing, or narrating a sequence of events using a set of drawings. Parts five and six test the candidate's ability to handle the functions and content associated with the Advanced and Superior levels by asking him or her to react appropriately to various topics and situations.

Stansfield (1991) summarizes the research conducted to date on the use of the SOPI and concludes that it is safe to say that the OPI and the SOPI test the same abilities. In five studies involving different languages, both tests were administered to the same individuals and each test was scored by two raters. Statistical comparison of the scores on the two test types show correlations of .89, .91, .93, .93, and .94. Stansfield further claims that the SOPI offers advantages as concerns reliability and validity. Since the SOPI is recorded and scored later, it is possible to select the most reliable raters. The test is also longer (45 minutes) than the OPI (20–25 minutes) and thus offers a more extensive sample of examinee speech. This, along with the fact that the speech sample elicited is not based on the skill of individual interviewers, offers the possibility of a more valid assessment. Finally, the SOPI is definitely more practical than the OPI in that it need not be administered by a trained interviewer, and it can be administered to more than one person simultaneously by a single administrator.

The best large-scale adaptation of the OPI is the recently introduced Texas Oral Proficiency Test (1991), now required for French, Spanish, and bilingual

Table 6-3
Sample Items from the Texas Oral Proficiency Test

Spanish: Sample Picture-Based Item	French: Sample Topic Item	Spanish: Sample Situation Item
You read in your test booklet and hear from the master tape:	You read in your test booklet and hear from the master tape:	You read in your test booklet and hear from the master tape:
Imagine that you are at a party in Cuernavaca, Mexico. You join a group of people who are describing their homes. One of the group, Marta, asks you to **describe a typical American home.** You may use the picture or your own experience as a source of ideas. You will have 15 seconds to prepare your answer. After Marta asks her question, you will have one minute and 20 seconds for your response. Remember to wait for Marta's question before you respond. (15 second pause) You hear from the master tape: ¿Cómo son los hogares en los Estados Unidos? (1 minute and 20 seconds for you to speak) Tone (5 seconds for you to complete your response)	An exchange teacher from Paris, Monsieur Martin, has come to you for advice on the first day of school. He will be teaching American students for the first time, and he would like to know how roll call is conducted in American class-rooms. After Monsieur Martin asks his question, **briefly explain to him the procedure for taking attendance in a typical American classroom.** (15 second pause) You hear from the master tape: Comment fait-on l'appel aux Etats-Unis? (55 seconds for you to speak) Tone (5 seconds for you to complete your response)	You are leading a group of 12 high school students on a tour of Mexico. When you arrive at a hotel in Mexico City, where you had already paid a deposit, the clerk tells you there are no rooms available. You ask to speak with the manager, Mr. Navarro. After he asks you what the problem is, **explain the situation to him. Ask him to remedy it, conveying both your feelings about what has happened and your urgent need to find accommodations for the group.** (15 second pause) You hear from the master tape: Buenos días, Me dijo el recep-cionista que quería hablar conmigo. ¿En qué puedo servirle? (55 seconds for you to speak) Tone (5 seconds for you to complete your response)

certification in Texas. The TOPT was developed by the Center for Applied Linguistics under contract with the Texas Education Agency. Nearly one thousand Texas educators were involved in the project. Test advisory committees in French and Spanish, composed of classroom teachers, other language specialists in the public schools, and college faculty, defined 38 speaking tasks of varying degrees of difficulty (e.g., "Introduce Yourself," "Lodge a Complaint," "Explain a Complex Process in Detail"). A survey of these speaking tasks was sent to 700 randomly selected teachers, who were asked to indicate whether, in their professional opinion, the level of ability required to perform this task was needed by teachers in their respective fields. Only those tasks that received a favorable rating by the teachers were included in the TOPT. Test items were then written, reviewed, and revised by advisory committees, followed by field testing and final revision.

The TOPT is a tape-mediated speaking test using two tape recorders, one for the master test tape and the other for the examinee response tape. The master tape times the test, which lasts approximately 45 minutes and includes about 20 minutes of timed pauses for speaking. All directions are read aloud in English on the tape and also appear written in English in the test booklet. Following a brief warm-up, the 15 TOPT items are divided into three groups of 5 in the following categories: picture-based items, topic items, and situation items. A sample item from each category is found in table 6-3.

Two specially trained raters score each test independently using four levels of the ACTFL Oral Proficiency Rating Scale: Intermediate–Mid, Intermediate–High, Advanced, and Advanced–High. An Advanced rating is required in order to pass the TOPT and receive Texas certification.

The Center for Applied Linguistics (CAL) offers the *TOPT Preparation Kit* (1991) to help familiarize potential candidates with this unique instrument. The *Kit* contains a complete description of the items that may appear on the test, detailed information about how the test is scored and what is required to pass it, ways to prepare to take the test, and strategies to use when taking it. Included with the *Kit* is a tape with a sample test on one side and examples of actual examinee responses at different score levels on the other side. The sample responses can help not only Texans about to take the test but anyone interested in determining his or her own level of proficiency. It would be most advantageous, for example, for university foreign language faculty to listen to and study these sample responses so that they become more aware of the type of proficiency needed to obtain certification.

In 1986, the Florida legislature enacted chapter 86-156, Laws of Florida, establishing the development and administration of subject-matter tests in more than eighty areas of initial certification, including French, German, Latin, and Spanish (LeBlanc 1990). Thanks to the efforts of numerous teachers at all levels of instruction, the state decided to develop its own set of tests instead of using existing instruments. The result was a 3½-year effort that included identifying teacher competencies, developing test items, and field-testing the instruments. According to Hallman (1991), who addressed the ACTFL Summer Institute on Teacher Education, the test is 2½ hours long and 25 percent is devoted to speaking. The latter section resembles the SOPI in that the questions are constant and the tapes are scored holistically by two independent raters using the Florida Oral Proficiency Scale, a modified version of the federal government and ACTFL scales. The test is administered simultaneously at ten sites and to date some three thousand individuals have taken it.

In addition to the work being done on the simulated oral proficiency interviews, the San Diego State University Foreign Language Resource Center is investigating the use of video stimulus in oral proficiency testing. The project's goal is to develop and research new elicitation techniques via video for group testing, with the intent of developing a *Visual-Oral Communication Instrument* (VOCI) (Bley-Vroman and Robinson 1991).

According to Uber Grosse and Benseler (1991), at least ten states require a certain minimum score on the National Teacher Examination (NTE) for certification. Although the NTE does not include a speaking segment, this is only temporary, as the Educational Testing Service, the publisher of the NTE, is in the process of developing a completely new series of tests entitled *The Praxis Series: Professional Assessments for Beginning Teachers,* which ETS hopes will assist states in the process of licensing teachers. This series of tests focuses on three critical areas of the teaching candidate's development: basic academic skills, subject-matter knowledge, and classroom performance. In her report on the ACTFL 1991 Summer Seminar on Teacher Education, Knop (1991) relates the comments of Susan Chyn of ETS concerning new foreign language subject-matter assessment in the Praxis series. The core of the examination will consist of a two-hour test of 140 multiple-choice items dealing with listening and reading comprehension, structure of the language, language and speech analysis, and culture. There will be three additional components: a 30-minute writing sample, a 30-minute speaking sample, and a one-hour written pedagogy segment involving items such as different ways to teach a particular lesson.

Given all the work that has been done in the field of foreign language proficiency assessment, even without mentioning the futuristic developments in computer-assisted and computer-adaptive testing, there is ample evidence that testing for language proficiency is not only a possibility but a necessity. It should indeed be required for certification purposes, but it should also be practiced among university majors after the sophomore year for its diagnostic value and at the end of the program for its summative value.

Culture and Civilization

In his article on what constitutes a well-trained modern language teacher, Freeman (1941) stated that modern foreign languages are a cultural study. "They are not an end in themselves; they are a tool—to sharpen our thinking, to enrich our expression, to help us understand history, literature, and other nations" (p. 305). Culture must become an integral part of second language learning and teaching. And culture must affect not only language learning but also the individual himself or herself; second language teachers have a unique opportunity to broaden the horizons of students, to help them better understand themselves, and in so doing help them understand others. Bowers and Flinders (1990) claim that in order to maintain affirming teacher–student relationships and an empowering learning experience, teachers need to understand the cultural and linguistic patterns that make up the ecology of the classroom. They maintain that "the term culture provides a way of understanding how nearly all aspects of human experience are based on taken-for-granted categories of understanding, patterns of social interaction, and prejudices of taste, sound, and color" (p. 19). The anthropologist Goodenough (1981) makes this point in a different way. "Culture," he writes, "consists of standards for deciding what is, standards for deciding what can be, standards for deciding how one feels about it, standards for deciding what to do about it, and standards for deciding how to go about doing it" (p. 62).

A classic debate among academics today opposes the proponents of culture as knowledge or information to those who view culture primarily as a process. In the words of Mueller (1991), the latter offer "mounting resistance to characterizing our own era through the pursuit, or the knowledge, of certain facts, the basis for defining previous eras. The search for method, the search for theory, is proposed as the modern way to knowledge" (p. 20). Within the view of culture as knowledge there is an even more intense debate over how that knowledge might be defined. We are witnessing not a "War of the Worlds" but a "War of the Canons." On one side we find Hirsch (1988), who defines cultural literacy as the storehouse of information possessed by educated readers of a particular society, and who proposes more than 5000 items that educated Americans should know. On the other side we find the proponents of "cultural or multicultural studies," who wish to replace the classical canon, which they describe as white, male, middle-class, and capitalist European, by a broadly defined and more representative collection of scholarly works. Patrikis (1987) reminds us that we now have an "embarrassment of choice: high culture, low culture, urban culture, suburban culture, rural culture, contemporary culture, the culture of past generations, women's culture, patriarchal culture, adolescent culture, children's culture" (p. 4).

It is motivating and intellectually stimulating to participate in the polemics currently permeating U.S. universities. No matter what individual universities or departments choose to emphasize, however, it is more important to reflect upon the fact that we are teacher educators and that prospective foreign language teachers are not so much concerned with the nature of culture in its own theoretical framework as they are with the *teaching of culture within the confines of the second language classroom.*

Crawford-Lange and Lange (1984) correctly point out that "when the acquisition and dissemination of elements of cultural information become the predominant teaching strategy, severe limitations are imposed on the learning of culture, especially the ability to recognize and understand cultural change over time" (pp. 141–42). Given the content and composition of contemporary textbooks, however, as well as the confining culture of the classroom, future teachers must be prepared to use both cultural knowledge and cultural process in their attempts to improve the cultural sensitivity of their students.

To most teachers culture has multiple meanings. Adaskou et al. (1990) distinguish four meanings of culture: the *aesthetic* sense (e.g., cinema and literature), the *sociological* sense (organization and nature of family, relations, customs, material conditions), the *semantic* sense (the conceptualization system that conditions perceptions and thought processes), and the *pragmatic* sense (e.g., background knowledge and social and paralinguistic skills) (pp. 3–4). On the other hand, Krasnick (1988) interprets culture from a receptive and productive point of view. He identifies four interactive dimensions of cultural competence: attitude (cultural sensitivity), knowledge (cultural awareness), skill (ability), and traits (e.g., tolerance and willingness). Finally, Allen's (1985) concept of cultural proficiency includes *information* (facts about the culture, behavior patterns, values, thought process, etc.), *experience* (process by which one can recognize, describe, evaluate, explain cultural phenomena), and *authenticity* (behavior and attitude of learner, e.g., socially and professionally).

The above concepts of culture differ in a variety of ways, but they all include both knowledge and process. Our prospective teachers need basic cultural information in order to make effective use of modern textbooks. More important, however, they need basic cultural information for use as a vehicle in learning the process of first discovering oneself and only later the "other" while at the same time developing a sensitivity for people and things that are different or foreign so that eventually they may arrive at acceptance of the "other."

AATF. It is within the domain of culture and civilization that the AATF document (AATF 1989) demonstrates its uniqueness and significant differences from the pronouncements of the other professional associations. Most important is the fact that the AATF does not include literature within the rubric of culture. Two committees produced separate chapters, one devoted to culture and the other to literature. The literature proponents did not wish to be subsumed within the area of culture "in view of the richness and wide influence of French and Francophone literature" (p. 17). Among the documents produced by the foreign language professional associations, the AATF has by far the most in-depth treatment of culture, including the following definition of cultural competence:

> Cultural competence is based on the concept of a culture as an organic whole made up of values, a grid through which one sees the world, habits of thought and feeling, and habits of interacting with certain social institutions and customs. The present evolution of a culture is strongly influenced by its past, including its proud achievements.
>
> Cultural competence can best be defined as a combination of three interrelated parts: the sociolinguistic ability to communicate, certain areas of knowledge, and certain informed attitudes.
>
> Cultural competence does include a body of knowledge and attitudes that supplements the understanding of a single culture area and its component societies. To be more than an amateur observer, one needs to know how to relate the heterogeneous surface manifestations to underlying core elements. One needs also a kit of methods and conceptual tools for observing and analyzing a culture: field study, direct and remote; the differentiation of subcultures; the analysis of space and time concepts; contrastive analysis. (p. 14)

Following this definition, the text describes eight informed attitudes, such as "intellectual awareness that 'different' does not mean 'wrong,' " then goes on to describe (1) the sociolinguistic ability and (2) the knowledge needed for the *basic* and *superior* levels of competence. Although useful if an institution is looking for examples of course objectives, it is at this point that the specificity of the document simply overwhelms. For example, one of the ten competencies listed in the knowledge segment of the *basic* level reads as follows: "can interpret simple menus, timetables, schedules, maps; manipulate the currency; knows which kinds of shops sell what kinds of merchandise, and knows where to go for information on such subjects" (p. 15). A comparable degree of specificity is found in the literature chapter:

> In order to attain a *superior* level of competence, teachers of literature need the historical, cultural, and literary background for the works to be studied including Biblical, mythological, and historical allusions. They should be aware of contemporary literature theory and a variety of critical approaches. (p. 17)

AATG.   Since the German standards (AATG 1992) are modeled on the generic standards set forth by the National Board for Professional Teaching Standards (1991), there is much less specificity concerning content knowledge. It is also interesting to note that the AATG document uses the term *studies* rather than *culture.* A segment of Standard 2 states:

> GERMAN TEACHERS KNOW GERMAN STUDIES
> Teachers of German have a strong background in the liberal arts. This includes the humanities as well as the social sciences and the natural sciences. They possess this background knowledge for the American as well as for the German-speaking world. Their knowledge of the German-speaking world pertains to both historical and contemporary developments.

ACTFL and AATSP.   The ACTFL (1988) and AATSP (1990) teacher-education program guidelines state that the program should provide the candidate opportunities to

1. discuss, research and reflect upon the daily living patterns, societal structure, institutions, and value systems of the people who speak the language;
2. explore the variability of cultural concepts;
3. obtain an overview of the literatures of the people who use the language with an emphasis on contemporary writers and an in-depth experience with some major author or theme;
4. obtain an overview of the cultures and civilizations from a variety of perspectives, including the historical, geographical, political, and artistic;
5. develop skills in processing information that promote the understanding and interpretation of cultures and civilizations. These include:
   a. observing, comparing and inquiring about cultural phenomena;
   b. analyzing and hypothesizing about cultural phenomena;
   c. synthesizing and determining the generalizability of cultural phenomena.

California Standards.   The preliminary draft of the California standards (Commission 1991) includes fourteen standards, eight of which are devoted to content. The following three are devoted to culture:

> *Standard 6: Knowledge of Culture*—The program enables teacher candidates to study geography, history, and contemporary social structures of

the target culture(s) and how these influence and shape cultural values and traditions.

Standard 7: Cultural Competencies—The program enables teacher candidates to function effectively within the target culture and fosters their ability to use the language in a manner considered culturally appropriate by native speakers.

Standard 8: Attitudes toward Culture—The program fosters in teacher candidates respect and understanding of the customs, traditions, and cultural values of the people who speak the target language.

Proposed Standards for FLES.   As seen in the chart that follows, Pesola (1991) identifies the cultural needs of the elementary school foreign language classroom in terms of cultural symbols, cultural products, and cultural practices and proposes several examples of elements with which the teacher would need to be familiar. In addition to these specifications, Pesola suggests that the elementary school foreign language teacher be familiar with the folk literature and contemporary children's literature of countries whose language is being taught. (See table 6-4.)

Achieving Culture: The College Major

Given the typical foreign language major at most universities, achieving the numerous goals set forth in the paragraphs above will indeed be a challenge

Table 6-4
The Pesola Cultural Elements
for the Elementary School
Foreign Language Classroom

Cultural Symbols	Cultural Products	Cultural Practices
Flags, insignia related to children's interests;	Significant examples of the visual arts (and artists);	Forms of greeting;
Significant national or geographic monuments;	Significant examples of the musical arts (and artists);	Celebration of holidays;
Symbols associated with holidays;	Important chracters, events, and themes from folk literature;	Use of gestures;
Good and bad luck symbols;	Traditional children's songs, rhymes, games;	Meals and eating practices;
Symbolic meaning of animals;	Traditional stories and legends;	Shopping;
Heroes from history and myth.	Examples of folk arts;	Favorite playtime and recreational activities;
	Currency and coins, stamps, and other realia;	Home and school life;
	Traditional and holiday foods.	Patterns of politeness;
		Types of and attitudes toward pets;
		How children and families move from place to place.

unless, like language, culture becomes an integral component of all courses taught. Crucial to the problem are the answers to the following questions: (1) Is the study of culture required for completion of the major? (2) Who will teach the culture course? (3) How often will culture be offered? (4) What is the content of the culture course? The answers to each of these questions will vary from institution to institution, but they will probably be less favorable to culture, the larger and more research-oriented the university. It would not be surprising to hear the following answers: (1) It is not a required major course. (2) It is taught by a nontenure line instructor who happens to be a native speaker. (3) It is offered when someone can be found to teach it. (4) It is often history or whatever the instructor wants to make of it.

During the past decade, some foreign language departments have increased their cultural offerings and some have even chosen to portray themselves as something other than literary. For example, at the State University College of New York, Cortland, the department is called the Department of International Communications and Culture. At Antioch College, the curriculum will soon require all undergraduates to become proficient in a foreign language and to study another culture firsthand, either in a foreign country or in the United States. Other departments have added cultural studies or a culture major to their undergraduate literature curriculum. The latter is especially evident among German departments, many of whom have established German Studies programs, as is reflected in the AATG standards, where all references to culture are encoded as "German Studies."

In order to achieve a minimum of the culturally oriented objectives, teacher-development programs must convince foreign language departments to offer a minimum of two culture courses, at least one of which must not be historical in nature. In addition, Lange (1991) suggests a course on children's and adolescent literature of the target language culture(s).

The percentage of culture content in the total curriculum can also be increased by using culture-based readings and authentic video as the core of conversation courses. Similar material should also be integrated in lower-division courses so that culture is a constant throughout the foreign language curriculum.

Finally, it is most important that all faculty serve as models of how to integrate culture and language teaching. They must reflect upon and eventually practice the ideas of Edwards (1992) concerning the learning of culture in the second language classroom. He notes that the major obstacle in learning culture is not only the fact that the learner arrives into the classroom already having absorbed the values and the everyday living patterns of his or her own culture, but also that the learner perceives these values and patterns as being the proper ones. In short, Edwards sees it as a "we versus they" situation, one that will not be altered with token amounts of good will, tolerance, and curiosity. In an attempt to overcome this obstacle, he suggests a six-step model for the teaching of a second culture: (1) awareness of one's own nonuniversal perspective, (2) differentiation (awareness that not only is the "other" different, but also that I am different with regard to the other), (3) exploration, (4) confrontation, (5) decentration (changing the center of . . .), and (6) surpassing oneself, accepting the "other."

One of the most important concepts in Edwards's model of second culture learning is the fact that the student is not ready to deal with some other culture's ways of living and thinking until he or she is willing to examine his or her own. Thus one must develop both an awareness of self and an awareness that others may be different and valued as well.

Achieving Culture: Study Abroad

There is little doubt that study, travel, and work abroad can make significant contributions to both the knowledge and the process of culture. Mullen (1992) argues that "no other experience can so successfully deconstruct the notion of monoculturalism, allowing a student to compare his or her own customs against those encountered abroad" (p. 32). In fact, few would deny that study abroad should be a mandatory component of teacher development.

Assessing Culture

If culture is to constitute an important component of the prospective teacher's education, it would behoove us to have instruments that can evaluate cultural knowledge, behavior, and attitudes. To date few materials have been prepared for assessing culture learning. For example, it was reported during the 1991 ACTFL Summer Seminar on Teacher Education that the Florida instrument devoted 9 percent of the test to culture, while the new ETS foreign language tests will devote approximately 13 percent to culture. Unfortunately, the suggestions that follow do not describe instruments that test culture but rather provide the reader with sources that suggest how to test culture. It thus becomes the responsibility of each teacher-education program to give credibility to its cultural component by creating and using assessment instruments.

Damen (1987) offers four types of evaluation techniques for culture testing: (1) self-assessment (checklists about attitudes, case studies, and discussion); (2) enactment (demonstrating what one has learned through role-plays and simulation); (3) production (a concrete product such as a report or an essay); (4) observation (demonstrating specific cultural skills or behavior observed by teacher or peers). Seelye (1984) devotes an entire chapter to testing culture, in which he discusses social distance scales, semantic differentials, criterion-referenced tests, standardized tests, simulations, and oral examinations. The most recent and up-to-date document is that of Lessard-Clouston (1992), who addresses the issues and offers numerous techniques and suggestions in the following domains: assessing knowledge of the target culture; assessing awareness/understanding of the target culture; and assessing skill/function in the target culture (pp. 332–38).

One of the most interesting initiatives in the area of assessment emanates from a project at the State University of New York sponsored by the Fund for the

Improvement of Post-Secondary Education (FIPSE). Lewis (1990) describes the project as a series of meetings over a three-year period during which two representatives from each of five SUNY campuses developed assessment strategies and instruments that were compatible with the curricular aims of each department. The foreign language group agreed to use the ACTFL *Proficiency Guidelines* (1986) as the organizing principle for all assessment, including culture and literature. This, of course, meant that they had to create guidelines for culture and literature, since the *Guidelines* do not treat those areas. The culture grid was divided into two major categories, culture/behavior and civilization/knowledge, each of which was subdivided further into content and skills. The descriptors for the Advanced level were as follows (Lewis 1990):

> *Cultural/Behavior: Content.* Etiquette; taboos and sensitivity; polite requests; invitations; gifts; apologies; introductions; use of telephone; purchasing and bargaining; routine banking.
> *Cultural/Behavior: Skills.* Demonstrates limited social competence; can deal with routine social situations; comprehends common social rules; does not offend but does miscommunicate; is aware of additional social patterns.
> *Civilization/Knowledge: Content.* Geographic, historical, artistic concrete facts in limited context; general current events and policies; field of personal interest.
> *Civilization/Knowledge: Skills.* Describes basic concrete historical, artistic, social phenomena; compares and contrasts; discusses a few aspects of home and foreign country. (p. 39)

Instruments for evaluating cultural competence as a skill included a combination of interviews, role-playing exercises, cultural vignettes with a choice of followup behaviors, and self-assessment devices. For assessing cultural knowledge they used a grid-completion instrument.

The most important outcome of a project such as that described above is not so much the assessment instruments themselves nor the collection and analysis of interesting data, but rather the potential of effecting a significant shift in departmental thinking, whereby the foreign language major is no longer viewed as a set of discrete courses to be covered or so many credits to be earned.

Language Analysis

We have maintained thus far that the prospective teacher must be able not only to communicate but also to do so under appropriate cultural circumstances. Now we ask that the good teacher also know about the language and about how it works. Knowledge of the language as well as knowledge of applied linguistics will help new teachers prepare more accurate presentations, interact more effectively with students, and evaluate pedagogical materials with greater discrimination. In addition to metalinguistic knowledge about the language itself, it is very important that prospective teachers also know about how foreign or second languages are learned. Although research in the area of second language acquisition does not concern itself directly with teaching, VanPatten (1992) rightfully affirms that teaching does indeed presume some understanding of learning and suggests that teacher-education students should be familiar with the following important second language acquisition research findings related to grammar:

1. Acquisition is not linear.
2. There are predictable stages of development and orders of acquisition.
3. Output is variable.
4. Learners need access to meaning-bearing, comprehensible input.
5. Fossilization or plateauing is a way of life.
6. Explicit instruction in grammar has little effect on acquisition. Acquisition is determined by the interaction of input and factors that are internal to the learner.

In addition, VanPatten (1992) recommends that future foreign language teachers gain knowledge of the following basic concepts in second language acquisition:

1. U-shaped curve
2. Universal Grammar
3. input processing
4. approximate system / interlanguage
5. learner language
6. contrastive analysis, error analysis, and performance analysis
7. psycholinguistic transfer
8. communicative transfer
9. communicative competence
10. second language acquisition variables: age, socio-affective, cognitive
11. acquisition *vs.* learning

Kramsch (1989) suggests that what needs to be taught is no longer the structure of language but foreign discourse in its cognitive and social dimensions. It is not enough to know grammar, syntax, and vocabulary if one wants to "function appropriately" in the foreign environment with native speakers of the language. Similarly, it is not enough to read fluently if one wishes to "understand" the intentions and implications of a written text (p. 5).

AATF. As was the case in culture and literature, the "applied linguistics" segment of the AATF Syllabus of Competence (AATF 1989) consists of a long list of very specific elements. To achieve the *basic* level of competence, teachers of French should know the following aspects of French: articulatory phonetics, phonology, sound–symbol correspondences; lexicology, lexicography, syntax, sociolinguistics, discourse, contrastive analysis, error analysis, the acquisition–learning distinction, cognitive style, and discourse analysis. Each of the above is then defined in further detail.

AATG. In the prologue to the "AATG Professional Standards for Teachers of German" (AATG 1992) there is mention of a metalinguistic competence as part of the teachers' linguistic abilities and awareness of theoretical models of second language acquisition and teaching as part of their professional abilities; the rubric "language analysis," however, is not discussed in the standards themselves.

ACTFL, AATSP. The ACTFL (1988) and AATSP (1990) guidelines define the language analysis component by stating that the program should provide the candidate opportunities to acquire and demonstrate

1. knowledge of the nature of language and the significance of language change and variation which occur over time, space, and social class;
2. knowledge of theories of first and second language acquisition and learning;
3. knowledge of the phonological, morphological, syntactical, and lexical components of the target language;
4. knowledge of how communication occurs in real life, to include: (a) the contribution of grammatical and lexical elements in expressing basic functions and notions of the target language within the context in which they occur, and (b) analysis of discourse and communication strategies. (ACTFL: 81–82; AATSP: 793)

Achieving Language Analysis

Traditional knowledge about the language, or grammar, has long been for many of us the only way we knew how to talk about a language. It consumed most of the lower-division courses, to say nothing of those taken in high school. Subsequently, it became the topic of discussion in one or two courses specifically called "grammar" and finally was often studied again in a course called "advanced grammar and composition" or "stylistics and composition." These courses still exist today, although it is to be hoped that some of the lower-division ones have been transformed into opportunities for greater functional use of the language. The AATF Syllabus of Competence (AATF 1989) recommends that language departments that educate future teachers should offer a course in phonetics, one in advanced grammar and composition, and one in applied French linguistics. In addition they recommend a second language acquisition course and a general applied linguistics course that would cover such things as contrastive analysis, error analysis, and learner systems.

Today's teacher-development programs must still include the metalanguage of grammar, especially since textbooks are still grammar-based and -sequenced. This metaknowledge must now extend beyond grammar, however; it must include the functions of various elements; it must expand to include discourse or grammar that goes beyond the sentence.

The Case for Latin

Enrollments in Latin language programs in schools, including elementary and middle schools, have been increasing since the late seventies. Unfortunately, however, there is a serious lack of available teachers. The various classical associations have done their utmost to remedy the situation, as is evidenced by recent publications (Burns and O'Connor 1987; Davis 1991; La Fleur 1987). In making recommendations for the teaching and learning of Latin, certain basic assumptions are made, some of which were not necessarily present in past Latin programs. They include: (1) Latin literature and documentary sources put teachers in direct contact with the Romans; (2) the learning of grammar *and* reading of Latin passages should be integrated (translation should be only *one* of many ways of accomplishing the understanding of a Latin text); (3) a knowledge of Roman history (including art and architecture) and Roman culture (lifestyles, values) is essential; and (4) the oral component of Latin is an important means of deepening a teacher's understanding of the language and literature.

Based on the above principles, Davis (1991) stipulates the competencies for the beginning Latin teacher:

- Language analysis: this competency demonstrates a knowledge of etymological application, vocabulary in context, and grammar and syntax.
- Reading comprehension: this competency demonstrates an ability to read and understand a straightforward passage of connected Latin prose or poetry.
- Culture and civilization: this competency demonstrates a knowledge of classical mythology, Roman literary history, Roman political history, Roman social history, and an awareness of Roman contributions to Western civilization.
- Oral proficiency: this competency demonstrates an ability to read Latin aloud with accuracy and expression and to use spoken Latin at a basic level in the classroom setting.
- Teaching methodology: this competency demonstrates an ability to use appropriate techniques for teaching language analysis, reading comprehension, culture and civilization, and oral proficiency. (p. 39)

Recommendations and Conclusion

Considering the number of sources cited in this document, as well as the number of issues discussed, it is only fitting that we conclude by making several recommendations, which will also serve as a brief summary of the chapter. These recommendations are in no particular order of importance.

1. It is recommended that funds be requested to emulate the actions of the National Council of Teachers of Mathematics and eventually produce a document that describes what the teaching of foreign languages ought to be

in the schools. Subsequently, the guidelines for foreign language teacher-education programs could be revised to reflect what should go on in the schools. (It should be noted that the College Board, the New England Collaborative, and ACTFL are currently launching a funded project to define outcomes and design assessment procedures to be used to articulate foreign language sequences.)

2. It is recommended that ACTFL, in cooperation with the AATs, be responsible for the one and only "guideline" document that would be officially used by NCATE for accreditation of teacher-education programs.

3. It is recommended that the AATs submit specific language documents to be used for national accreditation in cooperation with the standards set forth by the National Board for Professional Teaching Standards.

4. It is recommended that research be conducted to determine the pedagogical content knowledge (see Shulman 1987) of foreign languages. Is it the same for foreign language as it might be for history, science, or mathematics, or is it different, especially since the subject being taught is also the vehicle of instruction? Is this pedagogical content knowledge the same for each language?

5. It is recommended that research be conducted to identify the relationships, if any, between teacher subject-matter knowledge and/or competency and student achievement. (See Jarvis and Taylor 1990: 168.)

6. It is recommended that all university foreign language courses be taught in the target language.

7. It is recommended that all university foreign language courses include attention to the development of language proficiency.

8. It is recommended that study abroad be mandated for all prospective teachers.

9. It is recommended that foreign language teacher-education programs be built within a cultural context and that culture be included in all courses required in the foreign language department as well as in the college of education.

10. It is recommended that a national instrument be created to evaluate the knowledge and process of culture.

Considering the increase in foreign language enrollment during the past ten years, the development of programs in elementary schools, and the importance that foreign languages warrant in the worldwide intercultural community, the development of our future teachers cannot be left to chance. We need teachers who are fluent in the language they teach; teachers who understand and who are sensitive to both the students' culture and that of the target language(s); teachers who know what language is all about and what language learning is all about; and finally, teachers who have reflected upon the culture of the classroom and who are willing to share their knowledge and expertise with all learners. In the words of Kramsch (1989):

Within the foreign language education programs and the traditional linguistics or literature programs we must find a way to integrate the theory and the teaching of intercultural communication. This requires informing the teaching of foreign languages with all the theoretical insights gained in sociology, anthropology, psychology, political science, and even hermeneutics as they relate to the total verbal experience of the foreign language learner. (p. 8)

References, Subject-Matter Content

Adaskou, K., D. Britten, and B. Fashi. 1990. "Design Decisions on the Cultural Content of a Secondary English Course for Morocco." *ELT Journal* 44,1: 3–10.

Allen, Wendy W. 1985. "Toward Cultural Proficiency," pp. 137–66 in Alice C. Omaggio, ed., *Proficiency, Curriculum, Articulation: The Ties That Bind.* Report of the Northeast Conference on the Teaching of Foreign Languages. Middlebury, VT: Northeast Conference.

American Association of Teachers of French. 1989. "The Teaching of French: A Syllabus of Competence." *AATF National Bulletin* 15, Special issue, October.

American Association of Teachers of German. 1992. "Professional Standards for Teachers of German." Draft version. Cherry Hill, NJ: AATG.

American Association of Teachers of Spanish and Portuguese. 1990. "AATSP Program Guidelines for the Education and Training of Teachers of Spanish and Portuguese." *Hispania* 73: 785–94.

American Council on the Teaching of Foreign Languages. 1986. *Proficiency Guidelines.* Yonkers, NY: ACTFL.

————. 1988. "ACTFL Provisional Program Guidelines for Foreign Language Teacher Education." *Foreign Language Annals* 21: 71–82.

America 2000: An Education Strategy. 1991. Washington, DC: U.S. Dept. of Education.

Association of American Colleges. 1985. "Integrity in the College Curriculum: A Report to the Academic Community." Washington, DC: Association of American Colleges, Project on Redefining the Meaning and Purpose of Baccalaureate Degrees.

Bachman, Lyle F., and Sandra J. Savignon. 1986. "The Evaluation of Communicative Language Proficiency: A Critique of the ACTFL Oral Interview." *Modern Language Journal* 70: 380–90.

Ball, Deborah L., and G. Williamson McDiarmid. 1990. "The Subject-Matter Preparation of Teachers," pp. 437–49 in W. Robert Houston, ed., *Handbook of Research on Teacher Education.* New York: Macmillan.

Bley-Vroman, Robert, and Gail Robinson. 1991. "Foreign Language Resource Center." *ERIC/CLL News Bulletin* 15,1: 5–7.

Bowers, C. A., and David J. Flinders. 1990. *Responsive Teaching: An Ecological Approach to Classroom Patterns of Language, Culture, and Thought.* New York: Teachers College Press.

Brecht, R., D. Davidson, and R. Ginsberg. 1991. "The Empirical Study of Proficiency Gain in Study Abroad Environments among American Students of Russian: Basic Research Needs and a Preliminary Analysis of Data," in A. Barchenkov and T. Garza, eds. *Proceedings of the First Soviet–American Conference on Current Issues of Foreign Language Instruction.* Moscow: Vysshaja Shkola.

Buchmann, Margret. 1984. "The Priority of Knowledge and Understanding in Teaching," pp. 29–50 in Lilian G. Katz and James D. Raths, eds., *Advances in Teacher Education.* Vol. 1. Norwood, NJ: Ablex.

Burns, Mary Ann T., and Joseph F. O'Connor. 1987. *The Classics in American Schools.* Atlanta: Scholars Press.

Carroll, John B. 1967. "Foreign Language Proficiency Levels Attained by Language Majors near Graduation from College." *Foreign Language Annals* 1: 131–51.

Clifford, Ray T. 1991. "A Plan for Certifying Second Language Acquisition Programs." Paper presented at ACTFL Seminar: Teacher Education in the 1990s, Denver, 28–30 July.

Commission of Teacher Credentialing, State of California. 1991. "Preliminary Draft of Standards of Program Quality and Effectiveness for the Evaluation of Subject Matter Programs in Foreign Language." Sacramento: California Dept. of Education.

Crawford-Lange, Linda M., and Dale L. Lange. 1984. "Doing the Unthinkable in the Second-Language Classroom: A Process for the Integration of Language and Culture," pp. 139–77 in Theodore V. Higgs, ed., *Teaching for Proficiency, the Organizing Principle*. ACTFL Foreign Language Education Series, vol. 15. Lincolnwood, IL: National Textbook.

Damen, Louise. 1987. *Culture Learning: The Fifth Dimension in the Language Classroom*. Reading, MA: Addison-Wesley.

Davis, Sally. 1991. *Latin in American Schools*. Atlanta: Scholars Press.

DeKeyser, Robert M. 1991a. "Foreign Language Development during a Semester Abroad," pp. 104–19 in Barbara F. Freed, ed. *Foreign Language Acquisition Research and the Classroom*. Lexington, MA: Heath.

_____. 1991b. "The Semester Overseas: What Difference Does It Make?" *ADFL Bulletin* 22,2: 42–48.

Edwards, John. 1992. "Quelle Culture enseigner: réflexions et pratiques," in Robert C. Lafayette, ed., *Culture et Enseignement du français: réflexions théoriques et pratiques*. Paris: Didier Erudition.

Freeman, Stephen A. 1941. "What Constitutes a Well-Trained Modern Language Teacher?" *Modern Language Journal* 25: 293–305.

_____. 1949. "What about the Teacher?" *Modern Language Journal* 33: 255–67.

Goodenough, Ward H. 1981. *Culture, Language, and Society*. Redwood City, CA: Benjamin-Cummings.

Goodlad, John I. 1990. *Teachers for Our Nation's Schools*. San Francisco: Jossey-Bass.

Grannis, J. C. 1970. "The Social Studies Teacher and Research on Teacher Education." *Social Education* 34: 291–301.

"Guidelines for Teacher Education Programs in Modern Foreign Languages." 1966. *PMLA* 81,2: A-2, A-3.

Hallman, Clemens L. 1991. "The Florida Experience." Paper presented at ACTFL Seminar: Teacher Education in the 1990s, Denver, 28–30 July.

Hirsch, E. D., Jr. 1988. *Cultural Literacy: What Every American Needs to Know*. New York: Vintage.

Holmes Group. 1986. "Tomorrow's Teachers: A Report of the Holmes Group." East Lansing, MI: Holmes Group.

Houston, W. Robert, ed. 1990. *Handbook of Research on Teacher Education*. New York: Macmillan.

James, Dorothy. 1989. "Re-Shaping the 'College-Level' Curriculum: Problems and Possibilities," pp. 79–110 in Helen S. Lepke, ed., *Shaping the Future: Challenges and Opportunities*. Report of the Northeast Conference on the Teaching of Foreign Languages. Middlebury, VT: Northeast Conference.

Jarvis, Gilbert A., and Sheryl V. Taylor. 1990. "Reforming Foreign and Second Language Teacher Education," pp. 159–82 in Diane W. Birckbichler, ed., *New Perspectives and New Directions in Foreign Language Education*. ACTFL Foreign Language Education Series, vol. 20. Lincolnwood, IL: National Textbook.

Kalivoda, Theodore B. 1985. "The Language Training of Foreign Language Teachers: Some Directions for Curriculum Revisions." *ADFL Bulletin* 16,3: 13–17.

Knop, Constance K. 1991. "A Report on the ACTFL Summer Seminar: Teacher Education in the 1990s." *Foreign Language Annals* 24: 527–32.

Kramsch, Claire. 1989. "New Directions in the Study of Foreign Languages." *ADFL Bulletin* 21,1: 4–11.

Krasnick, H. 1988. "Dimensions of Cultural Competence: Implications for the ESL Curriculum." *TESL Reporter* 21,3: 49–55.

Lafayette, Robert C. 1987. "Joint France/LSU Summer Institute for Louisiana Teachers of French: Final Report." New Orleans: Louisiana Endowment for the Humanities.

La Fleur, Richard A., ed. 1987. *The Teaching of Latin in American Schools.* Atlanta: Scholars Press.

Lange, Dale L. 1991. "Implications of Recent Reports on Teacher Education Reform for Departments of Foreign Languages and Literatures." *ADFL Bulletin* 23,1: 28–34.

————, and William R. Sims. 1990. "Minnesota Foreign Language Teachers' Perceptions of Their Pre-Professional Preparation." *Modern Language Journal* 74: 298–310.

LeBlanc, Leona B. 1990. "Raising the Entrance Requirements: The Foreign Language Educator's Role in Implementing Florida's New Model for Teacher Certification." *Foreign Language Annals* 23: 511–15.

Lessard-Clouston, Michael. 1992. "Assessing Culture Learning: Issues and Suggestions." *Canadian Modern Language Review* 48: 326–41.

Lewis, Catherine Porter. 1990. "Assessing the Foreign Language Major at the State University of New York: An Interim Report." *ADFL Bulletin* 21,3: 35–39.

Lloyd-Jones, Richard. 1990. "What Teachers Need to Know about English," pp. 117–28 in David Dill and Associates, eds., *What Teachers Need to Know: The Knowledge, Skills, and Values Essential to Good Teaching.* San Francisco: Jossey-Bass.

Milleret, Margo, Charles W. Stansfield, and Dorry Mann Kenyon. 1991. "The Validity of the Portuguese Speaking Test for Use in a Summer Study Abroad Program." *Hispania* 74: 778–87.

Millman, M. M. 1988. "The Renaissance of Foreign Language Teaching in Alabama: A Case Study." *Foreign Language Annals* 21: 553–59.

Mueller, Marlies. 1991. "Cultural Literacy and Foreign Language Pedagogy." *ADFL Bulletin* 22,2: 19–24.

Mullen, Edward J. 1992. "Cultural Diversity and the Foreign Language Program: Foreign Language Departments and the New Multiculturalism." *ADFL Bulletin* 23,2: 29–33.

National Board for Professional Teaching Standards. 1991. *Toward High and Rigorous Standards for the Teaching Profession: Initial Policies and Perspectives of the National Board for Professional Teaching Standards.* 3d ed. Detroit: NBPTS.

National Council for Accreditation of Teacher Education. 1991. *NCATE Approved Curriculum Guidelines.* Rev. February 1991. Washington, DC: NCATE.

National Council of Teachers of English. 1986. *Guidelines for the Preparation of Teachers of English Language Arts.* Urbana, IL: NCTE.

National Council of Teachers of Mathematics. 1989. *Curriculum and Evaluation Standards for School Mathematics.* Reston, VA: NCTM.

————. 1991. *Professional Standards for Teaching Mathematics.* Reston, VA: NCTM.

Patrikis, Peter C. 1987. "Is There a Culture in This Language?" *ADFL Bulletin* 18,3: 3–8.

Pesola, Carol Ann. 1991. "Culture in the Elementary School Foreign Language Classroom." *Foreign Language Annals* 24: 331–46.

Petrie, Hugh G. 1987. "Teacher Education, the Liberal Arts, and Extended Education Programs." *Educational Policy* 11: 29–41.

Phillips, June K. 1989. "Teacher Education: Target of Reform," pp. 11–40 in Helen S. Lepke, ed., *Shaping the Future: Challenges and Opportunities.* Report of the Northeast Conference on the Teaching of Foreign Languages. Middlebury, VT: Northeast Conference.

"Qualifications for Secondary School Teachers of Modern Foreign Languages." 1955. *The Bulletin of the National Association of Secondary School Principals* 39: 30–33.

Seelye, H. Ned. 1984. *Teaching Culture: Strategies for Intercultural Communication.* 2d ed. Lincolnwood, IL: National Textbook.

Shulman, Lee S. 1987. "Knowledge and Teaching: Foundations of the New Reform." *Harvard Educational Review* 57: 1–22.

Smith, Philip D., Jr. 1970. *A Comparison of the Cognitive and Audiolingual Approaches to Foreign Language Instruction: The Pennsylvania Foreign Language Project.* Philadelphia: Center for Curriculum Development.

Stansfield, Charles W. 1989. "Simulated Oral Proficiency Interviews." *ERIC Digest* (December). Washington, DC: Center for Applied Linguistics.

————. 1991. "A Comparative Analysis of Simulated and Direct Oral Proficiency Interviews," pp. 199–209 in Sarinee Anivan, ed., *Current Developments in Language Testing.* Singapore: Regional English Language Center.

Texas Oral Proficiency Test 1991–1992: Registration Bulletin. 1991. Amherst, MA: National Evaluation Systems.

TOPT Test Preparation Kit. 1991. Preliminary ed. Washington, DC: Center for Applied Linguistics.

Uber Grosse, Christine, and David Benseler. 1991. "Directory of Foreign Language Teacher Preparation Programs in the United States: A Preliminary Report," pp. 27–45 in Robert M. Terry, ed., *Acting on Priorities: A Commitment to Excellence, Dimension: Languages '90.* Report of the Southern Conference on Language Teaching. Columbia, SC: Southern Conference.

VanPatten, Bill. 1992. "What Every Teacher Education Student Should Know about Second Language Acquisition." Paper presented at the Winterfest of the Illinois Council on the Teaching of Foreign Languages, Decatur, IL, February.

Wilson, S. M., Lee S. Shulman, and A. E. Reichert. 1987. "150 Different Ways of Knowing: Representations of Knowledge in Teaching," in J. Calderhead, ed., *Exploring Teachers' Thinking.* London, Eng.: Cassell.

7

The Pedagogical Imperative in Foreign Language Teacher Education

Barbara H. Wing
University of New Hampshire

A Rationale for the Pedagogical Imperative

Several years ago, Thomas Kean, then governor of New Jersey, proposed a solution to the teacher-education dilemma: select the best and the brightest of the students in colleges and universities, make sure they are well prepared in their major field, and place them in schools with highly competent cooperating teachers for a year of field experience (Sullivan 1983). At the end of the year, they should be ready to take their place in the ranks of beginning teachers, prepared by the crucible of hands-on experience.

Those who considered teacher-education programs to be a waste of time and money were attracted to Kean's proposal. They saw it as a way to increase the subject-matter competency of teachers while doing away with what they considered to be "Mickey-Mouse" courses in education. These critics of academic programs did not recognize the validity of studying teaching from both a theoretical and a practical perspective.

Kean's proposal, however, alarmed foreign language teachers and teacher educators. Many, indeed most, acknowledged that not all education courses are academically rigorous or even necessary. They also heartily agreed that language teachers need to achieve a higher level of proficiency in the target language and

Barbara H. Wing (Ph.D., The Ohio State University) is Associate Professor of Spanish and Chair of Spanish and Portuguese at the University of New Hampshire, where she teaches foreign language methodology and language courses, coordinates the Foreign Language Teacher-Education Program, and directs the UNH Study-Abroad Program in Granada, Spain. She edited the Northeast Conference *Newsletter* from 1986 to 1993 and has contributed chapters on teacher preparation to the ACTFL series and the Northeast Conference Reports, which she edited in 1986. She is a member of and has given workshops and papers at ACTFL, MLA, AATSP, and NHATFL, the New Hampshire organization.

attain a deeper level of understanding of the target cultures. Those areas of agreement were not the reason for their alarm: they objected on pedagogical grounds. They claimed, as does this chapter, that teachers need academic as well as clinical preparation in how to teach.

Why do language educators take this position? In the first place, because of the complexity of teaching a foreign language, the task is "in many ways unique within the profession of teaching" (Hammadou and Bernhardt 1987: 301). Factors such as the nature of the subject matter, the interaction patterns used in providing instruction, difficulties in increasing one's subject-matter knowledge, and the limited number of colleagues in the same field (Hammadou and Bernhardt 1987) make it unlikely that a year of field experience in one school will suffice, regardless of how good the mentor and the school may be. In the second place, the goals of foreign language teaching and the knowledge base that is currently being developed make it imperative that teachers examine the what, why, and how of classroom learning and instruction with a future-oriented perspective. Too often, what happens in classrooms reflects a perpetuation of the past rather than a vision for the future. The present volume contributes to the formation of such a vision.

This chapter focuses on those aspects of preparation and continuing development that comprise the "pedagogical content knowledge" of foreign language teaching. This knowledge, as defined by Shulman (1986), who conceptualized the term, consists of "the particular form of content knowledge that embodies the aspects of content most germane to its teachability" (p. 9). It is a term that unites subject matter and pedagogy in a more inclusive and symbiotic relationship than does the traditional term of "methodology." As a topic, it relates directly to the "professional" section of the ACTFL Program Guidelines for Foreign Language Teacher Education (ACTFL 1988). This discussion, which will be guided by, but not be limited to, the ACTFL Program Guidelines, will address recent developments and how the profession can meet the challenges it faces.

Professional Initiatives

In the past five years, significant progress has been made by foreign language teacher educators, in particular through the national and state professional organizations, toward identifying what it is that language teachers must know and be able to do. These efforts reflect concern with professional integrity and accountability. By stating the expected outcomes of teacher-education programs as clearly as possible, without being caught up in the minutiae of approaches and techniques, these organizations and agencies publicly acknowledge their responsibility to exercise control over the quality of language education in the United States in the twenty-first century.

When compared with earlier documents on teacher education (Freeman 1941; Paquette 1966; "Qualifications" 1955), the recent statements by ACTFL (1988) and the language-specific professional organizations—the American Association of Teachers of French (AATF 1989), the American Association of Teachers of German (AATG 1992), and the American Association of Teachers of Spanish and Portuguese (AATSP 1990)—reflect a higher level of sophistication, a broader range of knowledge and behaviors, and, perhaps most important, a clear emphasis on the teacher as creative decision maker. An analysis of the content knowledge as outlined in these documents is found in chapter 6 of this volume; a brief description of how pedagogical knowledge is treated will serve here as an introduction to the discussion of the pedagogical imperative. (The complete ACTFL Program Guidelines are found in the Appendix.)

The "Professional Development" section of the ACTFL Program Guidelines begins with five questions, which serve as a framework for a definition of the pedagogical content knowledge (p. 75):

1. "The question of *why:* understanding what it means to know another language and recognizing the values and benefits of such knowledge." Area I, "Rationale for Foreign Language Study," describes how programs must prepare teachers to keep up with changes in society and be effective advocates for the profession.
2. "The question of *who:* observing and analyzing learners and learning." Area II, "Theories of Child Development and Learning," addresses the importance of a balance of theory and practice, whereby preservice teachers examine human development, and especially language acquisition, in terms of both research findings and field experiences.
3. "The question of *what* and *when:* organizing the content of instruction to provide for effective teaching and learning." Area III, "Curriculum Development," treats the active involvement by teachers in the ongoing process of planning curricula.
4. "The question of *how:* providing appropriate, purposeful classroom experiences." Area IV, "Instruction," describes the progressive development, through clinical and field experiences, of the decision-making skills required for effective planning and managing of instruction in the classroom.
5. "The question of *where:* experiencing the system and setting in which formal education occurs." Areas V, "The Instructional Setting," VI, "Foreign Language in the Elementary School," and VII, "Foreign Language Education Faculty," address the environments in which teachers work and receive their initial preparation and ongoing support.

In each of the seven areas, the document provides (1) guidelines that describe the kinds of information and experiences deemed appropriate, (2) a brief discussion, and (3) a list of indicators by which foreign language teacher educators can assess their programs. The statements are not meant to be considered "minimal thresholds" for candidates or programs but are intended to be used as a framework for defining, assessing, and improving programs.

The AATSP "Program Guidelines for the Education and Training of Teachers of Spanish and Portuguese" (AATSP 1990) follows closely the "Professional Development" section of the ACTFL statement. In the AATF document,

"The Teaching of French: A Syllabus of Competence" (AATF 1989), the "Methodology" section identifies specific competencies and techniques (e.g., "culture assimilators") and recommends two methods courses, separated by a two- or three-year interval. The most recent statement, "Professional Standards for Teachers of German" (AATG 1992), identifies standards and indicators for outstanding teaching performance.

Efforts are currently under way by ACTFL and the AATs to come to a consensus that will represent the best thinking of the profession on what constitutes a well-prepared language teacher and a well-designed teacher-education program. Similarities in the pedagogical content area outnumber differences, which are characterized more by format and degree of detail than by substantive issues.

Some state foreign language associations have also developed statements on teacher preparation. For example, the report of the New York State Association of Foreign Language Teachers' Task Force on Teacher Preparation (Hume-Nigro and Webb n.d.) describes how classroom teachers collaborated with teacher educators to identify the competencies that language teachers need to demonstrate upon completion of student teaching. Of particular interest to the topic of this chapter is the emphasis on the need for in-depth exposure to principles of second language acquisition and to the development of partnerships of colleges and schools, not only in clinical experiences but also in the design and teaching of methods courses.

Another state initiative that is especially significant, given the increasing interest in foreign languages in the elementary schools (FLES) is "Elementary School (K–8) Foreign Language Teacher Education Curriculum," a project of the North Carolina Department of Public Instruction and the Center for Applied Linguistics (1992). Noting that "Currently, few U.S. institutions of higher education have faculty qualified to offer programs to prepare elementary foreign language teachers" (p. ii), the report describes fourteen competencies that were identified and prioritized by nearly 50 FLES trainers, teachers, and supervisors in a process that started in 1988. Among the top five are three pedagogical competencies: knowledge of instructional methods, knowledge of the K–12 foreign language curriculum and the elementary curriculum, and an understanding of second language acquisition in childhood (p. vii).

Implicit in all these statements is the assumption that the language teacher of the twenty-first century will need to develop pedagogical knowledge and competencies in college/university and in school partnerships that foster a synthesis of theory and practice, of course work and fieldwork, of content and process. Equally important is the underlying contention that the successful language teacher is not simply a fulfiller of an ever-increasing number of competencies, but rather a thinking, feeling decision maker who can identify and respond to the needs of real learners in the ever-changing classroom. Lange (1990) emphasizes this point when he argues that the term *teacher development* is more appropriate as a descriptor of the teacher's continual professional growth than *teacher training* (p. 250).

Foreign language teachers do indeed need pedagogical preparation, as the statements by national and state professional organizations and departments of education so clearly indicate. To understand the pedagogical imperative, we will need to consider:

- The nature of foreign language pedagogical content knowledge for the twenty-first century
- Acquisition of pedagogical content knowledge during the preparatory and career-development periods
- Assessment of pedagogical content knowledge for certification and professional development purposes
- Fulfilling the pedagogical imperative for the twenty-first century

Foreign Language Pedagogical Content Knowledge

What foreign language teachers need to know about teaching their subject matter ultimately depends on two factors: what students want and are expected to learn and how they can learn it most effectively in a classroom setting. The first factor, the goals to be realized, is relatively easy to define. The second, the processes by which the goals are achieved, is much more complex.

Foreign language teachers in U.S. schools and teacher educators in the colleges and universities are in considerable agreement that proficiency development, in its broadest sense, and cultural awareness, in its deepest sense, constitute the principal goals of language learning for grades K–12. Consensus is widespread, as seen by the types of materials used in classrooms, the workshops given at conferences, and especially in the reports in the popular press, that desirable outcomes include both the ability to communicate effectively with people of other language communities at a level of proficiency suitable to the task and an understanding of the factors that shape and define their cultures.

Consensus on how we achieve these goals, especially in the classroom setting, is not as easily achieved, nor is it likely to be, given the complexity of the question. How learners develop language proficiency and cultural awareness in the classroom depends on a set of interactive relationships in which the learner is the focal point. To be successful, learners must interact intentionally with (1) the language being learned, (2) the other players in the classroom experience, and (3) the instructional environment in which the learning is taking place. Figure 7-1 demonstrates these interactions.

When we consider what foreign language teachers must know about learners and their interactions with the other elements of this classroom model, we realize that prescriptions or lists of teaching behaviors will not suffice. Rather, foreign language teachers must develop, implement, and reflect upon a personal pedagogy that keeps the interactive relationships in focus and in balance. Teacher educators, in turn, must guide the prospective teacher in acquiring the knowledge, skills, and experiences that will facilitate this process.

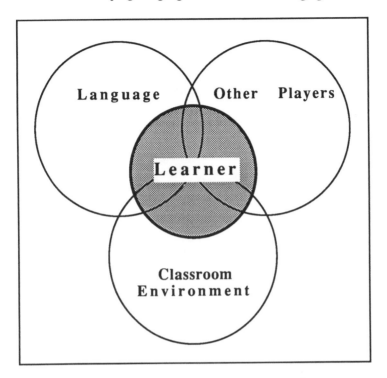

Figure 7-1. Model of Foreign Language Classroom Interaction

Central to the tasks of both the teacher and the teacher educator are familiarity with, respect for, and involvement in the ongoing search for answers to questions about how languages are learned in classroom settings. This search, which involves the cooperative efforts of classroom teachers and formal investigators, constitutes the vital activity of objective and replicable research. Foreign language teacher educators and teachers agree that an understanding of theory and research on language learning and teaching is essential to effective teaching (Hume-Nigro and Webb n.d.; North Carolina 1992).

Using the learner-centered model as a frame of reference, we will examine selected aspects of foreign language teaching pedagogical content that reflect the need to meld theory and practice in the preparation and continuing development of foreign language teachers.

The Learner

It is a truism to say that, while learners can learn without teachers, teachers cannot teach without learners. It is equally evident that teachers cannot teach effectively without understanding how learners learn. Much of what teachers need to know about learners will be studied in courses on the psychology of learning and the sociology of schooling. In these courses, teachers learn about the developmental stages of cognitive, affective, and psychomotor growth through which children and adolescents pass on their way to adulthood. They learn about how the brain functions, how short- and long-term memory operate, and how meaning and motivation are essential to learning. They also learn how affective factors influence how and what students learn. All this knowledge is extremely valuable to the language teacher, who must see the specific implications for teaching both in and about another language. In particular, two areas of generic research on learners that merit special consideration in the pedagogical preparation of language teachers are the factors of developmental stages and learning styles and strategies. They are important because language learning is not only a socially interactive process but also one that is clearly affected by individual characteristics and behaviors.

With the growing support for foreign languages in the elementary school, the factor of age, as a useful descriptor of developmental stages, assumes increased importance. When language teaching was primarily a function of the secondary school, teachers dealt almost exclusively with adolescent learners whose cognitive, affective, and psychomotor development was close to that of an adult. Curriculum development and instruction were influenced more by linguistic analysis of the subject matter than by an understanding of how learners function. Now, with FLES programs expanding and middle-school programs becoming more widely established, language teachers, and consequently teacher-education programs, need to address cognitive and affective development from preschool days through adolescence.

As Curtain and Pesola (1988) point out, an understanding of the principles of child development is essential to designing effective curricula and activities for elementary and middle-school learners. Of particular import to the language teacher is the work of Piaget (Wadsworth 1984), whose four sequential stages of development (sensory-motor intelligence from 0 to 2 years, preoperational thought from 2 to 7 years, concrete operations from 7 to 11 years, and formal operations from 11 to 15 years or older) have significant implications for how learners acquire both first and second languages.

A second factor related to the learner is the issue of language-learning styles, defined as innate characteristics that affect how one learns, and strategies, defined as techniques to accomplish the tasks of learning. Even in what is considered a homogeneous class, a wide range of learning styles and strategies prevails. Furthermore, the current practice of mainstreaming students makes it imperative that language teachers recognize the effects of different styles and help their students develop appropriate strategies to be successful.

Galloway and LaBarca (1990) review aspects of learning style related to how learners sense, act, interact, and think differently, but advise caution in interpreting results since research efforts are still in the exploratory stage. They also examine the relatively new field of strategy identification and practice in which researchers such as Cohen (1990) and Oxford (1990) are developing a research base and practical models for strategy training. Related to both styles and strategies is the research being done on language anxiety (Horwitz et al. 1986;

Horwitz and Young 1991), a new and important component of foreign language pedagogical content knowledge.

The Learner and the Target Language

In addition to understanding learners as thinking and feeling individuals who pass through generic developmental stages, foreign language teachers need to know what happens when learners interact with the subject matter, the target language. Within the rapidly growing field of research on language acquisition, three related yet distinct areas of investigation are being pursued. These three areas, while connected by the common denominator of language, are distinct because of the nature of the learning and the nature of the individual and environment in which the learning takes place.

- First language acquisition research, or L1 research, attempts to describe and explain how, as very young children, human beings develop the ability to communicate in the native language. Of the three types of acquisition research, this effort has the longest history. While there are similarities between the processes of first and second language acquisition, (e.g., the effectiveness of correction on the acquisition of structure), enough differences exist to limit the usefulness of this type of research in classroom foreign language learning situations.

- Second language acquisition/learning research (SLA/SLL) examines the processes and stages of learners who, already having mastered the native language, are developing competence in another language while living where the second language is the dominant mode of communication. The specific settings in which these individuals acquire or learn the second language may range from the linguistically unstructured workplace to a clearly defined program of instruction in a classroom setting, thus accounting for the two terms "acquisition" and "learning." Research on learning English as a Second Language (ESL) constitutes a principal topic of investigation in SLA. The extensive work done in this field, primarily in the United States and the United Kingdom, provides both models and methodologies that can be adapted to the foreign language classroom setting (cf. Richards 1990; Woodward 1991). In addition, a great deal of research is being done in Germany and France as a result of greater communication among nations and the influx of immigrants. We need to know more about their functional approach to this research.

- Foreign language learning (FLL) research, the most recently undertaken endeavor, investigates how languages that are not spoken in the community are learned in classroom settings. As VanPatten et al. (1987) point out, foreign language learners often differ significantly from second language learners, both in terms of individual motivation and opportunities to experience the target language and culture (p. 2). This area of research holds the most promise for providing school-based foreign language teachers with empirically derived information to guide their teaching practice. It also provides the greatest opportunity for teachers to contribute to the process of determining how languages are learned, as we shall see below.

All three areas of research on language acquisition draw on findings from other disciplines such as linguistics, psychology, and sociology. Likewise, all three are often assumed to be directly related to the teaching of language, whether native or second/foreign. Just as it is important that foreign language teachers study linguistics, psychology, and sociology, it is important that they be aware of and know how to use the findings of language-acquisition researchers. It is essential to recognize, however, that foreign language acquisition theory and research do not, per se, offer prescriptions on what to do in the classroom. As VanPatten (1992a; 1992b) notes, this type of research can help teachers, although it cannot provide definitive answers to questions such as what grammar to teach.

The Learner and the Other Players in the Classroom Game

In accord with the goal of developing proficiency in the foreign language classroom, learners must interact not only with the language but also with the other "players" in what Wittgenstein (1953) called the "classroom game." The significant other player in most classrooms has been and will continue to be the teacher. Traditional "rules" and expectations for fulfilling the roles of student and teacher have been well known by the participants, though not generally verbalized (Bellack et al. 1966; Fanselow 1977); with the implementation of instructional models that are more learner-centered than teacher-dominated, however, as in cooperative learning formats, role definitions are undergoing change. As these changes occur, research, including the action type in which teachers collaborate, will provide insights on the effects of student–student interactions. Foreign language teachers need to be aware of and act upon findings of this research.

Although both students and teachers will have to learn new roles, the teacher will continue to be responsible for creating opportunities for student interaction. In the foreign language classroom, one of the essential tools for stimulating such interaction is teacher talk. How the teacher uses the target language significantly influences how the students understand and use it. Research on teacher classroom talk reveals how modifications in rate of speech, frequency of pauses, pronunciation, vocabulary, and syntactical structure may affect comprehension (Chaudron 1988: 85). Questioning patterns and feedback techniques, especially in error correction, are two other important areas of teacher–student interaction that provide teachers with significant information on how students learn in the foreign language classroom (Chaudron 1988: 152).

The Learner and the Classroom Learning Environment

The teacher-centered foreign language classroom no longer suffices as the model for effective language learning. In recent years, the profession has come to realize the need for and value of alternative ways to structure the learning environment and provide the resources needed by active learners. Language teachers are learning, often from colleagues in other disciplines and at other levels of schooling, how to focus on the learner while maintaining the control that teachers must exercise if classrooms are to be dynamic and effective places in which to learn.

In structuring the foreign language learning environment, the teacher needs to be a manager who facilitates language acquisition; a resource developer who uses to the greatest advantage the target and native languages, materials, and technology; and an analyst who observes and evaluates what is happening in the classroom.

Managing the Classroom Environment.   The profession has made the case that foreign languages are for everyone, especially in the elementary and middle grades, but also in the secondary school. At each level language teachers need to be aware of and respond to the cognitive, affective, and psychomotor needs and developmental stages of their students. In addition, they must be prepared to deal with classes that are multigifted, multicultural, and multilevel.

Language teachers have found a powerful tool for dealing with the mix of ability, cultures, and levels in their classrooms. Cooperative learning, essentially a design for creating classroom environments that promote collaborative rather than competitive efforts among students, has attracted the attention of the profession (Bonaventura 1988; Gunderson and Johnson 1980). The work of Johnson et al. (1984) and of Slavin (1983) are being adapted to the foreign language classroom.

Effective implementation of cooperative learning techniques is dependent on a clear understanding of the basic elements upon which the approach is based. The principles of *positive interdependence, face-to-face interaction, individual accountability, and development of social skills* (Johnson et al. 1984: 8) embody a perspective of learning and teaching that emphasizes responsibility, both personal and collective, and communicative interaction. These principles have much in common with the goals of communicative language use; learners and teachers alike must realize, however, that social as well as linguistic skills have to be learned and practiced if cooperative learning is to be effective.

Using Language, Materials, and Technology.   The collaborative classroom described above is a propitious context for language learning; the character and quality of that learning, however, depends not only on how the environment is managed but also on the content that forms the basis for communicative interaction among students and between students and teachers. Thus, the language and materials and the way in which they are used in the classroom form a second aspect of the environment in which and with which the learner interacts.

Foreign language teaching was long dependent on didactic teaching materials designed to provide a step-by-step approach to the control of grammatical structures deemed necessary for becoming "fluent." These materials were generally contrived to include as many instances as possible of the particular vocabulary and structural items being addressed in the lesson. The fact that native speakers of the language did not express themselves as the characters in dialogues did was not a matter of concern. Today's proficiency-oriented goals, however, mandate the inclusion of "authentic speech" in the classroom. Students need to listen to and read what native speakers listen to and read under conditions where the task, not the material, is modified to fit the present stage of development of the learners. They need to experience authentic representations of the culture they are studying, and they need to hear different voices and different accents, regardless of how well their teacher speaks the target language. To meet these student needs for authentic language, teachers must be able to find and to use authentic materials in their classrooms.

Creating a collaborative context and incorporating authentic content require a working knowledge of how technology can re-create in the classroom the linguistic and cultural milieu of the target culture. The computer, video cassette and disk, and satellite TV have joined the overhead projector, audiotape player, and slide projector as tools for successful language learning. Teachers who cannot use these tools effectively are likely to find themselves wondering why their students are not motivated to realize the proficiency goals they have set.

Analyzing What Happens in the Foreign Language Classroom. The ACTFL Program Guidelines (1988) and the related statements of the specific language professional organizations emphasize the teacher's role as educational designer and decision maker. Fulfillment of this role is dependent on the capacity to reflect analytically on what happens in the classroom and to act upon those reflections.

The reflective approach to teaching, which guides the discussion in chapter 8 of this volume, represents a new model for foreign language teacher education. Drawing on "received knowledge" (a term that refers to the intellectual content of the profession, including research findings) and "experiential knowledge" (a term that refers to knowledge gained by practice of the profession), the effective teacher engages in a cycle of practice and reflection (Wallace 1991). This cycle may lead teachers themselves to engage in "action research," in which they collaborate with researchers to evaluate change in a systematic way. (See chapter 4 of this volume for a discussion of action research and other research paradigms.) This type of investigation is seen as holding great promise for teachers because it is practical and addresses locally defined problems (Bailey et al. 1991).

Summary

In this section on the nature of foreign language pedagogical knowledge, we have been selective rather than inclusive. Indeed, as Jarvis and Taylor (1990) state, "Pedagogical subject-matter knowledge for the neophyte foreign language teacher appears considerably more substantial than its traditional role in the curriculum would indicate" (p. 174). The intent here has been to highlight some of the more recent developments that show promise for the future rather than to reiterate the competencies that foreign language teachers must demonstrate.

In the next section we will consider how prospective foreign language teachers acquire knowledge and experience and how practicing teachers continue the process while actively involved in the classroom. The pedagogical development continuum implies that the beginning teacher needs both received and experiential knowledge that has been reflected upon in practice during field experiences in a constant iterative cycle. Equally important is the implication that the practicing teacher, whether in the first or fortieth year of teaching, will continue the process, not because certification standards require it but because to stop learning about teaching is, in effect, to stifle the learning process in both teacher and student.

Acquisition of Pedagogical Content Knowledge

A working consensus of what foreign language teachers need to know specifically about teaching their discipline is the first step toward more effective programs. The next step is to determine how the appropriate knowledge and experience is acquired and developed most effectively in both the preparatory and the practicing stages of a teacher's career. Implicit in the question of "how" are the following issues:

- *when* and *where* prospective teachers experience their pedagogical studies
- *what* constitutes an appropriate agenda for pedagogy courses and clinical experiences
- *who* determines the agendas and provides guidance and instruction to prospective foreign language teachers
- *how* practicing teachers continue to develop their pedagogical content knowledge

When and Where

Foreign language teachers, whether they realize it or not, begin their preparation for teaching in the first language class they take. From the moment they first say "Bonjour," "Guten Tag," or "Buenos días," their development consists of an amalgamation of ideas, feelings, opinions, and questions that is woven of both informal and formal experiences, first as language students and later as pedagogy students. This amalgamation forms the prospective teacher's pedagogical structure, a construct that can be compared to Ausubel's (1968) construct of cognitive structure. Just as each person's cognitive structure is unique, so is each teacher's pedagogical structure unique; yet individual cognitive and pedagogical structures share commonalities derived from received and experiential knowledge. The pedagogical content component of the foreign language teacher-education program provides a purposeful and structured format for the development of these commonalities. Traditionally, the formal development of pedagogical content knowledge began in the prospective teacher's senior year with a foreign language methods course in the college or university. This course was followed by a quarter or semester of student teaching in a public school. The degree of cooperation between the college and the school was characterized by great variability, as was the involvement of the college academic departments that were responsible for the subject-matter preparation of the student teachers.

Current practice varies widely, ranging from the traditional model to innovative programs that respond to recommendations made by the Holmes Group (1986, 1990), the Carnegie Task Force (1986), and the National Board for Professional Teaching Standards (1990), an outgrowth of the Carnegie Forum. These recommendations represent comprehensive efforts to reform teacher education in the United States. They specifically address the issue of when and where teacher education should take place by advocating much stronger ties among the schools, the colleges / departments of education, and the academic departments. They also propose a restructuring of teacher-education programs to shift the professional component to the graduate level, thus providing more time to develop the content area in an undergraduate major that includes both academic course work and experiences in areas where the target language is the principal means of communication.

Reform efforts are evident in three models, differentiated by when the prospective language teacher begins and completes the teacher-education program. These models of four-year, five-year, and post-baccalaureate programs are discussed in chapter 8 of this volume. In these models the pedagogical content component plays an important role from the moment the prospective teacher begins the program. In addition, close ties between the college / university and the schools, fostered by integrated clinical experiences, are a major feature of each model.

The question of whether five-year and post-baccalaureate programs will take hold and become major vehicles for teacher preparation is still to be answered. It is clear, however, that the old model of a college-based methodology course and a school-based semester of student teaching cannot prepare prospective language teachers adequately for their responsibilities as decision-making professionals in the complex setting of the U.S. school of the twenty-first century. The new models offer choices for an effective mix of content and process, school and university collaboration, foreign language pedagogy, and general teacher-education courses. They respond both to the call for reform as articulated in the reports cited and to the guidelines for foreign language teacher preparation.

The Foreign Language Methodology Agenda

The most structured contact with pedagogical content knowledge occurs in foreign language methodology courses. It is here that prospective teachers address the theoretical and practical aspects of "methodology," a term that is defined in the *Longman Dictionary of Applied Linguistics* as:

(1) the study of the practice and procedures used in teaching and the principles and beliefs that underlie them.

Methodology includes:

(a) study of the nature of LANGUAGE SKILLS (e.g., reading, writing, speaking, listening) and procedures for teaching them

(b) study of the preparation of LESSON PLANS, materials, and textbooks for teaching language skills

(c) the evaluation and comparison of language teaching METHODS (e.g., the AUDIOLINGUAL METHOD) (Richards et al. 1985)

In a later work, Richards (1990) describes methodology not as "a set of rigid principles and procedures that the teacher must conform to" but rather as "a dynamic, creative and exploratory process that begins anew each time the teacher encounters a group of learners" (p. 35). Such a definition emphasizes the decision-making responsibilities of all teachers, including the foreign language teacher educator who must plan the course that introduces students to methodology. It also supports the position that methodology courses exist to help prospective teachers develop their own teaching style and pedagogy rather than to indoctrinate them in the use of specific models and techniques (Combs 1989; Nunan 1991; Strasheim 1991).

Either explicitly or implicitly, the statements of professional organizations all support a foreign language methodology course (or courses) as opposed to a generic pedagogy course. While they differ in their approach to outlining pedagogical content knowledge, they all provide guidelines for developing an agenda for foreign language methodology courses for prospective teachers. Components of such an agenda that are common to all the statements include a rationale for foreign language teaching, an understanding of the learner's interaction with the elements of the foreign language classroom setting (see figure 7-1 above), and theoretical and practical knowledge of a reasonable sampling of the wide range of curricular and instructional possibilities in foreign language teaching. As indicated earlier and as noted by the participants in the 1991 ACTFL Summer Seminar on Teacher Education in the 1990s (Knop 1991b), consensus on specific competencies remains an issue.

Content, however, is not the only consideration in foreign language methodology courses. How we design and implement them is as important as the topics we decide to include in them. Process must be an equal partner with content, not only in the subject-matter preparation of prospective teachers, but also in their pedagogical preparation. Thus, the methodology agenda is not simply the pedagogical content knowledge that is taught but also the processes by which that knowledge is taught and learned.

Practicing What We Preach:
Cooperative Learning in the Methodology Course

In our methodology courses, teacher educators must practice what we preach. If we really believe that learners benefit from cooperative learning activities, we must not only tell our prospective teachers how to design and use them, we must show them by using these techniques ourselves. Pair and small-group activities, role-playing simulations, and even drill exercises need to be an integral part of the process agenda. One way to work them in is to have students participate in cooperative learning activities that involve the four skills actively in the target language, much as students would do in the classroom. A more innovative approach is to use a strategy called "loop input," devised by Woodward (1991) for use in her ESL methodology courses in England.

Using a Möbius strip as a model, Woodward proposes that "content = process = content" to illustrate and emphasize the symbiotic relationship that exists between the "what" and the "how" of teacher education. "Loop input" is the term she uses to describe what happens when a process that is appropriate for the foreign language classroom (such as the "jigsaw," a cooperative learning technique for reading and speaking) is used in the methodology course with content that is appropriate for a teacher-education situation. Instead of using a typical reading passage for a specific language class, Woodward has her students read and report to each other on segments of a selection that describes the jigsaw technique itself. Thus the methodology students learn from reflecting on both received knowledge (the information read and shared) and experiential knowledge (participation in the activity), and content and process complement each other. Loop input is well suited for use in multilanguage methods courses that must be taught in English and provides a model that teachers can readily apply to their specific language situation.

Practicing What We Preach:
Reflective Teaching in the Methodology Course

In similar fashion, if we believe that teachers need to engage in reflective teaching activities to improve their teaching and their students' learning, we must include such activities in the methodology course. Indeed, most teacher educators do reflect on their teaching by keeping abreast of new research and trends in education. This reflection, however, is generally undertaken privately or in encounters with other foreign language educators at professional meetings. Aside from the mandated teacher evaluations at the end of the course, it does not normally include student participation and input. By being willing to reflect openly with our students on what is happening in the methodology course, we provide yet another example of the interrelationship of content and process.

The foreign language methodology course offers students a unique opportunity to participate in a reflective teaching environment, to observe how a competent professional engages in reflection, and to take part in some of the decision making of the course. By sharing with students the process of building the syllabus through identification of their perceived needs and periodically evaluating the effectiveness of techniques and activities used, the foreign language methodologist models both the intent and the spirit of the content that is being taught.

Implementing a reflective teaching model in the foreign language methodology course signals a commitment on the part of the foreign language methodologist to personal and professional growth. It means doing new things in new ways, which is difficult if one believes that the methodologist's job is to "train" prospective teachers in the "right" way to stimulate learning in the classroom. It means taking risks, as proposed by Woodward (1991): "The wise trainer will choose a problem which she also has difficulty with, since this will give her the chance to improve. . . . Working on your own problems in an attempt to give ideas to a trainee with a similar problem can be a great way to empathy, honesty and better teaching" (p. 59).

Practicing What We Preach:
Meeting Special Needs in the Methodology Course

The norm in foreign language teacher-education programs in most universities is one multilanguage, multilevel methodology course, taught in English and usually taken before the student teaching or internship experience. This course must address the needs of students preparing to teach a range of languages, modern and classic, commonly and less commonly taught, across the spectrum of kindergarten through twelfth grade. While there are definite commonalities for all foreign language teachers, differentiated needs must be addressed. One area in which this is most apparent is foreign language teaching in the elementary school (FLES).

In 1985, the state of North Carolina mandated a kindergarten through grade 5 second language program for all public-school children, thus requiring the preparation of a large number of FLES teachers. Realizing that these teachers would need a FLES methodology course, as well as additional course work in child psychology, Mitchell and Redmond (1991) designed one that emphasizes integrated or content-based instruction (as in Curtain and Pesola 1988) and second language acquisition. In addition, it includes a practicum in which elementary-school children learn French or Spanish in a special class on the university campus taught by members of the methodology class. Not all foreign language teacher-education programs can afford to offer such a course, but an optional FLES component can be included in the regular methods course. Summer institutes are another common solution to the problem of limited resources (Hallman et al. 1992).

Another special need arises from the specific characteristics of different languages. While the challenges associated with teaching the less commonly taught languages, such as Russian, Arabic, and Japanese, and the classical languages such as Latin and Greek, come to mind first, it is clear that even languages of the same linguistic family, such as French and Spanish, have idiosyncratic aspects. The ideal, a language-specific methodology course, is beyond the hope of all but a few large foreign language programs. One way to address the problem within the methodology course is to provide for language-specific observation and consultation with other professors whose language classes reflect contemporary goals and practices. Another, within the clinical experience component of the program, is to bring together preparing and practicing teachers from different schools for workshops on language-specific topics.

Who Develops the Agenda and Provides the Guidance?

Acceptance of the premise that prospective language teachers should acquire their pedagogical knowledge in a variety of situations over an extended period of time through a series of integrated experiences means that several groups of professionals will play significant roles in the development and implementation of the agenda. These groups include

Foreign Language Teachers at the Elementary and Secondary Levels. These are the teachers who introduce students to the new world of a different language and culture. Through their own enthusiasm, effectiveness, and rapport with the students, they project a sense of the satisfaction and reward that teaching can bring. Indeed, as Morain (1990) observes, "Public school teachers hold unparalleled power over the future of foreign language study" (p. 23). Teachers at this level have the responsibility to develop to the highest level possible their own language skills and cultural understanding as well as their foreign language pedagogical content knowledge. Many of those who do will complete the role-model cycle by becoming the cooperating teachers and mentors of another generation of prospective teachers.

Foreign Language and Literature Professors at the College and University Level. Equally important in the development of the prospective teacher are the professors to whom the secondary teachers entrust their students. These professors must realize that they, too, are models for their students, both in terms of the content they choose to include in their courses and the processes by which they instruct the content. As we shall see in the final section of this chapter, this role is often not accorded priority status in postsecondary institutions.

Generic Teacher-Education Professors at the College and University Level. Like their colleagues in the foreign language departments, these professors influence the development of prospective teachers not only through what they teach but how they teach it. They provide the foundation for understanding educational theories, processes, and systems and the strategies for working with colleagues in other areas of the school.

Foreign Language Teacher Educators and Methodologists. Charged with the responsibility of guiding prospective teachers in the development of their own pedagogical structures, these professors may be found in both the department/school of education and the foreign language departments. Ideally, each institution that prepares teachers should have such a specialist in foreign language methodology on the faculty (Jarvis 1983: 240). As Phillips (1989) notes, because not all institutions can support such a position, new arrangements, such as consortial agreements that bring together students and specialist for immersion weekends or interim semesters, must be devised to provide the needed expertise (p. 35). The practice of assigning methodology teaching and supervisory tasks to young, unprepared, and inexperienced junior faculty members whose real interests lie elsewhere must not continue.

Foreign Language Cooperating Teachers and Master Teachers. The role-model cycle is completed when the prospective teachers return to the schools, at various stages in their preparation, for the clinical experiences that bond theory and practice. Ideally, their mentors are the teachers who have been recognized for their ability to inspire and instruct not only their own students but the student teachers and interns for whom they serve as cooperating and master teachers.

Collaboration and cooperation among these different constituencies is essential if foreign language teacher education is to improve. The old models, exemplified by the traditional prescriptive approach to supervision in which authority figures, whether at the university or school level, tell others what to do must be replaced by a more collaborative approach that recognizes the contributions that each individual and constituency can make. Initiatives that reflect this spirit of shared responsibility and decision making include the following:

- Since 1987, the state of Ohio has required that university-level instructors with teacher-education responsibilities spend an extended amount of time observing and teaching in elementary or secondary school classrooms. Bacon and Humbach (1989) report on an exchange in which (1) a university methods instructor observed and taught second- and third-year secondary-level Spanish classes and (2) the secondary teacher participated in several sessions of the methodology course. The benefits in terms of professional growth and validated curriculum reform far outweighed the procedural and personal concerns involved in undertaking such a project.

- Carnegie Project 30 is an association of now over thirty colleges and universities committed to teacher-education reform. In these institutions, faculties in arts and sciences and in education are working together on five themes, including pedagogical content knowledge, in an unusual collaboration. (See chapter 3 of this volume for the five themes.) Of particular note to foreign language educators is the position of the co-chair of the project, Daniel Fallon, that all teachers, not just foreign language teachers, should acquire language proficiency and live abroad (in Knop 1991b).

- The University of Northern Colorado is designing a Master Teacher/ Adjunct Professor Program (Sandstedt 1991) that will recognize school districts and cooperating teachers for the vital role they play in teacher education. Outstanding foreign language teachers, selected from nominees submitted by school districts, will not only serve as cooperating teachers but will also participate in special pedagogical workshops, be eligible for special tuition rates for the annual foreign language teacher-education summer institute, and teach the foreign language methodology course, when appropriate. By establishing better channels of communication, the program will help the university develop courses that will reflect more accurately the needs of the public schools and will provide the schools with consulting services in a broad spectrum of faculty expertise.

Continuing the Pedagogical Developmental Process

Foreign language teacher-education programs for prospective teachers lay the foundation for success as a beginning teacher. Practicing teachers must then continue the process of acquiring received and experiential knowledge in the reflective teaching cycle described above. Responsibility for providing opportunities to engage in professional development experiences is shared by local school districts, state departments of education through the office of the foreign language supervisor or consultant (if there is such a position), the foreign language professional organizations, and the institutions that prepare teachers. Despite the recognition that collaboration is the key to improved teacher education, little, if any, coordination among these entities occurs at the present time on the important issue of continuing development. Indeed, Draper (1988) reported that 55 percent of the state foreign language supervisors who responded to a survey conducted by the Joint National Committee for Languages (JNCL) neither maintained nor had access to information about inservice opportunities in their states. Clearly this situation has to change.

While the tendency is to group all practicing teachers in the same category when discussing inservice activities, research over the past two decades has highlighted the special needs of beginning teachers during what is called the "induction" period (Huling-Austin 1992). Specially designed programs, in which an experienced mentor plays a principal role, may have a positive effect on reducing the early attrition of beginning teachers (Odell and Ferraro 1992). Knop (1991a) has called for such an arrangement in the first few years of a teacher's career. Reports of formal induction programs for language teachers do not appear in the literature, quite likely because mentoring is assumed to occur, if it occurs at all, naturally on an informal basis because of the relatively small size of departments. The validity of this assumption has not been demonstrated, but it is clear that both beginning and more experienced teachers need the stimulation, knowledge, and support that well-planned inservice activities provide.

Two well-established vehicles for continued professional development currently are promoting connections among elementary, secondary, and postsecondary foreign language professionals, with an emphasis on collaboration and collegiality:

- The Extension Workshop Program, inaugurated in 1983 at the Central States Conference on the Teaching of Foreign Languages and the Outreach Training Workshop program, instituted in 1986 at the Northeast Conference on the Teaching of Foreign Languages, are examples of the concept of "teachers teaching teachers" (Riordan 1989). Selected foreign language teachers attend the annual conferences, receive training in presenting workshops on topics addressed at the conference, and return home to give a workshop to colleagues, thus disseminating information and enthusiasm about new developments in foreign language teaching.

- The Academic Alliance Project, which has overseen the establishment and growth of a national network of more than 130 local collaboratives of school and college foreign language faculty, exemplifies a bottom-up type of continuing teacher education that addresses the needs of its members. Collaboratives that include faculty from teacher-education institutions encourage participation by teacher candidates, thus providing yet another dimension to the clinical experiences component of their program. Agendas, while not limited to pedagogical content issues, emphasize a wide range of effective classroom activities, techniques, and materials.

Summary

The process of acquiring pedagogical knowledge and experience is one that extends throughout the career of the foreign language teacher. Attitudes and skills developed in the teacher-education program relative to where to find information, how to implement innovations and analyze results, and how to collaborate with students and colleagues to expand one's understanding of the learning process and one's repertory of effective techniques become the basis for a satisfying and successful career.

Acquisition, however, is not the end of the process of becoming an effective teacher. It becomes necessary at various points in one's career to assess one's knowledge and performance both for professional and personal reasons. In the next section, we will examine steps being taken to improve the assessment process in the pedagogical content area of foreign language teacher education.

Assessment of Pedagogical Content Knowledge _____

The issue of standards ranks high, if not first, on all calls for reform in teacher education, both generic (Holmes Group 1986, 1990; Carnegie Task Force 1986) and foreign-language-specific (Knop 1991b). There is general agreement that beginning foreign language teachers must demonstrate an acceptable level of proficiency in the target language and a broad knowledge of the culture(s) of the language, know how learners learn a foreign language in a classroom setting, and be able to choose from a basic set of strategies, techniques, and activities those that will create an appropriate learning environment for their particular students.

The question of how beginning teachers demonstrate an acceptable level of competence in general education and subject-specific areas is being debated and even legislated in many states. It is foreign language educators, however, who know the most about what subject-matter and pedagogical knowledge is essential for effective teaching. We are the ones who must take steps to ensure, through appropriate evaluative procedures and measures, that beginning and practicing teachers meet and, indeed, surpass the standards.

With the acceptance by the profession of the goals of proficiency-oriented instruction at the K–12 levels has come a concomitant concern about teacher language proficiency and subject-matter competency, a topic that is treated in chapter 6 of this volume. The question of how to assess foreign language pedagogical knowledge, a matter of equal importance, has just recently begun to receive attention by the profession.

Traditionally, beginning teachers have been assumed to have an appropriate level of pedagogical content knowledge if they completed an approved teacher-education program that included a methodology course (not always specific to foreign languages) and a student teaching experience. In addition, some states have required a standardized test, such as the National Teachers Exam, with a section devoted to methodology.

New initiatives in assessing the pedagogical content knowledge of foreign language teachers are emerging, largely as a result of the propositions of the National Board for Professional Teaching Standards (1990). These include the Praxis Series (ETS 1992) developed by the Educational Testing Service, and the proposed establishment by AATG (1992) of a German-language certification board that would place considerable emphasis on portfolio assessment.

"The Praxis Series: Professional Assessments for Beginning Teachers" (ETS 1992), which will eventually replace the National Teachers Examination required for certification by some states, are assessment instruments that include a core content module, two optional content area performance modules, and an optional content-specific pedagogy module. The Spanish series, available in 1993, is based on a job analysis by over eight hundred Spanish educators at all levels. In a one-hour test consisting of three 20-minute essays, the pedagogy module assesses the candidate's ability to understand topics such as planning for instruction, teaching and learning strategies, curricular materials and resources, evaluation techniques, and issues related to foreign language curricula and teaching (ETS 1992). The French and German series, likewise based on input from language-specific professionals, will be similar in content, though not identical to the Spanish series.

While it is difficult to predict the effectiveness of the Praxis Series and the extent to which it will be used, the instruments will provide a standard measure, developed by professionals conversant with contemporary goals, procedures, and theories of foreign language learning and teaching. The use of three "candidate-constructed-response questions" rather than a multiple-choice format in the pedagogy module is appropriate to the concept of teacher as decision maker and reflects a reform-oriented approach to assessing pedagogical content knowledge.

AATG, in its draft statement of "Professional Standards for Teachers of German" (1992), follows the outline of the National Board for Professional Teaching Standards (1990) in proposing five standards that "explicate the role of the outstanding German language professional" (p. 5). A unique component of the German standards is the requirement of a portfolio that documents the teacher's work in the classroom and in professional activities. Standard 3, "German Teachers Manage and Monitor Student Learning Effectively," specifically outlines a number of "performance-based indicators of competence" in the portfolio, including the following:

- Teachers provide representative samples of lesson plans and student work
- Teachers provide video recordings documenting pedagogical techniques, accompanied by annotated lesson plans
- Teachers provide testimonial letters from students, parents, school administrators and colleagues

The standards are meant to characterize the "outstanding" German teacher. As such, it is expected that teachers with a minimum of three to five years of experience will present themselves for assessment (Zimmer-Loew 1992). The standards can serve, however, as guidelines for the development of foreign language programs for both German and other languages. Because of the breadth and depth of the pedagogically and professionally oriented indicators, they provide guidance for the continuing development of practicing teachers as well.

The portfolio-based assessment procedure parallels a similar movement in assessing student work, especially in the elementary grades. As a vehicle for evaluating teacher-prepared and selected samples, it provides more valid and varied information about what teachers actually do in the classroom and in the profession. It does, however, require a significant commitment of time and energy on the part of both teacher and evaluators. Further refinement of the AATG draft statement will, no doubt, address this issue in what is an innovative and promising direction in foreign language teacher evaluation.

Fulfilling the Pedagogical Imperative for the Twenty-First Century

This discussion of the nature, acquisition, and assessment of foreign language pedagogical content knowledge for the twenty-first century has brought us far from Governor Kean's learn-by-doing immersion model of teacher preparation. It has focused on aspects of the professional development component that represent new directions and new initiatives for the profession. Realizing the potential of these new initiatives will require foresight, patience, and hard work by foreign language educators at all levels and in all capacities, as well as by colleagues in other disciplines who are also responsible for the welfare of the educational system.

As we undertake the education of foreign language teachers for the twenty-first century, we face three principal challenges in the area of professional development. The first is achieving a working consensus on a definition of pedagogical content knowledge and how it is most effectively learned by prospective and practicing teachers. The second is achieving real collaborative interaction among the several groups that play a role in developing pedagogical content knowledge. The third is creating policies and procedures for assessing the initial and continuing pedagogical content knowledge of teachers. Underlying all three challenges is the pressing need to make decisions based on research in foreign language teacher education.

The Challenge of Consensus

Consensus on the substance and processes of pedagogical content knowledge is a question of determining priorities rather than one of compiling lists of competencies. As this chapter has emphasized, foreign language teachers of the twenty-first century will have to be informed decision makers in classrooms that are constantly changing. The teacher-education program must prepare those teachers to design curricula and plan instruction that takes into account the needs and capabilities of all their students as well as the opportunities and the limitations inherent in the classroom setting. It must prepare teachers to use theory-based, reflective practice to deal with pedagogical problems and innovations that have not yet been identified.

Achieving consensus on priorities in pedagogical content knowledge is vital in a society as large and as mobile as that of the United States. It is also possible in a profession as specialized as foreign language education. At the national level, steps are already being taken by the language associations to review jointly their individual statements on teacher preparation. This and other efforts to come to consensus would be enhanced by the creation of a national commission on teacher education in foreign languages, as proposed at the 1991 ACTFL Summer Seminar (Knop 1991b).

Consensus on pedagogical priorities at the national level can and will provide direction for the profession. To be truly effective, however, this consensus must be translated into action in all foreign language teacher methodology courses and clinical experiences in both large and small foreign language teacher-education programs.

The Challenge of Collaboration

Collaboration in the professional preparation of prospective foreign language teachers and in the continuing development of practicing teachers involves all the teacher educators identified above in the discussion of the pedagogical agenda. A persistent challenge facing the profession is the development of collaborative efforts within and between institutions.

Within postsecondary institutions, barriers to cooperation exist as a result of traditional conceptions of responsibility and status. Even though lip service may be paid to the contention that the education of teachers is the responsibility of the entire college or university, the real priorities of foreign language and literature departments are evident in the curriculum for majors and the reward system for professors. In most programs, course offerings and recognition patterns perpetuate the traditional preeminence of the study and analysis of literature, relegating the preparation of teachers to a peripheral position. As Lange (1991) makes clear, department chairs have a responsibility to involve the faculty in discussions of course offerings and continued language development relative to the needs of prospective teachers as well as those of other students. Such discussions need to focus not only on subject-matter content, but also on the processes of learning and teaching a foreign language. The foreign language methodologist, who often is responsible for the coordination of the language programs, must be recognized by colleagues as a valuable resource for ensuring the progressive development of proficiency in all the four skills throughout the student's career in the department.

Foreign language and literature departments must also maintain a close working relationship with the teacher-education unit on their campus. Too often, there is little or no communication between the two areas. The foreign language specialist, whether located in education or foreign languages, must be recognized by both areas as the liaison person who coordinates the subject-matter and professional development components of the prospective teacher's program. When the position of language specialist does not exist in the institution, the chair of the foreign language department must designate and support a qualified and interested faculty member to serve as the liaison to ensure the viability of the foreign language teacher-education program.

Barriers to collaboration do not exist in postsecondary institutions alone, however. Efforts to increase cooperation between schools and colleges, a continuing goal of teacher-education programs, are often thwarted by different views on teaching and learning, role definitions, organizational structures, and reward structures within the two institutions (Winitzky et al. 1992). Exacerbating the dilemma is the traditional perception of a hierarchy of status and power that prevents faculties in schools and colleges from achieving equal partnership in the preparation and continuing education of teachers.

Collaboration is the key to effective foreign language teacher-education programs. It is also likely to be the most difficult challenge to meet because it must be initiated and maintained on the local level in every institution and school that prepares teachers. As a process, it is extremely time-consuming and often leads to frustration because of the dichotomy that exists between the need for coherence, on the one hand, and the desirability of participatory decision making, on the other. In attempting to foster collaborative efforts, frank admissions of problems encountered and as yet unresolved can be as illuminating as accounts of success (cf. Winitzky et al. 1992).

The Challenge of Assessment

Assessment, because of its close relationship to public accountability, ranks high on the priority list of those who view education from outside the profession. Accreditation of programs and certification of teachers are the vehicles by which states influence and even control curricular and instructional decisions in teacher education. The current efforts by the national and state foreign language associations and state boards of education to develop workable standards are an indication that foreign language educators accept responsibility for program design and implementation, on the one hand, and teacher competence, on the other. This challenge, especially as it relates to the area of pedagogical content knowledge, will require a high level of consensus and collaboration in the profession.

Research in Foreign Language Teacher Education

As we address the challenges of consensus, collaboration, and assessment, the basis upon which we make decisions is an important factor. Do we advocate a particular agenda because we have reliable evidence that it will be effective or simply because we think it is appropriate? In a comprehensive review, Bernhardt and Hammadou (1987) found that only 8 articles on foreign language teacher education out of a total of 78 published in the United States between 1977 and 1987 report the results of research studies. They conclude that the profession's research base consists of "perceptions of experienced foreign language educators" (p. 293) rather than the formal collection and analysis of data. The questions that Bernhardt and Hammadou pose in the area of pedagogical content knowledge form the basis of a research agenda that would provide answers to questions regarding the content and processes of the professional development area of a teacher's education. The profession must answer the call for expanded research efforts if foreign language teacher education is to change.

Conclusion

Meeting the challenges of consensus, collaboration, and assessment as they relate to the pedagogical imperative in the education of foreign language teachers, both prospective and practicing, requires that individuals, associations, and institutions emulate the microcosm of the foreign language classroom as it has been described in this chapter. Keeping in mind the interactions of the learner with the target language, with the other players in the classroom game and with the elements of the classroom environment, we must work cooperatively and reflectively on actualizing the content and process of professional development.

References, The Pedagogical Imperative in Foreign Language Teacher Education

American Association of Teachers of French. 1989. "The Teaching of French: A Syllabus of Competence." *AATF National Bulletin* 15, Special Issue, October.

American Association of Teachers of German. 1992. "Professional Standards for Teachers of German." Draft version. Cherry Hill, NJ: AATG.

American Association of Teachers of Spanish and Portuguese. 1990. "AATSP Program Guidelines for the Education and Training of Teachers of Spanish and Portuguese." *Hispania* 73: 785–94.

American Council on the Teaching of Foreign Languages. 1988. "ACTFL Provisional Program Guidelines for Foreign Language Teacher Education." *Foreign Language Annals* 21: 71–82.

Ausubel, David P. 1968. *Educational Psychology: A Cognitive View.* New York: Holt, Rinehart and Winston.

Bacon, Susan, and Nancy Humbach. 1989. "Putting the Foreign-Language Methods Class Back into the Classroom." *Hispania* 72: 1071–76.

Bailey, Kathleen M., Alice Omaggio-Hadley, Sally Sieloff Magnan, and Janet Swaffar. 1991. "Research in the 1990s: Focus on Theory Building, Instructional Innovation, and Collaboration." *Foreign Language Annals* 24: 89–100.

Bellack, Arno A., Herbert M. Kliebard, Ronald T. Hyman, and Frank L. Smith. 1966. *The Language of the Classroom.* New York: Teachers College Press.

Bernhardt, Elizabeth B., and Joanne Hammadou. 1987. "A Decade of Research in Foreign Language Teacher Education." *Modern Language Journal* 71: 289–98.

Bonaventura, Anna Maria. 1988. "Cooperative Learning: Facilitating Communicative Competence in the Foreign Language Classroom." *1988 Annual Meeting Yearbook.* Schenectady: New York State Association of Foreign Language Teachers.

Carnegie Task Force on Teaching as a Profession. 1986. *A Nation Prepared: Teachers for the 21st Century.* Rochester, NY: National Center on Education.

Chaudron, Craig. 1988. *Second Language Classrooms.* Cambridge, Eng.: Cambridge Univ. Press.

Cohen, Andrew D. 1990. *Second Language Learning: Insights for Learners, Teachers, and Researchers.* Boston: Newbury House (Heinle and Heinle).

Combs, Arthur W. 1989. "New Assumptions for Teacher Education." *Foreign Language Annals* 22: 128–34.

Curtain, Helena A., and Carol Ann Pesola. 1988. *Languages and Children—Making the Match: Foreign Language Instruction in the Elementary School.* Reading, MA: Addison-Wesley.

Draper, Jamie B. 1988. *State Activities Up-Date: Focus on the Teacher.* Yonkers, NY: American Council on the Teaching of Foreign Languages.

Educational Testing Service. 1992. "The Praxis Series: Professional Assessments for Beginning Teachers." Princeton, NJ: ETS.

Fanselow, John F. 1977. "Beyond Rashomon: Conceptualizing and Describing the Teaching Act." *TESOL Quarterly* 11: 17–40.

Freeman, Stephen A. 1941. "What Constitutes a Well-Trained Modern Language Teacher?" *Modern Language Journal* 25: 255–67.

Galloway, Vicki, and Angela Labarca. 1990. "From Student to Learner: Style, Process, and Strategy," pp. 111–58 in Diane W. Birckbichler, ed., *New Perspectives and New Directions in Foreign Language Education.* ACTFL Foreign Language Education Series, vol. 20. Lincolnwood, IL: National Textbook.

Gunderson, Barbara, and David Johnson. 1980. "Building Positive Attitudes by Using Cooperative Learning Groups." *Foreign Language Annals* 13: 39–43.

Hallman, Clemens L., Anne E. Campbell, and Gisela Ernst. 1992. "Development and Implementation of FLES Summer Institutes in Florida: A Functional-Collaborative Effort." *Foreign Language Annals* 25: 245–54.

Hammadou, JoAnn, and Elizabeth B. Bernhardt. 1987. "On Being and Becoming a Foreign Language Teacher." *Theory into Practice* 26: 301–6.

Holmes Group. 1986. "Tomorrow's Teachers: A Report of the Holmes Group." East Lansing, MI: Holmes Group.

————. 1990. *Tomorrow's Schools: Principles for the Design of Professional Development Schools*. East Lansing, MI: Holmes Group.

Horwitz, Elaine K., Michael B. Horwitz, and JoAnn Cope. 1986. "Foreign Language Classroom Anxiety." *Modern Language Journal* 70: 125–32.

Horwitz, Elaine K., and Dolly J. Young. 1991. *Language Anxiety: From Theory and Research to Classroom Implications*. New York: Prentice Hall.

Huling-Austin, Leslie. 1992. "Research on Learning to Teach: Implications for Teacher Induction and Mentoring Programs." *Journal of Teacher Education* 43: 172–80.

Hume-Nigro, Joanne, and John B. Webb, eds. n.d. "Investing in the Future of Foreign Language Teaching: A Design for Teacher Preparation." Report of the NYSAFLT Task Force on Teacher Preparation. Schenectady: New York State Association of Foreign Language Teachers.

Jarvis, Gilbert A. 1983. "Pedagogical Knowledge for the Second Language Teacher," pp. 234–41 in James E. Alatis, H. H. Stern, and Peter Strevens, eds., *Applied Linguistics and the Preparation of Second Language Teachers: Toward a Rationale*. Georgetown University Round Table on Languages and Linguistics. Washington, DC: Georgetown Univ. Press.

————, and Sheryl V. Taylor. 1990. "Reforming Foreign and Second Language Teacher Education," pp. 159–82 in Diane W. Birckbichler, ed., *New Perspectives and New Directions in Foreign Language Education*. ACTFL Foreign Language Education Series, vol. 20. Lincolnwood, IL: National Textbook.

Johnson, David W., Roger T. Johnson, Edythe Johnson Holubec, and Patricia Roy. 1984. *Circles of Learning*. Alexandria, VA: Association for Supervision and Curriculum Development.

Knop, Constance K. 1991a. "Reaction: Preservice and Inservice Teacher Education in the Nineties: The Issue Is Instructional Validity." *Foreign Language Annals* 24: 113–14.

————. 1991b. "A Report on the ACTFL Summer Seminar: Teacher Education in the 1990s." *Foreign Language Annals* 24: 527–32.

Lange, Dale L. 1990. "A Blueprint for a Teacher Development Program," pp. 245–68 in Jack C. Richards and David Nunan, eds., *Second Language Teacher Education*. New York: Cambridge Univ. Press.

————. 1991. "Implications of Recent Reports on Teacher Education Reform for Departments of Foreign Languages and Literatures," *ADFL Bulletin* 23,1: 28–34.

Mitchell, Jane Tucker, and Mary Lynn Redmond. 1991. "The FLES Methods Course: Key to K–12 Certification." *Foreign Language Annals* 24: 507–10.

Morain, Genelle. 1990. "Preparing Foreign Language Teachers: Problems and Possibilities." *ADFL Bulletin* 21,2: 20–24.

National Board for Professional Teaching Standards. 1990. *Toward High and Rigorous Standards for the Teaching Profession: Initial Policies and Perspectives of the National Board for Professional Teaching Standards*. 2d ed. Detroit: NBPTS.

North Carolina Department of Public Instruction and the Center for Applied Linguistics. 1992. "Elementary School (K–8) Foreign Language Teacher Education Curriculum." Washington, DC: ERIC Clearinghouse on Languages and Linguistics.

Nunan, David. 1991. *Language Teaching Methodology*. Hertfordshire, Eng.: Prentice Hall International.

Odell, Sandra J., and Douglas P. Ferraro. 1992. "Teacher Mentoring and Teacher Retention." *Journal of Teacher Education* 43: 200–204.

Oxford, Rebecca. 1990. *Language Learning Strategies: What Every Teacher Needs to Know*. Boston: Newbury House (Heinle and Heinle).

Paquette, André. 1966. "Modern Language Teacher Preparation: A Quarter Century of Growth." *Modern Language Journal* 50: 7–20.

Phillips, June K. 1989. "Teacher Education: Target of Reform," pp. 11–40 in Helen S. Lepke, ed., *Shaping the Future: Challenges and Opportunities*. Report of the Northeast Conference on the Teaching of Foreign Languages. Middlebury, VT: Northeast Conference.

"Qualifications for Secondary School Teachers of Modern Foreign Languages." 1955. *The Bulletin of the National Association of Secondary School Principals* 39: 30–33.

Richards, Jack C. 1990. *The Language Teaching Matrix.* Cambridge, Eng.: Cambridge Univ. Press.

————, J. J. Platt, and H. Weber. 1985. *Longman Dictionary of Applied Linguistics.* London, Eng.: Longman.

Riordan, Kathleen. 1989. "Teachers Teaching Teachers: An InService Model That Works." *Foreign Language Annals* 22: 185–88.

Sandstedt, Lynn A. 1991. "Foreign Language Teacher Education: A Reaction." *Foreign Language Annals* 24: 109–12.

Shulman, Lee S. 1986. "Those Who Understand: Knowledge Growth in Teaching." *Educational Researcher* 15,2: 4–14.

Slavin, Robert E. 1983. *Cooperative Learning.* White Plains, NY: Longman.

Strasheim, Lorraine A. 1991. "Preservice and Inservice Teacher Education in the Nineties: The Issue Is Instructional Validity." *Foreign Language Annals* 24: 101–7.

Sullivan, Joseph F. 1983. "Kean Offers Plans to Improve Education," *The New York Times,* Sept. 7, p. II, 5.

VanPatten, Bill. 1992a. "Second Language Acquisition Research and Foreign Language Teaching, Part 1." *ADFL Bulletin* 23,2: 52–56.

————. 1992b. "Second Language Acquisition Research and Foreign Language Teaching, Part 2." *ADFL Bulletin* 23,3: 22–27.

————, Trisha Dvorak, and James F. Lee, eds. 1987. *Foreign Language Learning: A Research Perspective.* Boston: Newbury House (Heinle and Heinle).

Wadsworth, Barry J. 1984. *Piaget's Theory of Cognitive and Affective Development.* 3d ed. White Plains, NY: Longman.

Wallace, Michael J. 1991. *Training Foreign Language Teachers: A Reflective Approach.* Cambridge, Eng.: Cambridge Univ. Press.

Winitzky, Nancy, Trish Stoddart, and Patti O'Keefe. 1992. "Great Expectations: Emergent Professional Development Schools." *Journal of Teacher Education* 43: 3–18.

Wittgenstein, Ludwig. 1953. *Philosophical Investigations.* Oxford, Eng.: Blackwell.

Woodward, Tessa. 1991. *Models and Metaphors in Language Teacher Training: Loop Input and Other Strategies.* Cambridge, Eng.: Cambridge Univ. Press.

Zimmer-Loew, Helene. 1992. Personal communication.

8

Reflecting on
Teacher Development

Elizabeth G. Joiner
University of South Carolina

[W]hat is truly constraining is to be the prisoner of unexamined traditions of teacher education which may never have had any real professional validity, or which may have lost whatever validity they once had through the passage of time. (Wallace 1991: 165)

Preamble

According to Webster, *reflection* is the throwing or turning back of thoughts (upon anything); meditation; or contemplation. If you, the reader of this chapter, are a graduate student preparing for an examination, it is unlikely that you will feel that you have time to pause and ponder this text as you read, to meditate or to contemplate its content in the light of your own experience and what you have learned in your program of graduate studies. Instead, you may be inclined to read it at the surface level, to look for names, dates, or facts for which you might be held responsible or which might serve to impress the examining committee. If you are a practicing teacher, you may be tempted to put this chapter aside because of pressing demands: classes to prepare, grade reports to complete,

---

Elizabeth G. Joiner (Ph.D., The Ohio State University) is Professor of French at the University of South Carolina, where she regularly teaches methods courses and supervises student teachers. In addition to teacher education, she has worked extensively on listening comprehension and authentic materials, both audio and video. She has authored numerous articles and books on a variety of topics in foreign language education, and her affiliations include ACTFL, the AATF, the MLA, the International Association of Learning Laboratories, and SCCFLT, the South Carolina state organization.

papers to correct, parents to call. If, on the other hand, you hold an administrative or supervisory appointment, you may be feeling the pressure of organizing a workshop or conference or wading through the mountains of paperwork associated with your position. In this fast-paced end of the twentieth century, time is, indeed, a most precious commodity.

And yet, taking the time to reflect, to ponder, to bring our considered thoughts and collective experiences to professional concerns is crucial if we are to address the problems that face education in general, and teacher education in particular, as we approach the third millennium. We have the good fortune to find ourselves in an era in which there is much support for educational reform from both within and without. If we are to take full advantage of this opportunity for change, we must be willing first to participate in thoughtful self-examination. You, the readers of this chapter, are invited to put aside for a time those demanding tasks that interfere with reflection and to join your thoughts, your experiences to those expressed in this chapter so that together we may participate as colleagues in thoughtful action that will result in positive and lasting change.

The Near Future and the Past Imperfect

At a recent Georgetown University Round Table, Galloway (1991) reported on an ACTFL project, the purpose of which was to create a staff-development program based upon observations of real-life teaching. In order to determine what teachers actually attended to as they watched classroom interactions, high school and college foreign language teachers were asked to view selected segments of videotaped classes and to record their observations of these classes for future discussion. When an analysis of the teachers' responses revealed that they tended to focus primarily on surface-level specifics and discrete behaviors, the researchers tried a new approach. Teachers were asked to view the video again, this time assuming the identity of a particular student; rather than taking notes as they had done before, they were to indulge themselves in the unlawful act of writing a note to a friend during class time. This new perspective resulted in a much deeper level of processing and, consequently, in a more fruitful discussion of the classroom interaction.

Similarly, in order to think more creatively, to escape the facile answer, the knee-jerk reaction, the obvious solution, we sometimes need to get beyond ourselves, to allow our minds to be stretched by projections into time or space or by the examination of situations similar to, but not identical with, our own. Let us, then, begin this chapter with a journey into the future. Try to imagine, if you will, the second language classroom of the year 2012, when the teachers who were certified in 1992 will have been in the profession for twenty years. Can you see the faces of the students? What do they look like? What are they doing? Is there a textbook? What materials are being used? How are they being used? What is the teacher doing? What technology is present? Can we even assume that second language learning will take place primarily in classrooms twenty years from now? Although we can attempt to project ourselves into the future and speculate about these and other questions, our best guesses may prove to be inadequate or even erroneous, for, as Schrier pointed out earlier in introducing chapter 5 of this volume, there is no guarantee that the future will bear any resemblance to the present. In fact, in a world that is fast becoming a global village, it is more reasonable to imagine that the future may be quite different from the present. Many of us will no longer be in the profession in the year 2012. Who will replace us and what legacy will we leave them? How can we prepare the future of the profession?

This question asked with new urgency in our rapidly evolving world is, in fact, not a new one at all. Rather, it is a question that has been asked by trade and professional groups for centuries, and each epoch has sought and found what it considered to be an appropriate response. To gain a different perspective on teacher education, then, let us leave our classroom of 2012 for a moment and journey backward in time to consider two traditional models of professional preparation. Our first stop on this journey in time and space is Italy. It is the seventeenth century and we are visiting a small village, the home of a well-known violin maker, whose fame has spread throughout the land. Because there is a demand for these stringed instruments and because the violin maker is a recognized master, many of the village youths seek to follow his example. They ask if they may watch the master, and, if they are among the fortunate few, they will become apprentices to whom the skills of the trade are entrusted and eventually passed on to future generations. Now, leaving Italy and moving ahead two centuries, let us travel to England to observe members of the British Medical Association, sitting in rapt attention as they listen to a report by Sir Joseph Lister, in which he outlines findings based on an extended investigation into the nature of inflammation. His lecture, "On the Antiseptic Principle in the Practice of Surgery," later published in volume 2 of the *British Medical Journal,* will establish him as the founder of antiseptic medicine.

The two examples of the transmission of knowledge and skills described above represent very different conceptions of how the future of a trade or profession may be ensured. The first, which is usually referred to as the craft model, focuses on skills that are passed on directly from master to apprentice through experience. Because it is essentially imitative, the craft model has been disparagingly compared to "sitting next to Nellie," Nellie being an experienced assembly-line worker (Stones and Morris as quoted by Wallace 1991: 6). Nevertheless, it is a model that has spanned numerous centuries and retains a certain appeal even today. We may, for example, observe that this model has much in common with the proposal of Governor Kean, elaborated in chapter 7 of this volume. The second model of professional training, one that has dominated for years not only the medical profession but also professions such as engineering, has been called the technical rationality (Schön 1987) or applied science (Wallace 1991) model. Deriving its authority from empirical science, this model seeks to make use of research-supported knowledge to achieve certain clearly defined objectives: experts transmit the knowledge to future and practicing professionals, who are expected to incorporate it into their practice.

The majority of teacher-education programs today represent variations of the applied science model. In fact, however, given the complexity both of second language acquisition and of teaching, a great deal of what we pass on to future and inservice language teachers is as much expert opinion as scientific knowledge, a fact that has led Wallace (1991) to suggest that a more accurate term for the knowledge transmitted via workshops and teacher-training programs is *received,* rather than *scientific,* knowledge. Student teachers during their "clinical" experience are expected to apply the received knowledge that they have encountered in their university methods classes to the "laboratory" of the school; practicing teachers are expected to modify their classroom practice to conform to the latest thinking of recognized experts in the field. The dissemination of the ACTFL Provisional Proficiency Guidelines (1982), drawn up by experts in the field, before they had actually been validated, is an example of the promulgation of received knowledge in our profession.[1]

Will either the craft model or the applied science model alone suffice as a prototype for second language teacher education if we are to prepare the capable decision makers of the future envisioned by Wing in chapter 7 or the agents of change called for by Hudelson and Faltis in chapter 2? It is highly unlikely. The essentially imitative craft model is more appropriate for perpetuating the past than for adapting to the future. The applied science model, too, may prove inadequate to the task of preparing tomorrow's teachers, for by separating research from practice it creates a dependence on experts that can, in the extreme, stifle individual initiative and stunt professional growth. Despite their shortcomings, however, both the craft and the applied science models may contribute to a new, more future-oriented conception of teacher education, one that recognizes that teachers must both adapt to and create change. This model is called the reflective model;[2] its goal is to promote within teachers the continuing self-development and self-renewal that normally characterize professionals.

In order to stress personal responsibility for ongoing professional growth, proponents of the reflective model normally speak of *teacher development* rather than *teacher training.* Wallace (1991), whose proposal for a reflective model of teacher development includes elements of both the craft and the applied science model, underscores the fact that the key to the model is *reflection on action,* and specifically reflection on the action that occurs in the process of teaching. This reflection may take several forms, but it typically involves examining action in the light of both knowledge and experience. As such, while it represents a significant shift away from the previous models of professional education, it does not totally reject them. Rather, the reflective teacher may, in attempting to understand a given action, bring together experience, theory, and data derived from quantitative research. As we continue to explore the future of teacher development, it will be important to keep in mind the three models briefly outlined here: the craft model, the applied science model, and the reflective model.

The Present Progressive: Part I

In our consideration of teacher education thus far, we have attempted to imagine the future and to revisit and learn from the past. It is time now to return to the present in order to expand our horizons by comparing our own concerns as teacher educators with those of others with similar, but not identical, goals. It is in a spirit of inquiry and reflection that the reader is invited to examine several current programs of professional development that were designed to provide exemplary professional preparation. Before we continue, a word of caution is in order. The descriptions that follow are summaries based upon reports that are of necessity incomplete, given the complexity of any program of teacher education. For this reason, the reader is encouraged to seek more detailed information from articles and books that have been written about these programs and from the contact persons listed in the references.

In spite of the necessary brevity with which they are described here, it will be clear that the programs selected represent a variety of designs whose strengths and weaknesses can be made apparent by comparing them with each other and with the programs of teacher development with which we are most familiar. No one program is intended as *the* model, nor would any given model be appropriate for all languages, students, teachers, and institutions. Indeed, they have been selected because each is different from the others; yet, all embody ways of addressing the issue of providing meaningful professional development.

The three programs that will be outlined first have been chosen in order to enable us to distance ourselves from preconceived notions of the way professional training *should* be conducted. The first will transport us from the United States to the United Kingdom, where we will reflect upon an ESL/EFL program; the second will bring us back to this continent for an examination of a Canadian response to the need for French teachers in a western province where fewer than 3 percent of the population is francophone. Finally, we will return to the United States but not to our customary teacher-education setting. Rather, we will step outside our profession to review a program designed to prepare managers for international business. It is hoped that these ventures outside our established educational contexts will provide new perspectives and raise significant questions that can help us evaluate both our traditional programs of teacher education and those that have been redesigned in response to the numerous reports that have called for dramatic change in the preparation of teachers.

Our first professional development program site is England, where Wallace (1991) reports on a four-year preservice course of study designed to prepare nonnative speakers of English to teach English in their home countries. In creating the program, five basic principles were followed. The designers believed that their program should, first of all, be relevant to the needs of the target population of eighteen-year-old future teachers and to the communities in which they would later teach. Further, the program should be both broadly educative and fully professional, should lead to increasing autonomy on the part of the trainees, and should be culturally broadening in that it should capitalise, as far as possible, on the trainees' presence in Britain to broaden their cultural horizons, while at the same time completely respecting the integrity of their own culture. (p. 147)

The program that resulted from this vision consists of four major strands: (1) the curricular areas, (2) the theory and practice of teaching and learning (TPTL), (3) school experience, and (4) academic counseling (p. 149). The two main curricular areas are English studies (language and literature) and a subsidiary subject; similarly, the TPTL courses are grouped into two main areas: learning and the learner (psychology, social context, types of learning, including computer-assisted instruction) and methodology (both TESOL and teaching of the second subject area). The academic counseling component consists of one 30-hour unit during each of the four academic years plus ten individual tutorials devoted to a culminating professional project, designed to help the participants integrate various elements of the four-year experience. Another integrative aspect of the program is the approach to assessment, which favors examinations designed to pull together learning from several related courses over examinations on individual courses. In addition, the students are evaluated on presentations and on the folios in which they write reflectively about their teaching experience.

A key element of this ESL program is the reciprocal relationship between the theory and practice of teaching and learning strand and the school experience, which consists of a total of twenty-four weeks with an extra two-week block for weak students. This experience is organized as follows: An initial one-week block in the home country is followed by a total of three weeks of experience spread throughout the first year in schools in the United Kingdom. In the second term of Year 2 there is a five-week block in a school in the UK. Students whose performance during that block is less than satisfactory are required to participate in a two-week remedial block in September of the third year. This completed, all students are considered to be ready for a twelve-week block in their home country at the end of that same year. The final year of the program contains an additional three-week experience, this time concurrent with classes, in a UK school.

Although much more could be said about this program, we risk becoming overwhelmed by detail and thus unable to see parallels between it and our own situation. Let us pause, then, and reflect upon some features of this program that might lead us to rethink our own approaches to teacher education.

1. Students who participate in this program receive the majority of their teacher preparation in a country where the target language is spoken rather than in their home country. Is this desirable/possible for U.S. students who wish to become foreign language teachers? What would be the role of teacher educators in the United States if the majority of the teacher-preparation program were taught on-site in Germany, for example? Could a program of faculty and student exchanges be arranged as in the European ERASMUS project?[3] What would be the effect on language skills and cultural understanding of four years of instruction in the target culture?

2. Students participating in this program learn how to teach an additional subject using English as the medium of instruction. They thus have a basis for implementing content-based instruction as a means of developing the linguistic and thinking skills of their future pupils. Can we design programs that will enable future language teachers in the United States to participate in this promising curricular innovation? What content areas might we explore? Is minoring in a content area sufficient or should there be specific instruction in that area conducted in the foreign language?

3. The extensive twelve-week block of teaching in the home country takes place not at the end of the four-year program but at the end of the third year in order to allow the student to reflect upon that experience and to integrate it into the professional project. Our typical program, as outlined in this volume, ends with student teaching. Is this situation inevitable or can programs be restructured to allow for a period of study and reflection subsequent to student teaching? Does alternating school experience with university courses enhance reflection on teaching?

4. The TPTL strand includes a strong technological component built around computer-assisted instruction. What sort of facilities and equipment would be necessary in order to implement such a component? What preparation would future teachers need in order to apply this technology to instruction?

5. Counseling, ever-present in this program, is often minimal in ours. Why did the creators of the program consider this component to be essential to their program? What would the effect of such a component be on our teaching majors?

6. The program design reflects five important principles. Which, in your opinion, are the most essential to a successful program? Which of the five principles seem to be the most closely related to the teacher-education programs with which we are familiar? Do our programs seem to be based on a carefully developed rationale or are we the prisoners of unexamined traditions of teacher education?

The program described above was an Honours Bachelor of Education Degree in TESOL intended for eighteen-year-olds who had completed a preuniversity course in the United Kingdom. For comparison, we will now consider an undergraduate teacher-education program in French as a Second Language taught at the University of Regina, Saskatchewan, and reported on by Moeller (1989). In this program, school experience begins during the first semester of the freshman year, with students spending one half day per week in classes ranging from K to 12. The second semester, the future teachers take the "Introduction to FSL Teaching," which is taught in French, along with major courses in French and in a teaching minor. During the following three semesters, the requirements for the French major and for their chosen minor are completed and students take an education elective taught in French as well. The "preinternship," or sixth semester, includes a combination of field-based and university-based activities structured around themes such as "learning styles" and "group work." These themes are addressed in each of the students' four courses (educational psychology, general education, French curriculum, French instruction) in order to provide an integrated experience. The seventh-semester internship begins with a week-long retreat for interns, cooperating teachers, and faculty advisers designed to foster an effective working relationship. The internship itself is divided into three phases: *orientation* (ten weeks of half-time teaching), *full-time teaching* (three weeks during which the intern assumes full responsibility for all classes), and *reflection* (three weeks of half-time teaching). The final semester of the program is devoted to the treatment of broad issues relating to society, language, and the educational system, with the majority of the classes being taught in French. According to Moeller, teachers from this program are in great demand.

As we look back on the outline of Regina's teacher-preparation program, we can identify some similarities, and a few differences, between it and the program described earlier by Wallace. Both are four-year sequences; both are highly structured; both offer not only major courses but also teacher-preparation courses conducted in the language being studied; both provide for a semester of class work after the lengthiest period of school experience. Even so, there are some significant differences with respect to time spent in an area where the target language predominates, types and length of school experience, and program design in general. Which features of each, we might wonder, could be most easily imported into the context of teacher-education reform within the United States?

Examining two undergraduate teacher-education programs from other countries has enabled us to distance ourselves from this society's entrenched traditions and long-standing attitudes toward the preparation of language teachers and to see how other societies go about reaching the goal that we espouse, that of preparing teachers of foreign and second languages. Another approach to reflection that we might use is the juxtaposition of two programs or processes with similar yet not identical goals. For example, we may gain perspective on our field and on our role as teacher educators by considering the way another profession prepares future professionals. This approach has been used by Barnett, Becher, and Cork (as quoted by Wallace 1991: 4), among others. As we continue our consideration of the professional preparation of teachers, an analysis of the Masters of International Business Studies Program at the University of South Carolina, ranked first in the nation for three consecutive years, will afford us the opportunity to step outside our own field and compare teacher-education programs with a program designed to form leaders in international business management.[4]

Like the undergraduate TESOL program discussed earlier, this course of study has four basic components: (1) an integrated business curriculum that includes the fundamentals of business but goes beyond these to encompass the special skills required by multinational enterprises, (2) specific foreign language training designed to enable future managers to communicate in at least one language other than their own, (3) a component of geopolitical studies, and (4) a six-month (seven in the case of Japanese and Korean) overseas internship. While these components, for the most part, are arranged in discrete blocks, an ongoing and integral part of the M.I.B.S. program is its series of international seminars and guest lectures, which enables the students to profit from the insights and experience of both corporate executives and foreign dignitaries.

The program contains a number of language tracks, and there are two-year and three-year sequences, depending on the time required to acquire the communicative skills necessary to conduct business in the language of specialization. Students are admitted once a year and must follow the program in sequence, beginning with a three-month intensive summer language course. Japanese students, who must complete a three-year course of study, begin with the summer language course at U.S.C., continue through an intensive business course organized into four- to eight-month modules throughout the fall and spring semesters while at the same time taking a language maintenance course, attend a university in Japan for ten months of additional language training, perform a seven-month internship in Japan, and return to the United States for nine weeks of final studies. On-campus recruiting of students by future employers begins in February, when the students return to the campus after their internships. In addition, résumé books are made available to more than 500 companies. Two-year programs follow a similar schedule, except that the preinternship overseas language training lasts four weeks rather than ten months.[5]

The M.I.B.S. Program is costly in the sense that, in addition to regular tuition, students must pay a one-time special matriculation fee of $4000 for South Carolina residents and $7400 for out-of-state students. They must also assume financial responsibility for travel to the internship site and any living expenses while there that exceed whatever living allowance may be provided by the company.

As we reflect on this program for business managers, we will no doubt be especially interested in the components dealing with language and culture. We might observe, for example, the following features:

1. The program recognizes that the time required for the attainment of a useful level of oral and written language skills (a) is lengthy and (b) varies with the language of specialization. Even the "easier" languages (French, German, Brazilian Portuguese, and Spanish) are developed through specific language instruction in both this country and the foreign country in which the students will do their internship. Students' language skills are further honed through the internship itself, which offers them an opportunity to use the language in a real professional situation. Is it possible to create or to restructure teacher-education programs in a way that recognizes that the time and experiences necessary to produce linguistic competency will vary according to language?[6] Can we, for example, envision a cadre of professional language teachers certified on the basis of linguistic competency instead of credit hours?

2. The experience abroad involves not simply studying but actually using the language in a realistic setting. How might we expand the study-abroad component of our programs to increase the opportunity to participate in the life of the people whose language is being studied? Might we organize teaching experiences in the foreign country for our interns?[7] How could other types of

abroad experience such as *au pair* work be recognized as contributing to the language skills and cultural awareness of future teachers?

3. The primary responsibility for cultural preparation is not entrusted to the foreign language faculty. "Culture," as we sometimes think of it, may be treated in the language component, but the geopolitical studies component is taught by specialists in government and international studies. This raises the question of just how legitimate culture courses offered by departments of foreign languages really are, given that they are often developed by people who have little or no preparation in this area beyond their own study and travel in the country in question. How can we strengthen the cultural preparation of future teachers when the culture courses that they take are most often taught by nonexperts? If we intend to offer culture courses, and indeed to require them for teaching majors, what steps need to be taken to ensure that they will be of the highest quality?

4. The M.I.B.S. program is interdisciplinary in that faculty from business, foreign languages, and government and international studies bring their expertise to the training of future international business managers. How can we make our teacher-education programs more interdisciplinary? Is it possible to identify faculty in other disciplines who are capable of teaching in the foreign language and who are willing to participate in the development of language teachers? What initiatives could result in improved teacher preparation through collaborative ventures with other disciplines?

5. It is clear that the future managers who enter the M.I.B.S. program recognize that they will be expected to use the language actively in their careers. How can we convince future language teachers that this is a necessity for them as well? Is it possible to place them with cooperating teachers who model on-the-job use of the foreign language and, if not, can we overcome the strong tendency of student teachers to teach languages the way that they have been taught, too often in classes dominated by the native language?

6. Students who enroll in the M.I.B.S. program are willing to invest a considerable amount of time and money in order to become international managers. Is it only financial gain that motivates them to do so or does the prestige of participating in a nationally recognized program also play a role? What incentives can we offer to prospective foreign language teachers?

7. The program begins with three months of intensive language training, provides continued language training during the two semesters of intensive business, and includes an additional period of intensive language training in the target country before the six-month internship. Would it be desirable to provide some intensive language experiences for future language teachers? How could these be organized and what would be their effect on our present curricula?

8. The intensive business courses are coordinated and scheduled interdependently in modules so as to enhance the students' perception of subject interrelationships. Is this a useful concept for rethinking content courses in the foreign language? Do future teachers integrate their courses on their own or do we need to provide some means of helping them to achieve this integration?

9. The M.I.B.S. program takes an active role in placing its graduates. Should we consider helping beginning language teachers find employment? What would be the result of on-campus recruitment and résumé books sent to selected school districts?

Before returning to the more familiar territory of language teacher education in this country, it may be worthwhile to pause and try to bring together in some way the three programs, two undergraduate and one graduate, two foreign and one domestic, two oriented toward teacher preparation and the third designed to prepare business managers, in some meaningful way. A simple first step would be to identify some of the features that the three programs we have examined have in common. One observation that we might make is that, while their design features are by no means identical, all three are highly structured courses of study designed for the purpose of developing highly qualified professionals. Further, all organize the course of study so that the future member of the profession will see relationships among its various components and achieve some degree of integration; all offer extensive work in the foreign language; all are somewhat inflexible in the sense that students must enter at the same point and follow a fixed sequence. These basic observations may serve as a starting point for readers who wish to compile a list of features of each program that seem particularly worthy of emulation. Another approach to reviewing this section would be to take the role of a student given the choice of participating in each of the three programs and to identify those features of each that would be particularly attractive or unattractive to the choice of a program of professional training.

The Present Progressive: Part II

In the previous section, we considered teacher education in the light of what is being done in other countries and in other professions. This section will present three innovative programs that have been designed by institutions in this country with the intention of preparing professionals capable of coping with the present and future challenges of language education. The three include a four-year, a five-year, and a fifth-year program. In order to reflect more critically on these programs, we might first flesh out our earlier conception of the foreign language classroom of the future by examining the projections of other experts in the field. With this purpose in mind, it may be helpful to consider recommendations contained in two articles by Tetenbaum and Mulkeen (1986) and Mulkeen and Tetenbaum (1987). In these articles, the authors discuss six very broad characteristics of the future "technological society" and subsequently draw implications for teacher education and propose a model for teacher development.

The model proposed by these educators contains nine key features. It is *field-based, problem-centered,* and *technology-driven.* It involves *experimental sharing* in that neophyte and experienced teachers, master teachers, college/university supervisors, and professorial staff participate in the identification and organization of resolutions to curricular and instructional problems. It is *developmental* in the sense that it must be designed to meet the needs of an increasingly sophisticated developing professional. Further, the model is *competency-based* and *expertly staffed* by a high concentration of professionals whose presence creates a *critical mass* within the school setting. Finally, the model is *open-ended* in that it suggests that professional development is never-ending and lifelong.

As was the case in the previous section, the programs outlined below are presented not so much as examples to follow but as subjects of reflection. Our approach to reflection in this case will be to keep in mind the key features of the model of teacher development summarized in the preceding paragraph and to view each program design in that light. To be perfectly fair, we should keep in mind that the program descriptions are not complete and that a given program should not be judged as lacking a characteristic simply because it is not mentioned in this chapter. Further, since all three are essentially preservice programs, although they may have an impact on the practicing teachers that serve as master or cooperating teachers, the developmental and open-ended features of the Tetenbaum–Mulkeen model may not be obvious.

In 1974, long before the various proposals for reform of teacher education that characterized the 1980s, the University of New Hampshire put into place a five-year program for preparing language teachers. In the sophomore year, prospective teachers complete a semester-long field placement, which involves both observation of, and limited participation in, instruction in a public school. The following year these same students normally spend at least a semester in a country where the target language is spoken. According to Wing (1992), this experience, during which many become involved in the teaching of English, not only improves the teacher candidates' language proficiency and cultural understanding but also strengthens their commitment to teaching as a profession. The fourth, or senior, year is devoted to completing the requirements for the language major while taking two or three courses in education, including a foreign language methodology course. In the fifth year, candidates intern in a public school with full responsibility for two courses through the whole year and a full-time teaching load for two weeks in the second semester. Weekly seminars for the language interns deal with pedagogical and administrative issues that arise in their classes.

A fifth-year, as opposed to a five-year, intensive program (two summer sessions plus a nine-month clinical experience) inaugurated at the University of Minnesota's Twin Cities Campus in the 1986–87 academic year culminates with a recommendation for certification (Lange 1990, 1991). Not targeted at any one specific language, the program is intended for those who have completed a bachelor of arts degree with a major in the language they intend to teach. The nine students admitted to the program during the first year included one in ESL as well as two in French, and three each in German and Spanish. Admission standards require a grade point average of 2.8 overall, and prospective students in the modern languages must have achieved oral proficiency equivalent to the advanced level as outlined on the ACTFL scale. Priority is given to those who have already had actual living and/or study experience in a country where the language of specialization is used. The three-month educational foundations component of the program includes seminars and courses dealing with traditional foundations subjects as well as certain topics, such as multicultural education, mandated by the state legislature.[8] In the nine months that follow this initial preparation, students participate in a clinical experience offered on-site within a school district and coordinated by a team that includes both university and school personnel. This experience, structured so as to progress through phases labeled *awareness, practice,* and *induction,* contains a research component that requires the student to examine the relationship of theory to practice. A report of the research project is presented during the terminal phase of the program, which takes place during the second three-month summer session. All students are required to take a three-hour, written comprehensive examination that requires them to relate theory to practice. A master of education degree is awarded after a year of teaching experience during which candidates videotape and analyze their progress at specified intervals.

One of the eight schools of the Renaissance Group, the University of Northern Colorado, is currently restructuring its four-year undergraduate teacher-preparation program in accordance with the Group's twelve principles.[9] The first year of the language teacher education program at that institution begins with general education and major courses but also includes a number of screening tests. Students who have achieved a 2.5 GPA may petition for admission to the core. At this point, foreign language faculty and faculty from the College of Education meet jointly to discuss each student individually. Those who are admitted enter a program designed to enhance meaningful learning by focusing on themes: Phase 2 (year 2) relates to the self and includes activities such as developing a written statement of one's personal philosophy of education and keeping a reflective learning log; Phase 3 (year 3), on the other hand, focuses on the learner and involves case studies that examine learners' social, physical, cognitive, psychological, and ethical development. After their admission to the program, the prospective teachers have a field experience every semester, culminating in a sixteen-week period of student teaching, which is followed by a capstone seminar. According to Sandstedt (1992), students in the Spanish track of this program are given an ACTFL Oral Proficiency Interview at the end of their junior year, and an advanced level is required in order for them to student-teach. Should the students fail to reach the required level, they may improve their skills through an intensive summer in Mexico or additional course work or conversation hours with native speakers. It is noteworthy that all nine of the Spanish faculty, including the literature specialists, have been trained to administer the OPI and that two are certified ACTFL testers.

In analyzing the 1987 version of the Minnesota program described above in light of the model of teacher development proposed by Tetenbaum and Mulkeen, Lange (1990) noted three shortcomings: the program was not technology-driven; it prepared no minority students; and the student–teacher relationship was not as democratic as would be desirable in a humanistically oriented program such as this one. As we reflect on this model as well as the New

Hampshire and Northern Colorado models, we should also take note of their obvious strengths and areas of consistency with the majority of the Tetenbaum and Mulkeen recommendations. It may also be helpful to assume once again the role of a student contemplating a career choice and review the programs from that point of view before proceeding to the next section.

From Surface to Deep Structure

In previous sections, we have focused primarily, although not exclusively, on the structure of the programs that we have analyzed. While program design is important, a good design in and of itself does not automatically guarantee the goals the designers wish to achieve. Indeed, focusing exclusively on the most obvious features of a program may cause us to overlook its deeper structure, i.e., what actually happens inside the program and gives it meaning.

At this point, it may be helpful to recall the three theoretical models briefly treated earlier in this chapter in order to see how a single design feature might be treated at a deeper level by each. If we take as an example microteaching, a common feature of many teacher-education programs, and examine it from the point of view of each model, we will see that the same program component can be approached in ways that represent very different attitudes.

In the craft model approach to microteaching, the future teacher might visit, or perhaps see on videotape, an actual class being taught by an experienced teacher. The recommendation would be: This is how it is done. Follow this model. In contrast, students being taught by an applied science model would see a demonstration class designed to incorporate the latest scientific and theoretical notions of what effective language teaching should be. The recommendation would be: This is how it should be done. Follow this model. The reflective model, as interpreted by Wallace (1991), would, on the other hand, treat the demonstration lesson not as an example to follow but rather as a starting point for analysis, discussion, and reflection. The approach would be: Here is a sample of language teaching. What are some strengths and weaknesses of what we have just seen? Let us examine the sample together and see what conclusions can be drawn.

In the absence of evidence from research, we can only theorize what might be the result of treating microteaching in each of the ways described above. Intuition would lead us to believe that a reflective approach would encourage inquiry and independence on the part of the future practitioner; that the results of research into teacher education often do not confirm our intuitive expectations, however, is suggested by the findings of a study undertaken by the National Center for Research on Teacher Learning (Kennedy 1991). The researchers, interested in determining whether various modifications in teacher-preparation programs had actually produced what their advocates intended, examined students in preservice, inservice, and induction programs as well as those seeking certification through alternative routes. Students selected for the sample were followed through the program in question and into their first year of teaching on their own. In all, more than 700 teachers and teacher candidates were studied.

A number of features of teacher-education programs were investigated in the study: subject-matter knowledge, multicultural preparation, mentoring, preservice programs, and alternative certification. In every case, there were some surprising findings. For example, courses created to help teachers better understand the cultures of various groups of students did not appear to enhance the ability of the teachers to instruct children who were members of these groups. The researchers speculate that because course content consisted primarily of generalizations about group characteristics and customs, the courses may, in fact, have inadvertently reinforced, rather than altered, latent prejudices, thus convincing future teachers that certain groups of students were unable to learn certain skills and knowledge.

In the case of mentoring and of alternative certification, findings were mixed but disappointing on the whole. Data revealed that mentors did help beginners with the emotional adjustment to teaching and, thus, may have reduced attrition among first-year teachers. On the other hand, many of the beginners became very traditional teachers, teachers who appeared to have learned neither how to improve the content they taught nor how to examine their own practices in a critical manner. (It is interesting to note that the researchers did find one mentoring program that was quite successful. Mentors in this program were released from full-time teaching in order to concentrate on their mentoring task, and they were given specific training both before and during their terms as mentors.) Like the typical mentoring programs, the two alternative certification programs were found to result in no improvement in teaching skills or self-examination. While the alternative certification programs were successful in attracting minority students into the profession, they did little more than enable these students to survive in the classroom and in the local school setting.

Reviewing the results of several well-intentioned efforts at reform that fell short of expectations has shown us that what seem to be the best of ideas on the surface may succeed or fail depending on how they are translated into reality. Similarly, looking at how one design feature, in this case microteaching, might remain constant and yet be approached quite differently in programs with different orientations has shown us that the content of change must be considered as well as its form. It will be helpful to keep these perspectives in mind as we examine one final example of teacher-education reform.

Generating Transformation

Thus far, we have highlighted preservice professional development. It is time now to bring the practicing teacher into the picture. The final program that we will examine and reflect upon here has brought together, and continues to bring together, inservice teachers along with preservice teachers and teacher educators in an attempt to address a need for qualified FLES teachers. As such, it will serve as an example of an effort to effect widespread, rather than merely local, change.

The original impetus for the project in question came from two mandates by the state of North Carolina, whose legislature decided (1) that by 1989, all teacher educators in that state should be certified to teach in grades K–12 and (2) that by 1993, all public school students in the state should be required to study a second language from kindergarten through grade 5 and have the opportunity to continue language study through grade 12. In response to this legislation, a statewide committee, spearheaded by the North Carolina Department of Public Instruction, was formed to develop K–12 teacher competencies and student evaluation measures as well as guidelines for K–12 second language teacher-preparation programs. (See North Carolina 1992.) As a result of the work of this committee, composed of college and university teacher educators, elementary and secondary school teachers, and local level supervisors from all eight educational regions of the state, North Carolina now has a curriculum for grades K–8, and twenty-three institutions of higher education have had their FLES teacher-education programs approved by the Department of Public Instruction. In the meantime, the state's children have benefited from the attention focused on them during the project.

The North Carolina FLES project is especially interesting as a model for effecting widespread change.[10] The groundwork for the project began in early 1988 when the original committee[11] began to meet to draw up competencies. By November of the following year, the co-sponsors of the project, the Department of Public Instruction and the Center for Applied Linguistics, had received a grant from FIPSE (Fund for the Improvement of Postsecondary Education) to support the development, over a period of three years, of a national model for a university teacher-training program for elementary school foreign language teachers. Helena Curtain's evaluation report (1992), based on on-site visits and interviews with the participants, is highly positive and concludes that the project met or exceeded its five goals:

1. to improve the ability of North Carolina foreign language teacher educators to train future elementary school foreign language teachers
2. to facilitate collaboration among foreign language teacher educators and practicing FLES teachers
3. to provide training in FLES methods instruction for 22 teacher educators and 14 FLES teachers
4. to build a statewide capacity to expand opportunities for professional development by training project participants to become trainers
5. to disseminate the teacher-education curriculum and model to other interested districts and states

According to Toussaint (1992), the keys to the success of this project are the following:

1. Allow sufficient time to prepare for a major change. By starting in 1988 to prepare for a mandate that will go into effect in 1993, the Department of Public Instruction and its statewide committee had the time to proceed thoughtfully and to avoid hasty, patchwork solutions. Their next area of concentration is the middle school.
2. One person should assume the responsibility for leadership and coordination of the project. Because of the participation of the Center for Applied Linguis-

tics, there were co-directors of the North Carolina project; however, only one of these was consistently present within the state.

3. The project leader should select a committee composed of a manageable number of capable people. Care should be taken to ensure geographical representation as well as representation from all groups who will ultimately participate in the project. In this case, classroom FLES teachers, local supervisors from the eight school districts, college and university teacher educators, and representatives from the North Carolina Department of Public Instruction were included in the initial group of twenty-four.

4. The project should build on established strengths. North Carolina had already drawn up guidelines (North Carolina 1992) for teacher preparation for ESL as well as a set of competencies for ESL teachers. These already validated documents served as the starting point for the working paper on FLES presented to the committee at their first meeting.

5. Projects seeking funding are more likely to meet with a favorable decision if they can demonstrate that they have already begun to address the area of desired change on their own. It is very likely that the fact that a steering committee had already been meeting regularly for a year to draw up a set of competencies for FLES teachers contributed to FIPSE's decision to fund the project.

6. Committee meetings should be focused, and every meeting should result in a product. If possible, those who participated should leave the meeting with something tangible that resulted from their deliberations. For this project, all meetings were planned for two or three days in order to allow sufficient time for discussion of issues and drafting of documents.

7. Limitations must be recognized and priorities set. According to the project report (Curtain 1992), the most difficult aspect of establishing the FLES curriculum was deciding which were the most crucial competencies, given the limited time and resources available. The painful task of rank-ordering fourteen competencies, all of which were considered essential by members of the committee, resulted in the following top five priorities: (a) proficiency in the foreign language, (b) knowledge of instructional methods, (c) knowledge of the K–12 foreign language curriculum, (d) an understanding of second language acquisition in childhood, and (e) knowledge of elementary school principles and practices.

8. For maximum impact, change must extend beyond the initial group. The North Carolina project brought together college and university teacher educators with experienced FLES teachers for a number of periods of observation, planning, and co-teaching in the schools. A ripple effect was created as teacher educators who participated in the first year of the project were paired with new teacher educators and FLES teachers. This ever-widening circle of change has resulted in the initial group's doubling of its membership and thus its influence.

9. Assessment must be built into the project. In this case, the competencies have been validated, the project itself has been evaluated, and tests for assessing the

skills of students who have participated in the FLES programs are in the process of being piloted.

It is the American way to measure success by the attainment of predetermined goals; unfortunately, this attitude may cause us to overlook unforeseen yet important outcomes of the process of change. A closer look at the North Carolina project will make this clear. Over the years of working together with a common purpose, the statewide committee has bonded into a very close support group not only on a professional but also on a personal level. Members of the committee have increased their participation in professional meetings, and a number of them have published in professional journals. Several have been chosen as Educator of the Year, or some variation thereof, by either their local school, their school district, or the state, and one has received a grant from the National Science Foundation to produce a series of laser discs for use in the preparation of FLES teachers to teach scientific concepts through the medium of a foreign language.

In short, this statewide effort has resulted not only in a successful FLES program that can serve as a national model but also in increased professional activity and better self-esteem on the part of those who participated in it. Comments to the evaluator also indicate that the collaborative approach embraced by the committee has resulted in mutual trust and respect among teacher educators and classroom teachers, an attitude that is, unfortunately, not always the norm. Because of their feeling of accomplishment, their sense of purpose, and their joy in collaboration, the committee members are eager to continue their work even in the absence of FIPSE funding; furthermore, as we have seen above, the original project has begun to spawn additional fundable projects. The whole has become greater than the sum of its parts.

The Future Imperative

In an article on reflective teaching, Bartlett (1990) quotes Paolo Freire's observation that "reflection without action is mere verbalism whereas action without reflection is activism—doing things for their own sake" (p. 213). There is much activity today in the field of teacher education in general and language teacher education in particular, but activity alone is not sufficient. One of the purposes of this volume has been to provide information that could serve to channel the energy of our profession into thoughtful action rather than unthinking activism. This being the case, this chapter, and this volume, should logically end with a series of recommendations and a call to action. For reasons that will be explained below, I have chosen to take another course.

Certainly teacher education needs reforming; few would contest that fact. The imperative for our profession, however, is not so much to establish what should and could be done as to determine how to bring to reality the proposals for change that have been enunciated many times and in many places for at least half a century. Some of these recommendations occur in the form of guidelines adopted in recent years by various professional organizations; others are contained in articles and priorities papers written during the past fifteen years (Grittner 1980; Jarvis and Taylor 1990; Joiner 1980; Jorstad 1980; Lange 1990, 1991; Phillips 1989; Strasheim 1991; Wing 1984); still others have appeared in the earlier chapters of this volume. A sobering fact is that the more recent proposals for reform bear a striking similarity to those published in 1941 (Freeman), 1955 ("Qualifications"), and 1966 ("Guidelines"). To be sure, some of the contemporary articles, in keeping with demographic shifts and technological developments, place greater emphasis on technology, multiculturalism, the recruitment of minorities, and study abroad as imperatives for teacher development; nevertheless, the familiarity of many of the recommendations contained in publications from previous eras reminds us that, in spite of isolated achievements, we have failed decade after decade to bring about substantive and lasting national change in the preparation and certification of language teachers. It is this reality that we must address if the future is to be more than a replication of the past, which has known too many short-lived triumphs.

While it is tempting to blame the educational establishment or lack of funds or poor public support for our spotty success in the area of teacher-education reform, we should perhaps explore other explanations. Two primary hypotheses come to mind: One is that we have not understood well enough the process of change and have thus underestimated its complexity. Another is that the isolation and fragmentation of our profession alluded to by Tedick et al. and Schrier earlier in this volume have prevented the crystallization of a vision of language teacher education shared by those who are most closely involved in this important endeavor.

In a recent presentation, Met (1992) brought to the attention of foreign language supervisors a model of the change process developed by Mary Lippitt of Enterprise Management, Ltd. This paradigm proposes five necessary components of effective change: a *vision* of what is needed or desired, the *skills, incentives,* and *resources* necessary to achieve the vision, and an *action plan* that brings together the other components in an effective way. All components are necessary for the vision to be realized in a timely fashion. If vision, skills, and resources are present, and if there is an action plan, *gradual change* may occur even in the absence of incentives. On the other hand, according to this analysis, the absence of any other component will defeat all attempts at change. To see how this works, let us remove one component at a time from the process. If we delete the component of a clear vision, which normally serves as the starting point for change as well as its focus, the process will ultimately deteriorate into *confusion.* Even if a vision, incentives, resources, and an action plan are present, the absence of skills will lead to little more than *anxiety.* Where all other components are present, a lack of resources will cause the change process to terminate in *frustration.* Finally, vision, skills, incentives, and resources cannot be mobilized in the absence of an action plan. The expected result of this combination of components is a series of *false starts* doomed to lead nowhere.

Change is a difficult and often painful process that may begin in enthusiasm yet end in despair if the key precursors to change outlined above are not present (figure 8-1). We have all experienced anxiety, frustration, and confusion; and we have all known false starts. While the North Carolina FLES initiative and a number of innovative teacher-education programs seem at this point to be thriving, many excellent efforts at reform over the years have faltered and withered on the vine. As we have seen above, the *sine qua non* of change is a clear vision of the desired end product, but vision alone will not suffice. Whether the change in question involves an individual teacher educator or an entity such as an institution, a school system, a state, or a professional organization, skills, incentives, and resources must be mobilized through an action plan in order for successful change to result.

Change may be initiated at the national level, as exemplified by the proposal for a national teaching certificate, or at the state level as in the case of the legislation that gave birth to the North Carolina FLES project. On the other hand, it may simply arise from the foresight of a group of committed professionals at an individual institution or from an individual teacher educator who chooses to restructure a methods course. Whatever the case may be, the most lasting and far-reaching change is likely to result from a shared vision, one in which those involved willingly participate and in which they can feel some ownership. For this reason, it is especially important to take steps to combat the isolation and fragmentation that characterize our field.

The diversity of our profession with its many languages, cultures, and areas of specialization is both a strength and a weakness. Within our language departments are housed specialists in literature, civilization, applied and theoretical linguistics, language education, and second language acquisition. The group of individuals involved in the preparation of a future language teacher will also include specialists in education and at least one cooperating teacher in a school. If all who participate in teacher preparation can direct their talents toward a common goal, the program will gain from the richness of their diverse repertoires. If, on the other hand, they remain locked in their areas of special interest, the fragmentation of the field may impede any efforts at improvement.

Fragmentation is at least in part responsible for the isolation felt by some members of our profession. One thinks of the lone teacher educator in a department dominated by specialists in literature or the single foreign language teacher in a rural high school, who may be the only person in the community who speaks or understands a foreign language, of the Latin teacher whose counterparts in the modern languages are unaware of the contribution the study of a classical language can make to global education,[12] of the ESL or bilingual education teacher whose colleagues in foreign languages fail to see that the fields of second and foreign languages have a great deal in common. Related to isolation is the lack of respect for certain members of the profession based on status within various established hierarchies. Frequently, the specialist in language education is considered to be less important in the departmental hierarchy than the literary scholar. Language specialists housed in colleges of liberal arts may consider the education specialists across the way to be somehow intellectually inferior. University supervisors of student teachers may accuse

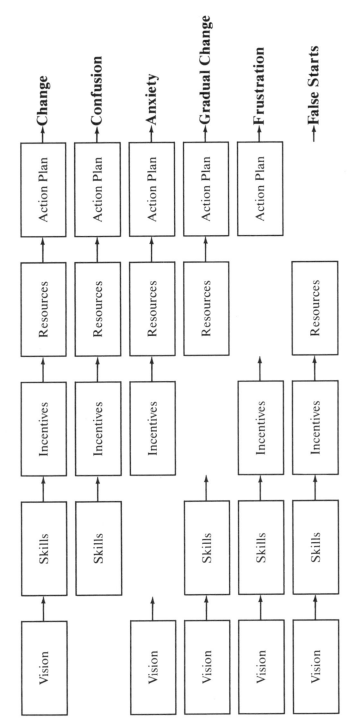

Figure 8-1. Managing complex change.

cooperating teachers of not reading and keeping up in the field; while practitioners in the schools may counter that the university-based experts in pedagogy have fled the realities of the classroom and ensconced themselves in an ivory tower.

If we are to formulate a vision of the future and bring that vision to reality, we must adopt an attitude of open-mindedness and outreach that will invite other potential participants in teacher education to share in our vision. We, of all professions, should not be guilty of stereotyping our colleagues as "literature people" or "education people" or "high school people" as if there were no individual differences within those groups. Rather, our approach should be to replace attitudes of condescension and mutual distrust with attitudes of collaboration based upon mutual respect in the pursuit of common goals. What we must do is to put aside labels and preconceived notions and reach out to those individuals within any group who are sympathetic to our vision or can be enlisted in our cause. One method of building bridges would be to identify and emphasize arenas of change that tend to cut across disciplines and areas of specialization. A case in point is study abroad, which is seen in a positive light by language, literature, and culture specialists as well as by specialists in education and practicing teachers.[13] Still another is FLES, which enjoys not only professional but also considerable public support at the moment. If we elaborate a vision in which many people can share and if we invite collaborative participation in the change process rather than imposing change from above, we will be more likely to see reform become a reality.

Conclusion

We began this chapter with the dictionary definition of the word *reflection* and throughout these pages we have gradually discovered a more specific interpretation of this term, one that is embodied in the concept of *reflective teaching*. A reflective approach basically seeks to cultivate in both future and practicing teachers the kind of inquiring mind and critical attitude that will foster continued professional development throughout the career; it also implies a collaborative approach that assumes mutual respect among the various participants involved in teacher education, be they practitioners, researchers, supervisors, or students. As such, it may be expected to create a fertile seedbed in which change can germinate, take root, and thrive. This, no doubt, is one of the reasons that the words *reflection* and *reflective* are liberally sprinkled throughout the pages of this volume on teacher-education reform.

The authors of earlier chapters have offered us their vision of tomorrow's schools and tomorrow's teachers. They have seen a multicultural learning environment in which language education is the key to communication and cultural understanding. They have presented a picture of teachers who are not only proficient in language and culturally and technologically aware but who are also decision makers and agents of change. They have seen the profession as one that is evolving and will continue to evolve as our research base is broadened and we learn more about both language acquisition and the art and craft of teaching. They have recognized the necessity of change and acknowledged the many organizations and entities that must be considered if real change is to take place.

As we end this volume and begin to elaborate our personal visions of change in teacher education, or to ask ourselves how we can use our skills to contribute to the visions elaborated in this volume, the following quotation from the extensive literature on educational change is worth contemplating:

> Educational change is fundamentally dependent upon change in people's attitudes, understanding, skills, and behavior. The changes which occur in terms of buildings, instructional materials, school organization, curriculum content, operational processes and school purposes are in reality but manifestations of change in the persons responsible for those elements of programming. (Edmonds, Ogletree, and Wear as quoted by Wu 1988: 13)

The viewpoints of the authors of previous chapters and the examples of success-ful change described in this chapter can serve to inspire additional initiatives and to give focus and unity to efforts already under way. It is important to remember, however, that the changes proposed in these pages, as well as those that have arisen from other sources, are more likely to be realized if they are supported by reflective, action-oriented teachers who feel that they are capable of acting rather than being acted upon. The initial catalyst for reform may come from within or without, but if change is to be lasting, we must prepare teachers who are not only proficient in language and knowledgeable about culture and literature, but who are flexible, thoughtful, inquiry-oriented, and self-directed professionals. We can afford neither to act without thinking nor to think without acting. Both are necessary if constructive change is to be effected and if that change is to endure.

Notes

1. Dandonoli and Henning (1990) used French and English as a Second Language in their validity studies of the *Guidelines* and of the oral interview process. This report is listed in the references below.
2. The term *reflective* has been variously defined. For a more complete discussion of these variations, see Bartlett (1990), Lange (1990), and Schön (1987). For this paper, I have chosen to accept the definition proposed by Wallace (1991).
3. The Barrière article (1991) in the references mentions specifically grants for future teachers of foreign languages within the framework of ERASMUS. Other articles in the same volume describe European initiatives that may be of interest to those engaged in teacher reform efforts.
4. Technically, it is the Department of International Business that is compared to other such departments in a survey of Deans of Schools of Business conducted annually by *U.S. News and World Report;* however, the first-place ranking is largely attributable to the M.I.B.S. program. Information concerning the M.I.B.S. program was obtained from Virginia Holcomb, Assistant Director for Corporate Relations and Communica-tions, Graduate Division, College of Business Administration, University of South Carolina.

5. Other three-year tracks such as Korean and Arabic also require almost a full year of language and culture training in the foreign country.

6. Clifford (1987) outlines a number of differences between language instruction in government language schools and in the academic setting. A chief difference is that the government schools recognize the fact that the number of hours required to achieve proficiency varies according to language and organize their curriculum accordingly.

7. Glisan and Phillips (1988) describe a three-week elementary classroom field experience in Jalapa, Mexico, or Nancy, France.

8. In its January/February 1992 issue, *Change* magazine reported that more than a third of all American colleges and universities have a multicultural general education requirement and that more than half of all colleges and universities have added multicultural elements to their course offerings.

9. The Renaissance Group (1989) is composed of presidents and deans of education from a small number of institutions with a major commitment to teacher education.

10. The University of Florida Functional-Collaborative Model, another noteworthy FLES-related state effort, is described in Hallman et al. (1992). Central to the Florida model are summer institutes for FLES teachers.

11. Information regarding this project was provided by L. Gerard Toussaint, Consultant, Second Language Studies, North Carolina Department of Public Instruction, who worked closely with the committee. The recommendations are based on his observations of the change process in action.

12. Abbot (1991) specifically mentions the need to bridge the separation between teachers of modern and classical languages. For a discussion of the role of classics and global education, see the Summer 1991 issue of *Prospects,* copies of which may be obtained by writing to the Department of Classics, Randolph-Macon College, Ashland, VA 23005.

13. The National Endowment for the Humanities, which has traditionally favored literature and civilization over language in its funding decisions, has awarded a three-year $940,000 grant to Connecticut College to fund a national fellowship program beginning in 1992 for independent summer study abroad for foreign language teachers in elementary and secondary schools. Each fellow selected on the basis of a national competition will receive a $3,750 stipend to cover six weeks of study or individual research abroad.

References, Reflecting on Teacher Development

Abbot, Martha G. 1991. "Priority: Classics; Critical Instructional Issues in the Classics for American Schools." *Foreign Language Annals* 24: 27–37.

American Council on the Teaching of Foreign Languages. 1982. *Provisional Proficiency Guidelines.* Yonkers, NY: ACTFL.

Barrière, Charles. 1991. "A Linguistic Response to 'Europe, 1992': The Lingua Program," pp. 20–27 in Gerard L. Ervin, ed., *International Perspectives on Foreign Language Teaching.* ACTFL Foreign Language Education Series, vol. 21. Lincolnwood, IL: National Textbook.

Bartlett, Leo. 1990. "Teacher Development through Reflective Teaching," pp. 202–14 in Jack C. Richards and David Nunan, eds., *Second Language Teacher Education.* New York: Cambridge Univ. Press.

Clifford, Ray T. 1987. "Language Teaching in the Federal Government: A Personal Perspective." *Annals of the American Academy of Political and Social Science* 490: 137–46.

Curtain, Helena A. 1992. "Improving Elementary School Foreign Language Teacher Education: Center for Applied Linguistics/North Carolina FIPSE Project Evaluation Report." Unpublished manuscript.

Dandonoli, Patricia, and Grant Henning. 1990. "An Investigation of the Construct Validity of the ACTFL Proficiency Guidelines and Oral Interview Process." *Foreign Language Annals* 23: 11–22.

Freeman, Stephen A. 1941. "What Constitutes a Well-Trained Modern Language Teacher?" *Modern Language Journal* 25: 255–67.

Galloway, Vicki. 1991. "Reflective Teachers," pp. 65–75 in James E. Alatis, ed., *Linguistics and Language Pedagogy: The State of the Art.* Georgetown University Round Table on Languages and Linguistics. Washington, DC: Georgetown Univ. Press.

Glisan, Eileen W., and June K. Phillips. 1988. "Foreign Languages and International Studies in Elementary School: A Program of Teacher Preparation." *Foreign Language Annals* 21: 527–33.

Grittner, Frank M. 1980. "How to Break Out of the Never-Ending Circle of Retraining: A Self-Adjusting Mechanism for the 1980s," pp. 72–77 in Dale L. Lange, ed., *Proceedings of the National Conference on Professional Priorities.* Yonkers, NY: ACTFL Materials Center.

"Guidelines for Teacher Education Programs in Modern Foreign Languages." 1966. *PMLA* 81,2: A-2, A-3.

Hallman, Clemens L., Anne E. Campbell, and Gisela Ernst. 1992. "Development and Implementation of FLES Summer Institutes in Florida: A Functional-Collaborative Effort." *Foreign Language Annals* 25: 245–54.

Jarvis, Gilbert A., and Sheryl V. Taylor. 1990. "Reforming Foreign and Second Language Teacher Education," pp. 159–82 in Diane W. Birckbichler, ed., *New Perspectives and New Directions in Foreign Language Education.* ACTFL Foreign Language Education Series, vol. 20. Lincolnwood, IL: National Textbook.

Joiner, Elizabeth G. 1980. "Preservice Teacher Education: Some Thoughts for the 1980's," pp. 78–80 in Dale L. Lange, ed., *Proceedings of the National Conference on Professional Priorities.* Yonkers, NY: ACTFL Materials Center.

Jorstad, Helen. 1980. "Inservice Teacher Education: Content and Process," pp. 81–85 in Dale L. Lange, ed., *Proceedings of the National Conference on Professional Priorities.* Yonkers, NY: ACTFL Materials Center.

Kennedy, Mary M. 1991. "Some Surprising Findings on How Teachers Learn to Teach," *Educational Leadership* 49,3: 14–17.

Lange, Dale L. 1990. "A Blueprint for a Teacher Development Program," pp. 245–68 in Jack C. Richards and David Nunan, eds., *Second Language Teacher Education.* New York: Cambridge Univ. Press.

————. 1991. "Implications of Recent Reports on Teacher Education Reform for Departments of Foreign Languages and Literatures." *ADFL Bulletin* 23,1: 28–34.

Met, Myriam. 1992. "Supervising for Change." Plenary address presented at the MLA Professional Development Institute on Current Issues in Foreign Language Teaching, Athens, Georgia.

Moeller, Paulette C. 1989. "The Making of a Foreign Language Teacher—Regina Style." *Foreign Language Annals* 22: 135–44.

Mulkeen, T. A., and T. J. Tetenbaum. 1987. "An Integrative Model of Teacher Education and Professional Development." *Educational Horizons* (Winter): 85–87.

North Carolina Department of Public Instruction and the Center for Applied Linguistics. 1992. "Elementary School (K–8) Foreign Language Teacher Education Curriculum." Washington, DC: ERIC Clearinghouse on Languages and Linguistics.

Phillips, June K. 1989. "Teacher Education: Target of Reform," pp. 11–40 in Helen S. Lepke, ed., *Shaping the Future: Challenges and Opportunities.* Report of the Northeast Conference on the Teaching of Foreign Languages. Middlebury, VT: Northeast Conference.

"Qualifications for Secondary School Teachers of Modern Foreign Languages." 1955. *The Bulletin of the National Association of Secondary School Principals* 39: 30–33.

Renaissance Group. 1989. *Teachers for the New World: A Statement of Principles.* Cedar Falls: Univ. of Northern Iowa.

Sandstedt, Lynn A. 1992. Personal communication.

Schön, Donald A. 1987. *Educating the Reflective Practitioner: Toward a New Design for Teaching and Learning in the Professions.* San Francisco: Jossey-Bass.

Strasheim, Lorraine A. 1991. "Preservice and Inservice Teacher Education in the Nineties: The Issue Is Instructional Validity." *Foreign Language Annals* 24: 101-7.

Tetenbaum, T. J., and T. A. Mulkeen. 1986. "Designing Teacher Education for the Twenty-First Century." *Journal of Higher Education* 57: 621-36.

Toussaint, L. Gerard. 1992. Personal communication.

Wallace, Michael J. 1991. *Training Foreign Language Teachers: A Reflective Approach.* Cambridge, Eng.: Cambridge Univ. Press.

Wing, Barbara H. 1984. "For Teachers: A Challenge for Competence," pp. 11-45 in Gilbert A. Jarvis, ed., *The Challenge for Excellence in Foreign Language Education.* Report of the Northeast Conference on the Teaching of Foreign Languages. Middlebury, VT: Northeast Conference.

————. 1992. Personal communication.

Wu, P. C. 1988. "Why Is Change Difficult? Lessons for Staff Development." *Journal of Staff Development* 9,2: 10-14.

Appendix: ACTFL Provisional Program Guidelines for Foreign Language Teacher Education

These guidelines should be used with caution. They do not represent a statement of minimum thresholds and therefore neither supplant nor correspond in purpose to current accreditation and monitoring instruments. Though professional consensus on minimal indicators may ultimately be gleaned from the statements in this document, these guidelines are intended to serve a program development function; that is, to represent forward-looking view as to what knowledge, skills and experiences are deemed by the profession as holding the most promise for the preparedness of foreign language teacher candidates. The discussion which follows each set of guidelines is for the purpose of helping you assess your institution's preparation of foreign language teachers from several perspectives, draw conclusions regarding the overall effectiveness of the program and plan for future improvements.

The guidelines contained herein focus on three areas in the preservice preparation of foreign language teachers:

a) Personal Development: the knowledge and skills derived from a strong liberal arts education

b) Professional Development: the knowledge and skills derived from education and experience in the art and science of pedagogy

c) Specialist Development: the knowledge and skills associated with being a specialist in the language and culture to be taught in the classroom.

These guidelines were developed pursuant to a three-year grant to ACTFL from the Department of Education. They are provisional only and require at this point scrutiny, discussion and commentary from all sectors of the foreign language teaching profession.

ACTFL wishes to thank the following committee members who gave so generously of their time, energy and thoughts in the development of this document:

Jeannette Bragger—Pennsylvania State University
Robert DiDonato—Miami University, Oxford, Ohio
Gregory Duncan—Georgia Department of Education

T. Bruce Fryer—University of South Carolina
Neil Granoien—Defense Language Institute
Gilbert Jarvis*—The Ohio State University
Dorothy Joba—South Glastonbury (CT) High School
Carl Johnson—Texas Education Agency
Constance Knop—University of Wisconsin
Robert Lafayette*—Louisiana State University
Dale Lange—University of Minnesota
Frank W. Medley, Jr.*—University of South Carolina
Myriam Met—Montgomery County (MD) Public Schools
Alice C. Omaggio—University of Illinois
June K. Phillips*—Tennessee Foreign Language Institute
Lynn Sandstedt—University of Northern Colorado
C. Edward Scebold—ACTFL
Stanley Shinall—University of Illinois
Vicki Galloway—Project Director

*Committee Chairperson

Personal Development

Programs designed to prepare foreign language teachers should include a strong liberal arts component to foster the personal and intellectual development of the candidate. The range of course offerings should include the humanities, social and behavioral sciences, natural sciences, mathematics and the arts. The educator is first and foremost an educated individual. Therefore, this sequence of studies should be well planned and broad enough to permit candidates to develop the processes and skills essential to experiencing success, satisfaction and intellectual growth in teaching and in life.

Area I: Communication

Guidelines
The coursework and experiences that comprise the liberal arts curriculum will develop:
1. Effective communication skills and strategies in English, including:
    a) listening for the implied and intended meaning as conveyed by verbal and nonverbal signals;
    b) conveying thoughts orally in a clear manner appropriate to the audience being addressed;
    c) reading a variety of texts and deriving a meaning consonant with the writer's intention;
    d) writing clearly and concisely in a style appropriate to the intent of the task;
    e) tailoring language (both oral and written) for a variety of audiences.

2. Strong interpersonal skills, including:
   a) an awareness of the perspective of one's audiences;
   b) a sense of the appropriateness and effectiveness of behaviors within a range of social and professional contexts;
   c) flexibility of thought in situations which offer a variety of interpretations and options;
   d) recognition or creation of alternative resolutions to conflict.

Discussion
An essential characteristic of an effective teacher is the ability to communicate well with a wide variety of audiences, using both written and spoken language. Toward this end, the Liberal Arts program should provide a broad spectrum of activities and experiences that will enable the candidates to practice these skills.

Indicators   of program consistency with these guidelines include:
- the availability of coursework in English communication skills and strategies;
- opportunities for students to develop oral and written language skills across the disciplines;
- the availability of coursework and instructional approaches designed to develop skills in interpersonal relations and group dynamics;
- planned opportunities for contact with a variety of audiences;
- guidance in determining listener / reader frame of reference and perspective;
- guidance in determining speaker / writer frame of reference and perspective;
- provision of simulation or case-study opportunities to provide for individual discovery, analysis and problem solving;
- opportunities for writing on topics related to foreign language pedagogy.

Area II: Acquisition and Use of Knowledge

Guidelines
The coursework and experiences that comprise the liberal arts curriculum will develop:
1. An awareness of information sources and the ability to:
   a) identify information sources and assess source reliability;
   b) evaluate the thoroughness of reporting and the strength of arguments, and distinguish between fact and opinion.
2. The ability to analyze and synthesize new information with emphasis on the development of critical-thinking and study skills, including:
   a) identifying issues or problems and their causes, securing relevant information and relating, comparing or quantifying data from various sources;
   b) making decisions which are based on logical assumptions and which incorporate all pertinent information;
   c) recognizing personally appropriate and effective strategies for different types of learning.

3. The ability to work with and learn from a variety of media and technologies.

Discussion
The liberal arts component of the teacher's education should not only provide information, but foster intellectual curiosity in order to encourage individuals to become seekers of knowledge. This intellectual curiosity will most likely arise from experiences that help potential teachers acknowledge their responsibilities to themselves for their own learning. A knowledge base that does not remain static and confined but that continually expands and enriches perspectives will be that of the teacher who is able to bring the world into the classroom and to link the classroom to the world. The above statements, therefore, relate to skills that contribute to an ability and desire to learn. As such, they are not limited to programmatic issues of course offerings but to types of in-class experiences and opportunities—ways in which instruction is delivered. What is learned through the liberal arts study may ultimately be less important than how it is learned.

Indicators of program consistency with this guideline include:
- the availability and accessibility in all areas of study of a variety of types of information sources, print and nonprint;
- encouragement of the use of multiple sources for obtaining information, including the exploration of non-traditional information sources;
- the provision in all areas of study of criteria for and guidance in evaluating the accuracy, authenticity and completeness of information;
- instructional approaches which include clearly structured tasks that allow for learner independence in investigation and performance;
- programs in all subject areas that are designed to offer not only discrete information but also linkage and integration of concepts to provide for continual expansion of knowledge;
- opportunities for questioning and speculating in a context that acknowledges and supports a variety of appropriate answers;
- inclusion of interdisciplinary coursework or the planned incorporation of cross-disciplinary application of concepts;
- availability of and opportunities to use computers as information delivery and organization systems.

Area III: Leadership

Guidelines
The coursework and experiences that comprise the liberal arts curriculum will develop:
1. initiative, the desire and ability to start projects independently and take action beyond what is necessarily called for;
2. skills in planning and organizing time, resources, setting and sequence of activities for goal-derived task accomplishment;
3. utilization of both tactical and strategic decision-making.

Discussion

Teachers are expected to assume the responsibility of leadership, both within and outside their own disciplines. The above statements thus refer to the development of special skills and characteristics that are necessary for knowledgeable and articulate individuals to carry out these leadership roles and to serve as classroom models for future leaders. Within the classroom, these skills translate into purposeful and planned instruction through clearly defined goals and a well-established yet flexible course of action to achieve these goals. Good leaders are good strategic decision-makers, able to plan alternative courses of action when time is available. They are also good tactical decision-makers; equipped to see options, take actions and commit themselves in ongoing situations, where time for deliberation is limited and extensive information gathering is inappropriate.

Indicators of program consistency with these guidelines include:

- coursework and seminars treating leadership characteristics and identifying individual leadership style;
- opportunities to participate in shared decision-making activities on a range of topics and with varying degrees of constraint imposed on the group;
- coursework in and practice with time and resource allocation and management for the attainment of specified goals and objectives;
- instructional approaches that focus on identification of the probable consequences of specific courses of action;
- opportunities to set performance goals, to plan courses of action and make decisions that will result in realization of the goals;
- opportunities to participate in structured exercises and activities that focus upon the need for individual initiative, divergent thinking and spontaneous decision-making;
- opportunities to participate in social and professional activities beyond the classroom that call upon the candidate to exercise varying degrees of initiative, information gathering and processing, planning and organizing, goal-setting, shared and individual decision-making and attainment of closure during the process.

Professional Development

Programs for the development of foreign language teachers should have a plan and clearly-stated policies for recruitment, selection and admission. The criteria for these should be published and available to potential applicants who wish to seek admission.

Introduction

The professional development component of the candidate's preservice education is composed of coursework and experiences that relate to the individual in the role of "teacher."

Guidelines in this section focus on programmatic aspects that prepare candidates to respond to major questions in planning and implementing foreign language instruction:

1. The question of "why": understanding what it means to know another language and recognizing the values and benefits of such knowledge.
2. The question of "who": observing and analyzing learners and learning.
3. The question of "what" and "when": organizing the content of instruction to provide for effective teaching and learning.
4. The question of "how": providing appropriate, purposeful classroom experiences.
5. The question of "where": experiencing the system and setting in which formal education occurs.

Area I: Rationale for Foreign Language Study

Guidelines
Programs provide instruction in the purposes for and benefits of foreign language study that includes:

1. information about the impact of competence in foreign languages on modern society and on one's own personal development;
2. emphasis on the importance of foreign language as it relates to the needs and interests of specific communities;
3. opportunities to develop skills in conveying the benefits of proficiency in another language to many different audiences (students, parents, administrators, business and community);
4. opportunities to integrate this rationale in curricular and instructional decision-making.

Discussion
Programs have a responsibility to equip prospective teachers with information to help them become effective advocates for their profession. Teachers will be expected to keep abreast of future research and to interpret changes in society as they affect the role of foreign language study. Good programs will also provide opportunities for candidates to have direct experiences interacting with persons from other cultures.

Indicators   of program consistency with this guideline include:
- availability of resource materials on rationales and language policy issues;
- opportunities for candidates to communicate the purposes and benefits of language study to others;
- planned interactions with people from cultures with language policies different from those in the United States;
- student participation in professional meetings on this topic.

Area II: Theories of Child Development and Learning

Guidelines
Programs provide instruction in child development, models and theories of learning and their relationship to the development of foreign language competence. This includes information about:

1. theories of physical, emotional, cognitive and linguistic development of children and adolescents;
2. the interrelationship of these processes in terms of developing competence in a foreign language and its relationship to other subject areas in the curriculum of schooling.

Discussion
It is important that programs present theories and models proposed to explain learning in general and that this information be related to models hypothesized for foreign language learning through curricular or instructional linkage. Achieving this requires that instruction be closely related to field experiences with the full range of student populations for which certification is sought. These direct experiences include contacts with students of varying ages, abilities, aptitudes and physical conditions as well as diverse school settings (e.g., urban, suburban, rural), diverse socioeconomic and subcultural settings (e.g., teenage parents, latch-key children, non-English speaking areas) and serve to analyze and link theories to the realities of the classroom and other elements of the school curriculum.

Indicators of program consistency with this guideline include:
- courses and materials showing treatment of human development concepts as well as their relationships to foreign language learning;
- planned and frequent opportunities to relate general learning theory to specific aspects of foreign language learning and foreign language teaching behavior through individual projects or cross-college collaborative efforts;
- schedules of opportunities in the curriculum for observing and working in diverse school settings.

Area III: Curriculum Development

Guidelines
Programs provide instruction in the theories and processes of curriculum development and their application to foreign language education. This includes information about:

1. the role of curricular design in adapting the nature of the discipline to learner needs, interests and characteristics;
2. the objectives and characteristics of different curricular models and their applicability in foreign language education;

3. the rights and responsibilities of the teacher in making decisions about foreign language program planning.

Discussion
Programs emphasize the teacher role in curricular design and provide information about ways in which curricula are developed both in terms of processes and models. Foreign language curriculum planning is viewed as being ongoing, open to change and a function of teacher involvement across levels, languages and disciplines. Aspects of professional development should include exploration of issues such as needs assessment, articulation, consensus, learner expectations, measurability and the role of textbooks and other instructional materials as resources in achieving curricular goals.

Indicators   of program consistency with these guidelines include:

- materials and syllabi that treat diverse models, objectives and program formats;
- opportunities to link knowledge of curriculum design and learning theory to specific foreign language program-planning efforts;
- opportunities for writing objectives and lesson plans for achieving goals;
- opportunities to evaluate materials in terms of their match with curricular objectives;
- field experiences in which curricula and lesson plans can be implemented.

Area IV: Instruction

Guidelines
Programs provide opportunities to acquire decision-making skills related to planning, managing and evaluating instruction. This includes information about and experiences in:

1. identifying the purpose and theoretical underpinnings of a variety of teaching strategies and anticipating the learning outcomes that result;
2. making critical decisions regarding planning for instruction, selecting materials, sequencing and executing learning activities;
3. evaluating effectively the total teaching-learning process, including daily interaction with students, continuous assessment of student learning and self evaluation.

Discussion
Programs build the essential decision-making skills of prospective teachers by providing a knowledge and experience base for instruction which is derived from an up-to-date understanding of the second-language learning and teaching process. Programs provide for a weighing of advantages and disadvantages of alternative decisions so that candidates realize their role in achieving appropriate student behaviors. Programs are responsible for showing how research and experimentation have refined the practices of the past so that preservice teachers

are aware of the necessity of continuous professional growth through inservice involvement.

Indicators   of program consistency with these guidelines include:

- availability and accessibility of current literature in the areas of foreign language education, research on effective teaching and effective schools;
- multiple opportunities to select and experiment with instructional strategies and to evaluate results;
- structured formats for observing, assessing and hypothesizing about classroom decisions through video taped or live classroom observations;
- coursework and experience in devising appropriate testing techniques;
- coursework in and effective models of classroom management: using grouping strategies, structuring tasks, giving directions, maximizing use of class time;
- practice in establishing progression in classroom activities;
- regular use of professional journals in the field of general and language-specific foreign language pedagogy;
- opportunities for use of learning/teaching devices: overhead projectors, video, computer software, language lab facilities;
- exploration of sources of instructional materials.

Area V: The Instructional Setting

Guidelines
Programs provide information about and experience in the secondary educational system, to include:

1. information about the roles and responsibilities of public schools in United States society;
2. examination of the roles and services of school district/state personnel: principals, guidance counselors, superintendents, school boards, foreign language supervisors and State Department of Education personnel;
3. awareness of protocols, reporting mechanisms and rules governing the various functions of schools;
4. clinical and field experiences which provide contact with a wide range of students, settings, other subject areas and the many non-instructional aspects of life in schools;
5. a plan for integrating clinical and field experiences into all phases of the candidate's preparation;
6. procedures of and practice in self assessment.

Discussion
Programs may vary considerably in form and duration, but a common goal exists in an integrated approach which gradually increases the candidate's involvement in classroom decision-making. The tasks and responsibilities of prospective

teachers build toward a culminating experience consisting of a sustained period of responsibility that reflects a full teaching load.

Indicators   of program consistency with these guidelines include:

- a plan that defines the number, scope, expectations and activities of clinical and field experience;
- clearly stated criteria for selection of cooperating teachers;
- clearly stated role descriptions for cooperating teachers, student teachers and university supervisors during field experience;
- evidence of planned contacts for the candidates with master foreign language teachers, school administrators, students and teachers in other subject areas;
- evidence of a full range of experience for grades for which certification is sought;
- frequent communication with the public schools.

Area VI: Foreign Language in the Elementary Schools

Guidelines

For programs preparing teachers to teach foreign languages in elementary schools, the following additional guidelines are appropriate:

Programs provide information about and experience in the elementary educational system to include:

1. an understanding of first language development and its relation to second language learning in childhood;
2. the ability to teach reading and writing as developmental skills to learners acquiring literacy skills in their first language;
3. familiarity with the children's literature appropriate to the target culture;
4. knowledge of the elementary school curriculum and ability to teach or reinforce elementary school curricula through or in a foreign language;
5. knowledge of elementary school principles and practices and the ability to apply such knowledge to foreign language instruction.

Discussion

The preparation of elementary school foreign language teachers insures that candidates can integrate foreign language within the context of the total elementary school program. Teacher candidates develop an understanding of the developing child, and particularly, the development of language and literacy skills in childhood. Sound foreign language instruction builds upon first language development in both the oral and written modes. Further, teachers are prepared to reinforce, enrich or directly teach the elementary school content areas through the medium of the target language. Prospective elementary school foreign language teachers are enabled to perform their roles and responsibilities through extensive preservice experiences at appropriate grade levels.

Indicators of program consistency with this goal include:
- faculty who have demonstrated excellence in teaching foreign language in the elementary grades, in addition to demonstrating the requisite knowledge and skills necessary to prepare prospective teachers;
- a plan which provides teacher candidates with prolonged and substantive field experiences at the appropriate grade levels;
- clearly stated role descriptions for cooperating teachers, student teachers and university supervisors during field experience;
- evidence of planned contacts for the candidates with master foreign language teachers, school administrators, students and teachers in other subject areas;
- evidence of a full range of experience for grades for which certification is sought;
- frequent communication with the public schools.

Area VII: Foreign Language Education Faculty

Guidelines
The faculty responsible for the foreign language education component of the candidate's professional development will:

1. be proficient in a foreign language;
2. have preparation and expertise in foreign language pedagogy;
3. have a record of excellence in language teaching;
4. maintain clear relationships with foreign language and education faculty and with school administrators and teachers.

Specialist Development

Introduction

The guidelines for specialist education detailed below address the areas of Language, Culture/Civilization and Language and Communication Processes. The first set of guidelines focuses on the functional use of the four language skills—listening, speaking, reading and writing. The second deals with the acquisition of knowledge and appreciation of the totality of the foreign language culture and civilization. The third area concentrates on conceptual knowledge of the target language itself as well as a basic understanding of the principles of linguistics. For each of these components the program will provide pre-assessment, formative assessment, feedback, appropriate remediation and summative evaluation. Program guidelines and the applicable evaluative measurements should be provided to candidates early in their program of study. Among the components of program implementation should be experiences incorporating application of technology (i.e., computers, film, video) to the aforementioned guidelines, as well as study abroad or its equivalent.

Area I: Language Proficiency

Guidelines
The foreign language teacher education program provides the candidate opportunities to develop competence in the following skills to the degree indicated:
1. Speaking:
    a) satisfy the requirements of a broad variety of everyday, school and work situations;
    b) discuss concrete topics relating to particular interests and special fields of competence;
    c) display some ability to support opinions, explain in detail and hypothesize;
    d) use communicative strategies, such as paraphrasing and circumlocution;
    e) use differentiated vocabulary and intonation to communicate fine shades of meaning.
2. Listening:
    a) understand the main ideas of most speech in a standard dialect;
    b) comprehend extended discourse of a general nature on a variety of topics beyond the immediate situation;
    c) understand some culturally implied meanings beyond the surface meanings of the text.
3. Reading:
    a) follow essential points of written discourse in areas of special interest and knowledge;
    b) comprehend facts in texts and make appropriate inferences;
    c) understand parts of text which are conceptually abstract and linguistically complex, texts which treat unfamiliar topics or situations and texts which involve aspects of target language culture;
    d) comprehend a variety of texts, including literary texts and demonstrate an emerging awareness of the aesthetic properties of language and literary style.
4. Writing:
    a) write routine social correspondence and join sentences in simple discourse of at least several paragraphs in length on familiar topics;
    b) write cohesive summaries and resumes;
    c) write narratives and descriptions of a factual nature, drawing from personal experience, readings and other verbal or non-verbal stimuli.

Discussion
It is incumbent on foreign language teacher education programs to provide the kinds of experiences, both in and out of the classroom, which will permit the candidate to develop functional performance in the language at a level equivalent to the Advanced Plus level on the ACTFL Proficiency Guidelines in listening, speaking and reading, and at the Advanced level in writing.

Programs should be examined in terms of progressive and continuous attention to the development of language proficiency. Approaches which confine language and grammar study to lower levels with culture and literature at higher levels may be less effective in producing the levels of language use outlined above.

Indicators   of program consistency with this guideline include:

- the presence of written goals for each level of language study and accurate placement instruments;
- opportunities to hear, speak, read and write authentic language in all foreign language courses;
- the presence of language courses which focus on the totality of communication in addition to those which focus specifically on culture, grammar, literature and pronunciation;
- a clearly articulated sequence of courses that balances culture, grammar, language use and literature throughout the major's course of study;
- opportunities for intensive language experiences in this country and / or through study or living abroad programs;
- use of appropriate evaluative instruments to measure candidate performance. An example of such would be the Oral Proficiency Interview to measure the speaking component;
- effective use of available technology for providing authentic language models and efficient learning.

Area II: Culture and Civilization

Guidelines
The foreign language teacher education program provides the candidate opportunities to:

1. discuss, research and reflect upon the daily living patterns, societal structure, institutions and value systems of the people who speak the language;
2. explore the variability of cultural concepts;
3. obtain an overview of the literatures of the people who use the language with an emphasis on contemporary writers and an in-depth experience with some major author or theme;
4. obtain an overview of the cultures and civilizations from a variety of perspectives, including the historical, geographical, political and artistic;
5. develop skills in processing information that promote the understanding and interpretation of cultures and civilizations. These include:
   a) observing, comparing and inquiring about cultural phenomena;
   b) analyzing and hypothesizing about cultural phenomena;
   c) synthesizing and determining the generalizability of cultural phenomena.

Discussion
As specialists in the area of foreign language, candidates entering the teaching profession must not only be linguistically proficient but culturally proficient as well. Programs designed to develop cultural awareness will not only include information about the cultures of the people who speak the language but acknowledge the limitations and datedness of any corpus of information. To this end, programs should integrate a broad range of experiences designed to

acquaint candidates with the everyday life and artistic accomplishments of peoples, as well as the independent ability to "process" and interpret cultural phenomena encountered directly or vicariously. In addition, programs should be designed to allow candidates to see the relationships that necessarily exist between language, literature and culture in both the native and target cultures.

Indicators of program consistency with this guideline include:

- materials and instructional approaches which present authentic cultural contexts;
- course requirements in the area of culture and civilization as well as literature;
- opportunities to acquire knowledge and contact with cultures, literatures and civilizations of countries other than the "mother country";
- opportunities to experience the cultures, literatures and civilizations in their own environment;
- opportunities to study children's and adolescent literature of both target and "mother" cultures where appropriate;
- opportunities to enroll in courses in other departments (history, anthropology, sociology, art, etc.) for content not available in the foreign language department;
- opportunities to use modern technology (computers, film, video, interactive video, etc.) to study cultures, literatures and civilizations;
- instructional approaches that utilize simulation, incident analyses and other discovery and problem-solving techniques geared toward the explanation and resolution of cross-cultural conflict.

Area III: Language Analysis

Guidelines
The program provides the candidate opportunities to acquire and demonstrate:

1. knowledge of the nature of language and the significance of language change and variation which occur over time, space and social class;
2. knowledge of theories of first and second language acquisition and learning;
3. knowledge of the phonological, morphological, syntactical and lexical components of the target language;
4. knowledge of how communication occurs in real life, to include:
   a) the contribution of grammatical and lexical elements in expressing basic functions and notions of the target language within the context in which they occur;
   b) analysis of discourse and communication strategies.

Discussion
It is important that programs prepare candidates to understand how the elements of and the totality of language in order that they be able not only to explain grammar and know when and how to analyze and correct learner errors, but also

to understand and implement appropriate discourse strategies and establish meaningful contexts necessary for teaching communication. Programs should thus be evaluated in terms of how they are preparing future teachers to view and explain grammar as it contributes to real-life communication.

Indicators   of program consistency with this guideline include:

- instructional approaches that reflect language as it is used to perform functions in real-life contexts;
- opportunities to examine and use communicative strategies associated with the acts of reading, writing, speaking and listening;
- opportunities to examine features of discourse;
- opportunities to examine cultural connotations at the word level and at the discourse level;
- opportunities for coursework in foreign language or other departments in at least one of the following areas: communication theory, second-language acquisition, discourse analysis, psycholinguistics, socio-linguistics, applied linguistics.

Index to Persons Cited

Index to Major Topics Cited

NTC PROFESSIONAL MATERIALS

ACTFL Review

Published annually in conjunction with the American Council on the Teaching of Foreign Languages

NEW PERSPECTIVES, NEW DIRECTIONS IN FOREIGN LANGUAGE EDUCATION, ed. Birckbichler, Vol. 20 (1990)

MODERN TECHNOLOGY IN FOREIGN LANGUAGE EDUCATION: APPLICATIONS AND PROJECTS, ed. Smith, Vol. 19 (1989)

MODERN MEDIA IN FOREIGN LANGUAGE EDUCATION: THEORY AND IMPLEMENTATION, ed. Smith, Vol. 18 (1987)

DEFINING AND DEVELOPING PROFICIENCY: GUIDELINES, IMPLEMENTATIONS, AND CONCEPTS, ed. Byrnes, Vol. 17 (1986)

FOREIGN LANGUAGE PROFICIENCY IN THE CLASSROOM AND BEYOND, ed. James, Vol. 16 (1984)

TEACHING FOR PROFICIENCY, THE ORGANIZING PRINCIPLE, ed. Higgs, Vol. 15 (1983)

PRACTICAL APPLICATIONS OF RESEARCH IN FOREIGN LANGUAGE TEACHING, ed. James, Vol. 14 (19

CURRICULUM, COMPETENCE, AND THE FOREIGN LANGUAGE TEACHER, ed. Higgs, Vol. 13 (1981)

Professional Resources

CENTRAL STATES CONFERENCE TITLES (annuals)

A TESOL PROFESSIONAL ANTHOLOGY: CULTURE

A TESOL PROFESSIONAL ANTHOLOGY: GRAMMAR AND COMPOSITION

A TESOL PROFESSIONAL ANTHOLOGY: LISTENING, SPEAKING, AND READING

THE COMPLETE ESL/EFL RESOURCE BOOK, Scheraga

ABC'S OF LANGUAGES AND LINGUISTICS, Hayes, et al.

AWARD-WINNING FOREIGN LANGUAGE PROGRAMS: PRESCRIPTIONS FOR SUCCESS, Sims and Hamm

PUZZLES AND GAMES IN LANGUAGE TEACHING, Danesi

GUIDE TO SUCCESSFUL AFTER-SCHOOL ELEMENTARY FOREIGN LANGUAGE PROGRAMS, Lozano

COMPLETE GUIDE TO EXPLORATORY FOREIGN LANGUAGE PROGRAMS, Kennedy and DeLorenzo

INDIVIDUALIZED FOREIGN LANGUAGE INSTRUCTION, Grittner and LaLeike

LIVING IN LATIN AMERICA: A CASE STUDY IN CROSS-CULTURAL COMMUNICATION, Gorden

ORAL COMMUNICATION TESTING, Linder

ELEMENTARY FOREIGN LANGUAGE PROGRAMS: AN ADMINISTRATOR'S HANDBOOK, Lipton

PRACTICAL HANDBOOK TO ELEMENTARY FOREIGN LANGUAGE PROGRAMS, Second edition, Lipton

SPEAK WITH A PURPOSE! Urzua, et al.

TEACHING LANGUAGES IN COLLEGE, Rivers

TEACHING CULTURE: STRATEGIES FOR INTERCULTURAL COMMUNICATION, Seelye

TEACHING FRENCH: A PRACTICE GUIDE, Rivers

TEACHING GERMAN: A PRACTICAL GUIDE, Rivers, et al.

TEACHING SPANISH: A PRACTICAL GUIDE, Rivers, et al.

TRANSCRIPTION AND TRANSLITERATION, Wellisch

YES! YOU CAN LEARN A FOREIGN LANGUAGE, Goldin, et al.

LANGUAGES AT WORK (VIDEO), Mueller

CULTURAL LITERACY AND INTERACTIVE LANGUAGE INSTRUCTION (VIDEO), Mueller

For further information or a current catalog, write:
National Textbook Company
a division of *NTC Publishing Group*
4255 West Touhy Avenue
Lincolnwood, Illinois 60646-1975 U.S.A.